New Directions in German Studies

Vol. 29

Series Editor:

IMKE MEYER

Professor of Germanic Studies, University of Illinois at Chicago

Editorial Board:

KATHERINE ARENS
Professor of Germanic Studies, University of Texas at Austin

ROSWITHA BURWICK
Distinguished Chair of Modern Foreign Languages Emerita,
Scripps College

RICHARD ELDRIDGE
Charles and Harriett Cox McDowell Professor of Philosophy,
Swarthmore College

ERIKA FISCHER-LICHTE
Professor Emerita of Theater Studies, Freie Universität Berlin

CATRIONA MACLEOD
Edmund J. and Louise W. Kahn Term Professor in the Humanities
and Professor of German, University of Pennsylvania

STEPHAN SCHINDLER
Professor of German and Chair,
University of South Florida

HEIDI SCHLIPPHACKE
Associate Professor of Germanic Studies,
University of Illinois at Chicago

ANDREW J. WEBBER
Professor of Modern German and Comparative Culture,
Cambridge University

SILKE-MARIA WEINECK
Professor of German and Comparative Literature,
University of Michigan

DAVID WELLBERY
LeRoy T. and Margaret Deffenbaugh Carlson University Professor,
University of Chicago

SABINE WILKE
Joff Hanauer Distinguished Professor for Western Civilization and
Professor of German, University of Washington

JOHN ZILCOSKY
Professor of German and Comparative Literature, University of Toronto

Volumes in the series:

Vol. 1. *Improvisation as Art: Conceptual Challenges, Historical Perspectives*
by Edgar Landgraf

Vol. 2. *The German Pícaro and Modernity: Between Underdog and Shape-Shifter*
by Bernhard Malkmus

Vol. 3. *Citation and Precedent: Conjunctions and Disjunctions of German Law and Literature*
by Thomas O. Beebee

Vol. 4. *Beyond Discontent: "Sublimation" from Goethe to Lacan*
by Eckart Goebel

Vol. 5. *From Kafka to Sebald: Modernism and Narrative Form*
edited by Sabine Wilke

Vol. 6. *Image in Outline: Reading Lou Andreas-Salomé*
by Gisela Brinker-Gabler

Vol. 7. *Out of Place: German Realism, Displacement, and Modernity*
by John B. Lyon

Vol. 8. *Thomas Mann in English: A Study in Literary Translation*
by David Horton

Vol. 9. *The Tragedy of Fatherhood: King Laius and the Politics of Paternity in the West*
by Silke-Maria Weineck

Vol. 10. *The Poet as Phenomenologist: Rilke and the New Poems*
by Luke Fischer

Vol. 11. *The Laughter of the Thracian Woman: A Protohistory of Theory*
by Hans Blumenberg, translated by Spencer Hawkins

Vol. 12. *Roma Voices in the German-Speaking World*
by Lorely French

Vol. 13. *Vienna's Dreams of Europe: Culture and Identity beyond the Nation-State*
by Katherine Arens

Vol. 14. *Thomas Mann and Shakespeare: Something Rich and Strange*
edited by Tobias Döring and Ewan Fernie

Vol. 15. *Goethe's Families of the Heart*
by Susan E. Gustafson

Vol. 16. *German Aesthetics: Fundamental Concepts from Baumgarten to Adorno*
edited by J. D. Mininger and Jason Michael Peck

Vol. 17. *Figures of Natality: Reading the Political in the Age of Goethe*
by Joseph D. O'Neil

Vol. 18. *Readings in the Anthropocene: The Environmental Humanities, German Studies, and Beyond*
edited by Sabine Wilke and Japhet Johnstone

Vol. 19 *Building Socialism: Architecture and Urbanism in East German Literature, 1955–1973*
by Curtis Swope

Vol. 20. *Ghostwriting: W. G. Sebald's Poetics of History*
by Richard T. Gray

Vol. 21. *Stereotype and Destiny in Arthur Schnitzler's Prose: Five Psycho-Sociological Readings*
by Marie Kolkenbrock

Vol. 22. *Sissi's World: The Empress Elisabeth in Memory and Myth*
edited by Maura E. Hametz and Heidi Schlipphacke

Vol. 23. *Posthumanism in the Age of Humanism: Mind, Matter, and the Life Sciences after Kant*
edited by Edgar Landgraf, Gabriel Trop, and Leif Weatherby

Vol. 24. *Staging West German Democracy: Governmental PR Films and the Democratic Imaginary, 1953–1963*
by Jan Uelzmann

Vol. 25. *The Lever as Instrument of Reason: Technological Constructions of Knowledge around 1800*
by Jocelyn Holland

Vol. 26. *The Fontane Workshop: Manufacturing Realism in the Industrial Age of Print*
by Petra McGillen

Vol. 27. *Gender, Collaboration, and Authorship in German Culture: Literary Joint Ventures, 1750–1850*
edited by Laura Deiulio and John B. Lyon

Vol. 28. *Kafka's Stereoscopes: The Political Function of a Literary Style*
by Isak Winkel Holm

Vol. 29. *Ambiguous Aggression in German Realism and Beyond: Flirtation, Passive Aggression, Domestic Violence*
by Barbara N. Nagel

Ambiguous Aggression in German Realism and Beyond

Flirtation, Passive Aggression, Domestic Violence

Barbara N. Nagel

BLOOMSBURY ACADEMIC
NEW YORK • LONDON • OXFORD • NEW DELHI • SYDNEY

BLOOMSBURY ACADEMIC
Bloomsbury Publishing Inc
1385 Broadway, New York, NY 10018, USA
50 Bedford Square, London, WC1B 3DP, UK
29 Earlsfort Terrace, Dublin 2, Ireland

BLOOMSBURY, BLOOMSBURY ACADEMIC and the Diana logo
are trademarks of Bloomsbury Publishing Plc

First published in the United States of America 2019
Paperback edition first published 2021

Copyright © Barbara N. Nagel, 2019

For legal purposes the Acknowledgments on p. x constitute
an extension of this copyright page.

Cover design by Andrea Federle-Bucsi
Cover image: Redembrace 2 by Jacques Lezra, 2018. By kind permission of the artist.

All rights reserved. No part of this publication may be reproduced or
transmitted in any form or by any means, electronic or mechanical,
including photocopying, recording, or any information storage or retrieval
system, without prior permission in writing from the publishers.

Bloomsbury Publishing Inc does not have any control over, or responsibility for,
any third-party websites referred to or in this book. All internet addresses given
in this book were correct at the time of going to press. The author and publisher
regret any inconvenience caused if addresses have changed or sites have
ceased to exist, but can accept no responsibility for any such changes.

Library of Congress Cataloging-in-Publication Data
Names: Nagel, Barbara Natalie, author.
Title: Ambiguous aggression in German realism and beyond: flirtation,
passive aggression, domestic violence / Barbara N. Nagel.
Other titles: German realism and beyond: Flirtation, passive aggression, domestic violence
Description: New York: Bloomsbury Academic / Bloomsbury Publishing Inc., 2019. |
Series: New directions in German studies ; Vol. 29 |
Includes bibliographical references and index.
Identifiers: LCCN 2019013190 | ISBN 9781501352713 (hardback) |
ISBN 9781501352737 (epdf)
Subjects: LCSH: German fiction–19th century–History and criticism. | German
fiction–20th century–History and criticism. | Ambiguity in literature. | Flirting in
literature. | Aggressiveness in literature. | Family violence in literature. |
Affect (Psychology) in literature. | Realism in literature. | Literature,
Modern–Themes, motives.
Classification: LCC PT771 .N34 2019 | DDC 833/.809353–dc23
LC record available at https://lccn.loc.gov/2019013190

ISBN: HB: 978-1-5013-5271-3
PB: 978-1-5013-8145-4
ePDF: 978-1-5013-5273-7
eBook: 978-1-5013-5272-0

Series: New Directions in German Studies
Typeset by Integra Software Services Pvt Ltd.

To find out more about our authors and books
visit www.bloomsbury.com and sign up for our newsletters.

For Daniel—nobody with whom I would rather think

Contents

Acknowledgments		x
Author's Note		xii
One	Introduction	1

Flirtation

Two	"Love Exploded on a Time Fuse": Flirtation and Critical Theory from Realism to #MeToo	19

Passive Aggression

Three	Twice-Read Love Letters: The Ambiguities of Epistolary Violence	43

Domestic Violence

Four	Home in Hiding: Scenes of Domestic Violence	71

Symphonic Aggression

Five	"What Murderously Peaceful People There Are": On Aggression in Robert Walser	103
Six	Conclusion	139
Bibliography		143
Index		153

Acknowledgments

Let me start by acknowledging how much joy it gave me to write this book—for the pleasures of writing are seldom the subject of acknowledgments. I have been fortunate to have been able to work on this project for seven years, while receiving a paycheck and benefits. I want to extend my gratitude to those who gave me a chance and a contract: Susanne Lüdemann, for whom I had the pleasure to work at the Ludwig-Maximilians-University in Munich, and the Department of German at Princeton—Brigid Doherty, Devin Fore, Mike Jennings, Joel Lande, Tom Levin, Inka Mülder-Bach, Adam Oberlin, Sally Poor, Jamie Rankin, the Graduate Students, Joseph Vogl, Johannes Wankhammer, Nikolaus Wegmann—not to forget Janine Calogero, Pat Heslin, Lynn Ratsep, Fiona Romaine, and Ed Sikorski. I greatly cherish the freedom, collegiality, and support in this department.

I would like to thank members of the intellectual communities at the LMU, the German departments at Princeton, Yale, Northwestern, Rutgers, and Columbia Universities, NYU in Berlin, the Department of Comparative Literature at the Free University, the Center for the History of Emotions in Berlin, and the graduate seminar "Affects of Realism" at Princeton for taking the time and mental energy to think through my project with me.

A stay at the American Academy in Berlin was instrumental in bringing the manuscript into its final form. One year later, I feel acute homesickness for this place, and dearly miss the congenial atmosphere created by Michael Steinberg and the people working at the American Academy. I could not have had a more productive and pleasurable time with the fellows and their partners and families, especially Amy Remensnyder and Linda Heuman, Drew Hicks and Kelli Carr, Carole Maso, Ran Ortner and Rebecca Roffey.

For intellectual support, invitations, cooperations, discussions, and feedback on chapters, thanks to: Anthony Adler, April Alliston, Lisa Andergassen, Michael Auer, Ian Balfour, Rüdiger Campe, Peter Coviello, Stanley Corngold, Ute Frevert, Florian Fuchs, Michael

Gamper, John Hamilton, Martin Harries, Nadine Hartmann, Maha El Hissy, Nancy Hoffman, Wolfgang Hottner, Katharina Ivanyi, Desmond Jagmohan, Regina Karl, Annette Keck, Mona Körte, Sabine Kranzow, Michael Levine, Paul North, Sarah Pourciau, Iris Roebling-Grau, Amy Rowland, Anette Schwarz, Teresa Shawcross, Mareike Stoll, Ulrike Vedder, Barbara Vinken, Arnd Wedemeyer, Mai Wegener, Henrik Wilberg, Jenny Willner, and Georg Witte.

It has been wonderfully energizing to find an editor like Imke Meyer who took on the manuscript with such verve and who found such good reviewers; I would like to extend my gratitude to Kirk Wetters as well as to Peter Rehberg for their insightful comments and for sacrificing their time. Spencer Hadley's exactitude and calm in assembling the bibliography and index is something to live up to. Jacques Lezra has helped me out more than once in life, this time by offering one of his incredible paintings for the cover of this book. For his continuous mentoring I feel happily indebted to Paul Fleming; heartfelt thanks too to Judith Kasper for having involved me in projects when it required a leap of faith; for her friendship and sustained engagement with my work I bow down to to Claudia Hein. Finally, we all write with an audience in our head—I owe it to Daniel, his enthusiasm and intellectual care, and his extraordinary editing, that I get to enjoy writing so much; for I can be certain that there will be someone who listens, laughs, and engages.

Author's Note

Citations from primary texts are provided in the original German and generally set in the footnotes. For the main text, I have consulted available English translations, which have been slightly modified when necessary.

> It is as though there were a hidden trap here to force ambiguity to reveal its own traps, and as though in surrendering unreservedly to ambiguity, literature were attempting to keep it—out of sight of the world and out of the thought of the world—in a place where it fulfils itself without endangering anything. Here ambiguity struggles with itself.
>
> Maurice Blanchot, "Literature and the Right to Death"

One Introduction

> "(it is impossible to say how many emotions there are; they are without number)"[1]
> *Longinus*

Our main words to describe emotional states suggest that we have clarity about them: "love," "hatred," "anxiety," "sorrow," etc. The reality, however, tends to be more complicated, as we are often faced with gestures and utterances that are more difficult to interpret and that might leave us wondering: "Was that just an insult?" "Was that a flirt?" Or, "was that aggression?" In these cases, the experience of well-defined emotion becomes—to the degree it is available at all—a phenomenon of belatedness. The central thesis of *Ambiguous Aggression* is that three interlocking, contested forms of social violence that are currently in circulation—flirtation, passive aggression, and domestic violence—first received voice and form in the nineteenth century. In order to understand this circulation, my book traces their literary-historical genealogy in German realism and beyond: German realist and late realist texts present an abundant archive for studying aggression in its full rhetorical complexity—troped aggression, aggression with a degree of self-reflexivity. By grasping these social forms of violence through their literary mediation I seek to develop an analytical vocabulary for them. Literature, in this regard, is both singular and exemplary: although not every moment of social violence is structured as exquisitely as a sentence from Fontane, the analysis of the literary form grants insight into the logic of the social form. My work thus engages with the new socio-political formalism by Caroline Levine or Anna Kornbluh,[2] though my work is distinctive in bringing this approach to bear on forms of violence in particular.

---

1 Longinus, "On Sublimity," in *Classical Literary Criticism*, ed. D. A. Russell and Michael Winterbottom (Oxford/New York: Oxford University Press, 1989 [1972]), 143–187, at 166–167.

2 Caroline Levine, *Forms: Whole, Rhythm, Hierarchy, Network* (Princeton, NJ: Princeton University Press, 2015); Anna Kornbluh, *The Order of Forms: Realism, Formalism, and Social Space* (Chicago, IL: University of Chicago Press, 2019).

2   Ambiguous Aggression

Realism's position within literary history is, according to Fredric Jameson, characterized by "affect" taking over the space previously inhabited by "named emotions."[3] Affects have the capacity to register "the sliding scale of the incremental, in which each infinitesimal moment differentiates itself from the last by a modification of tone and an increase or diminution of intensity."[4] Accepting the messiness of affect after Romanticism, this book is neither about emotionality as such, nor about emotionality as a result of "the birth of the subject" or of interiority; it is even less about the alleged waning of affect that would accompany "the end of the subject." Rather, what happens in realism is the literary opening up of everyday life, and its small, new codes of expression, which first allow ambivalent aggression to emerge. One of the goals of my book is to trace the literary-historical emergence of this new intricacy in realist and modernist writers of German language such as Annette von Droste-Hülshoff, Adalbert Stifter, Theodor Storm, Theodor Fontane, Gerhart Hauptmann, Robert Walser, and Franz Kafka, covering a historical period from the second half of the nineteenth century until the beginning of the twentieth. As this book explores small social forms of ordinary life it also listens to female voices, or better, to females who ever so slightly raise their voices—Emilie Fontane, Lisa Walser, Felice Bauer, Milena Jesenská—in order to be heard by their male, authorial companions.

The book is divided into three sections: "Flirtation," "Passive Aggression," and "Domestic Violence." The first part takes up flirtation and its associated terrors; the second part aims to give a historical and literary account of passive aggression; the third analyzes literary scenes of domestic violence. In the case of the first two ambiguous aggressions—flirtation and passive aggression—one might wonder about the *aggression* part of the equation, i.e., "what is so aggressive about a harmless flirt?" Or: "is passive aggression really so aggressive after all?" In the case of domestic violence, by contrast, it is the *ambiguity* that is in question: what does it mean or imply to call domestic violence "ambiguous"? Some readers might be scandalized by the suggestion that there is anything ambiguous about physical violence. Yet, this provocation strikes me as necessary in order to make palpable the perfidious effects of family violence—a sort of violence that hides itself behind virtuous concepts (love, justice, pedagogy) even as it is interrelated with other forms of structural violence (state violence, racial

---

3   Fredric Jameson, *The Antinomies of Realism* (London/New York: Verso, 2015 [2013]), 29.
4   Ibid., 42.

violence, heteronormativity). The long final analysis chapter on Robert Walser has the function of bringing together the reflections on flirtation, passive aggression, and domestic violence, meditating on their interdependence and their further development in the epoch of modernism.

Speaking of Walser, a word about the the period-designation in the title—*German Realism and Beyond*—is in order, and in particular a word about the "beyond." The preposition is meant in a temporal way, i.e., the "beyond" accounts for the historical unorthodoxy of reading realist authors alongside modernist ones like Walser and Kafka—not to mention modernist theorists like Georg Simmel, Ernst Bloch, Siegfried Kracauer, and Walter Benjamin. One can smooth out this temporal transgression by highlighting Walser's and Kafka's strong affinities to realism: Kafka famously modeled his own writing after Flaubert and Dickens (as well as after Fontane, but more about that later). Walser shared Kafka's admiration for Flaubert and held his compatriot, the realist Gottfried Keller, in high esteem;[5] Walser also claimed to write in a purely realist manner, insisting for instance that *The Assistant* (*Der Gehülfe*) was "a completely realist novel. I didn't need to invent anything. Life took care of that."[6] But even more interestingly, Walser aspired to "act like the sober realist"[7] even in his daily life, as he confided to his guardian Carl Seelig.

And yet, all of this only kicks the problem further down the field. To begin with, both "realism" and "modernism" are vague attempts at cutting time into pieces. If the notion of "modernism" arguably lacks the relative conceptual coherence of that of "realism,"[8] then German "realism" in turn appears to be quite idiosyncratic when viewed in the greater context of European realisms, most notably French realism (to some the realist Flaubert but definitely Baudelaire are already considered to constitute modernism); this is true in terms of the uncertainty

---

5 Carl Seelig notes that Walser was strikingly conversant in regard to Flaubert's characters: *Wanderungen mit Robert Walser* (Frankfurt/M.: Suhrkamp, 2017), 99.

6 Ibid., 60.

7 Ibid., 57 and 97.

8 One that was admittedly contested by Jakobson's "On Realism in Art," in *Language in Literature*, ed. Krystyna Pomorska and Stephen Rudy (Cambridge, MA: Havard University Press, 1997), 19–27. Jakobson mocks the way in which *every* new art movement claims greater "realism" for itself. Implicitly identifying the avant-garde with realism, Jakobson couldn't yet know that the avant-garde would become to serve as a defining feature of (post-)modernism: see Peter Bürger's *Theorie Der Avantgarde* (Frankfurt am Main: Suhrkamp, 1974) and Andreas Huyssen's *After the Great Divide: Modernism, Mass Culture, Postmodernism* (Bloomington: Indiana University Press, 1986).

of its time-span⁹ as well as the negligible role that phenomena such as industrialization or the city play in German realism in comparison to its European analogues, as Erich Auerbach criticized in his legendary take-down of German realism, from which its reputation never really recovered.¹⁰ Instead of rehashing this Western European-comparatist debate and developing another variation departing from the ever-same humanist premises, which would then result in the ever-same rankings of *"Which national realism wins the contest of being 'the most political?',"* the more recent scholarship on certain realist authors has changed the coordinates of the comparison by substituting time for space: it interrogates German realism in regard to its structural and aesthetic affinities to modernism.¹¹ One of the things that motivates a temporal comparison of this kind is an awareness that one period only becomes graspable through the next period, insofar as the act of drawing the boundary to the period means one is no longer *in* the period. This is to say that Walser and Kafka help us understand what realism is or was and that indeed at certain moments they are more realist than the realists. Only someone who takes realism naïvely as the promise of the real instead of an "effect of the real"¹² or as "double exposures"¹³ of repeatedly failing attempts to fix the real, will not register the continuities that exist between realism and, say, Kafka's looping scenes of interpretation or Walser's insistence on revisiting the same motives and constellations in the serial mode of his prose pieces.

Both Kafka and Walser reframe realism, showing once more the non-self-identity of realism that causes it to pop up at different places and times; hence, Devin Fore can write on *Realism after Modernism*¹⁴ or

---

9   One agrees that the beginning of German realism is marked by the failed revolution of 1848; however, the question of where it ends causes much debate; Andreas Huyssen concludes in *Bürgerlicher Realismus* (Stuttgart: Reclam, 1974), 9–24 that "it is impossible to find a satisfying solution for the epoch-problem" (9); see also Helmuth Widhammer, *Die Literaturtheorie des deutschen Realismus (1848–1860)* (Stuttgart: Metzler, 1977) and Todd Kontje, *A Companion to German Realism: 1848–1900* (Woodbridge: Boydell and Brewer, 2002).
10 Erich Auerbach, *Mimesis. Dargestellte Wirklichkeit in der abendländischen Literatur* (Bern: Francke, 1994 [1946]), 478–480.
11 Peter Uwe Hohendahl/Ulrike Vedder, "Zur Einleitung," in *Herausforderungen des Realismus. Theodor Fontanes Gesellschaftsromane*, ed. Ibid. (Freiburg i.Br.: Rombach, 2018), 7–22, at 10.
12 Roland Barthes, "The Reality Effect (1968)," in *The Rustle of Language*, trans. Richard Howard (Berkeley/Los Angeles: University of California Press, 1989), 141–148.
13 Eric Downing, *Double Exposures: Repetition and Realism in Nineteenth-Century German Fiction* (Stanford, CA: Stanford University Press, 2000).
14 Devin Fore, *Realism after Modernism: The Rehumanization of Art and Literature* (Cambridge, MA/London: MIT Press, 2015).

Jacques Rancière can recall that modernism's "inaugural moment has often been called *realism*, which does not in any way mean the valorization of resemblance but rather the destruction of the structures within which it functioned."[15] What we may take from all of this is that "the ordinary is a moving target" as Kathleen Stewart writes in *Ordinary Affects*, thus rephrasing the problem; she continues: "Not first something to make sense of, but a set of sensations that incite."[16] *Ambiguous Aggression in German Realism and Beyond: Flirtation, Passive Aggression, Domestic Violence* is after something that exceeds realism and spills over into the modernist era, namely a heightened skepticism about the readability of affect and an intensified effort to capture those new, confusingly ambivalent affective constellations. And this stupendous capacity for ambivalence with all that it entails—doubt, uncertainty, all its negativity—indeed distinguishes German realism from (relatively) melodramatic realism à la Zola or Dickens.[17] Just take this short but emotionally multi-faceted description of some village people's reaction to two young lovers in Keller's *A Village Romeo and Juliet* (1871):

> The spectator's amazement was a very peculiar mixture of pity with misery, of contempt for the debauchery and depravity of the parents and of envy towards the good fortune and unity of the couple.[18]

Likewise, in Theodor Storm's *Viola Tricolor* (1874), the author takes several lines just to give a detailed account of the gestures and competing negative emotions experienced by a young stepmother:

> Ines turned away and stepped to the window; she felt the tears welling up in her eyes. An inextricable mixture of bitter feelings burrowed its way through her breast; homesickness, self-pity, remorse for her lovelessness towards the child of the

---

15 Jacques Rancière, *The Politics of Aesthetics: The Distribution of the Sensible*, trans. Gabriel Rockhill (New York: Continuum, 2007 [2000]), 24.
16 Kathleen Stewart, *Ordinary Affects* (Durham, NC/London: Duke University Press, 2007), 93.
17 Needless to say, there exist exceptions—most notably perhaps, Jane Austen's prose of ambivalence; see Daniel M. Gross, "Mixed Feelings in Jane Austen's *Sense and Sensibility*," in *Uncomfortable Situations: Emotion Between Science and the Humanities* (Chicago, IL: Chicago University Press, 2017), 111–129.
18 Gottfried Keller, *Romeo und Julia auf dem Dorfe* (1871), *Die Leute von Seldwyla*, vol. 1 (= *Sämtliche Werke. Historisch-Kritische Ausgabe*, vol. 4, ed. Walter Morgenthaler) (Zürich: Stroemfeld, 2000), 74–159, at 144: "Die Verwunderung dieser Zuschauer war ganz seltsam gemischt aus Mitleid mit dem Unglück, aus Verachtung der Verkommenheit und Schlechtigkeit der Eltern und aus Neid gegen das Glück und die Einigkeit des Paares."

beloved man; she herself didn't know everything that now came over her ... [19]

What Keller calls "a very peculiar mixture" or what Storm, in even stronger terms, calls an "inextricable mixture" of affects, we could also conceptualize under the psychoanalytical notion of "ambivalence." Although both Keller and Storm still make reference to the old, romantic "named emotions," they present these in so many competing layers that it becomes impossible to draw a synthesis—which means we are dealing with something different from the early modern struggles between strong passions, as displayed in Petrarch or Shakespeare.

I therefore side with Brian Massumi, who highlights the importance of the category of affect (rather than that of emotion), without, however, according with his somewhat hyperbolic idea of an absolute "openness"[20] of affect. The reason for my hesitation in this regard is that what Massumi's Deleuzian evocation of "the escape of affect" or "the continuity of affective escape"[21] jettisons is the readability of affect. According to Massumi, affects can be perceived but not really analyzed. By comparison, my point is that with the nineteenth century affects become increasingly difficult to read, at least to decode—nevertheless, this does not mean that we could simply stop reading affects, contenting ourselves with "The Autonomy of Affect." Eugenie Brinkema programmatically postulates the reintroduction of close reading into affect studies: "Affect is not a place where something immediate and automatic and resistant takes place outside of language. The turning to affect in the humanities does not obliterate the problem of form and representation. Affect is not where reading is no longer needed."[22] Thus, my preference for the notion of "ambiguity" over that of "openness" is also to be understood as a nod to William Empson's *Seven Types of Ambiguity* and more generally to Empson's persistent attempt (however desperate it may seem at times) to distill a technical vocabulary that helps us to

---

19 Theodor Storm, *Viola Tricolor* (= *Sämtliche Werke: Novellen 1867–1880*, vol. 2, ed. Karl Ernst Laage) (Frankfurt/M.: Deutscher Klassiker Verlag, 1987), 131–163, at 143–144: "Ines wandte sich ab und trat an das Fenster; sie fühlte, wie ihr die Tränen aus den Augen quollen. Ein unentwirrbares Gemisch von bitteren Gefühlen wühlte in ihrer Brust; Heimweh, Mitleid mich sich selber, Reue über ihre Lieblosigkeit gegen das Kind des geliebten Mannes; sie wußte selber nicht was alles jetzt sie überkam."
20 Brian Massumi, "The Autonomy of Affect," *Cultural Critique* 31 (autumn 1995): 83–109, at 96.
21 Ibid., 97.
22 Eugenie Brinkema, *The Forms of the Affects* (Durham, NC/London: Duke University Press, 2014), xiv.

detect, describe, and ultimately enjoy literary ambiguity—even if the object of this ambiguity is aggression.

All this is actually very much in the sense of the time we are speaking about: the late nineteenth and twentieth century, an extended timespan when the fervor for introspection that arose in the eighteenth century gains its full momentum and is translated into the field of psychology; here, psychology finally emancipates itself from philosophy and, in the words of the historian Ute Frevert, "makes a powerful *entrée* into all sorts of domains: from industrial relations to commercial advertising, from individual therapy to political communication. In its wake, emotions gained attention and permeated public discourse as well as private conversations among lovers, friends, and family."[23]

As I have already begun nodding to various kindred projects, my earlier formulation of the "readability" of affect echoes Rüdiger Campe's phrase "the readability of man in his life,"[24] as well as of his seminal hypothesis that a transition took place in the seventeenth and eighteenth centuries from the old rhetorical doctrines of affect to a more individualized, hermeneutic approach to reading "expressions": "Up until far into the nineteenth century one hears people insistently talking of 'the expression of the moods', 'the language of passions' or 'the semiotics of affect.'"[25] *Ambiguous Aggression* picks up on how the literary history of emotions unfolds afterwards in realism and modernism. How did the lessening of the readability of emotions alter literary thinking about affects and their staging? If the early modern period is all about rhetoric and if romanticism is all about subjectivity and expression, then what happens after the demise of these paradigms? This book is based upon the assumption that realism distances itself from the romantic frenzy of "expressing emotions" by breaking, as Jameson noted, with the idea of "named emotions," and by turning to "affect" instead—thereby equally rebuking the idea of "expression," as Rei Terada has elucidated.[26] Whereas Romanticism strives for radical subjectivity, realism aspires towards objectivity. Now, the two paradigms that carry the burden of the realist aspiration are, as Lukács and

---

23 Ute Frevert, *Emotions in History—Lost and Found* (Budapest/New York: Central European University Press, 2011), 17.
24 Rüdiger Campe, *Affekt und Ausdruck. Zur Umwandlung der literarischen Rede im 17. und 18. Jahrhundert* (Tübingen: Niemeyer, 1990), x.
25 Ibid.
26 In her discussion of the category of affect in Spinoza via Deleuze, Rei Terada clarifies: "Affect is heuristically important because it faces both in and out, and therefore clinches the univocity of expression." *Feeling in Theory: Emotion after the "Death of the Subject"* (Cambridge, MA: Harvard University Press, 2003), 118–119.

Barthes each taught us in different ways, description and the detail.[27] Here rhetoric comes more to the fore again (and I am well aware that insisting with Barthes on *the rhetoric of realism*[28] presents no small provocation, at least to more conservative scholars of realism).[29] The shift from expression (back) to rhetoric becomes even more apparent in (post-)modernism where the technical or scientific approach to affect is further advanced by increasingly sophisticated forms of narrative perspective (point of view, focalization)—what Denise Riley calls "the gulf between the ostensible content of what's said, and the affect which seeps from the very form of words—in short, unexamined rhetoricity is at stake."[30] This obscure rhetoricity or technicity produces something like a psychology of the text. So, if realism undertakes the atomization of affect in the name of objectivity, then the modernist authors in turn present an interiorization of atomization, thus cutting against objectivity by radicalizing perspective.

---

27 The two most famous discussions of the role of the detail and the function of description for realism are those by Georg Lukács, "Erzählen oder beschreiben? Zur Diskussion über Realismus und Naturalismus (1936)," and Roland Barthes, "L'Effet de réel (1968)." Although one might think that for a "materialist" like Lukács the detail would be of paramount importance, he disappoints such a facile account of materialism, accusing the detail of a certain fetishism in "Erzählen oder beschreiben? Zur Diskussion über Realismus und Naturalismus (1936)," in *Begriffsbestimmung des literarischen Realismus*, ed. Richard Brinkmann (Darmstadt: Wissenschaftliche Buchgesellschaft, 1969), 33–85; following Lukács, the detail disrupts the narrative function, which again enables identification and thus the coming to (class-)consciousness. Although Barthes's "The Reality Effect" most likely was not influenced by Lukács, the text is from 1968 and marks Barthes's break with structuralism. As the world became more and more political, Barthes chooses to speak of a "reality effect" instead of a given "reality," and thus implicitly rejects any simple belief in "truth" or "reality" or the idea of an "objective" history (146).

28 According to Barthes, realism is subject to two constraints: first, the constraint of the aesthetic/rhetoric on description (every description has to end at some point); second, the constraint of the descriptive on the aesthetic/rhetoric: one has to motivate realism, one has to motivate description, which means that one cannot simply bring a list without context but has to ground the description in an activity of describing. This is what hypotyposis does—*the rhetoric of realism*, so to speak (145).

29 In *Die Literaturtheorie des deutschen Realismus (1848–1860)*, Helmuth Widhammer proclaimed an end of rhetoric in realism, subtitling this death certificate with the presumably "pragmatic communication-structure [of realist texts] that allows for the effortless decoding by the recipient" (vi, see also 3). Contrary to Widhammer's claim, my objective in this book is to show that it is not without making a considerable effort that one may surmise the complexities of realist affect.

30 Denise Riley sees the function of rhetoric in safeguarding us from overtly psychological readings: *Impersonal Passion: Language as Affect* (Durham, NC/London: Duke University Press, 2005), 2.

Introduction 9

I have already gestured towards the exceptional status of German realism by calling it "idiosyncratic" in comparison to other realisms. Really, at the time of its emergence, the new German realism referred to itself as "poetic" or "bourgeois realism"—an early indicator that it was a tamed version of realism, i.e., not the French realism of the working class but a realism by the bourgeoisie for the bourgeoisie. After the failed revolution of 1848, German politics resumed in the era of reaction in a decidedly anti-revolutionary manner, and the success of Bismarck's *Realpolitik* broke the liberal bourgeoisie's resistance for good. Which is to say, whoever is looking in German realism for radical responses to the challenges of (a belated) industrialization and modernization will be disappointed; but those who take an interest in carefully balanced, rhetorical negotiations of social violence will discover a rich corpus. In these realist texts, we can thus witness the questioning of old feudal forms, orders, and codes of social behavior that nonetheless remained mostly intact. Realist and late realist texts present an abundant archive for studying the complexity and rhetoricity of aggression: troped aggression, aggression with a degree of reflexivity. While in the scholarship these kinds of reflections on social aggression are usually undertaken in relation to spectacular events—e.g., the duel, adultery—my analysis focuses on the most mundane social forms for negotiating aggression. It picks up on what Friedrich Theodor Vischer, one of the most-read nineteenth-century German theorists of art, coined as the "frosting over of modes of interaction,"[31] or what one of Fontane's narrators described (and circumscribed) as "[n]o thunderstorms, just little words with the poison content of half a mosquito bite, or instead silence, muteness, sulking …. Those are the forms."[32] Similarly, the Austrian writer Adalbert Stifter—one of the most prolific representatives of German realism—famously stated that he was not interested in grandiose emotions but rather in the "gentle law" (*das sanfte Gese[t]z*) that guides human beings, forcing them to control and to moderate the expressions of their affects:

> A whole life full of justice, simplicity, efficacy, mastering oneself, reasonableness, effectiveness in one's circle, admiration of the

---

31 "[D]ie Erkältung der Umgangsformen," Friedrich Theodor Vischer, "Theorie des Romans," in *Theorie des bürgerlichen Realismus*, ed. Gerhard Plumpe (Ditzingen: Reclam, 2009), 240–247.
32 Theodor Fontane, *Frau Jenny Treibel, Short Novels and Other Writings*, ed. Peter Demetz, trans. Ulf Zimmermann (New York: Continuum, 1982), 237; in German: "'Kein Donnerwetter, nur kleine Worte mit dem Giftgehalt eines halben Mückenstichs, oder aber Schweigen, Stummheit, Muffeln …. Das sind so die Formen, *Frau Jenny Treibel oder „Wo sich Herz zum Herzen findt"* (= *Grosse Brandenburger Ausgabe*, vol. 14, ed. Tobias Witt) (Berlin: Aufbau-Verlag, 2005 [1892]), 139.

beautiful, combined with cheerful, tranquil effort, I consider great; mighty movements of temperament, frightful outbursts of anger, the lust for vengeance, the inflamed spirit that strives for activity, tears down, changes, destroys, and in its excitement often throws away its own life, I consider not greater, but smaller, for these things are as much products of individual and one-sided forces as storms, fire-spewing mountains, and earthquakes. We want to try to observe the gentle law that guides the human race.[33]

The imperative to moderation, at once poetic[34] and social, leads to the competition between dimmed-down emotions—a competition that itself is the precondition for intense emotional ambiguity.

On the methodological level, this book combines a historical approach with a formal one. My analysis proceeds genealogically (in Nietzsche's sense of the word) in that the literary examples highlight residues of aggressivity within the cultural history of sublimation and asks if sublimated aggression (still) is potential aggression. Thus, the study leans on major philosophical-theoretical reflections on the subject

---

33 Adalbert Stifter, "Preface to *Many-colored Stones*," trans. Jeffrey L. Sammons, *German Novellas of Realism*, vol. 1, ed. by Jeffrey L. Sammons (New York: Continuum, 1989), 1–6, at 3. "Ein ganzes Leben voll Gerechtigkeit Einfachheit Bezwingung seiner selbst Verstandesgemäßheit Wirksamkeit in seinem Kreise Bewunderung des Schönen verbunden mit einem heiteren gelassenen Sterben halte ich für groß: mächtige Bewegungen des Gemüthes furchtbar einherrollenden Zorn die Begier nach Rache den entzündeten Geist, der nach Thätigkeit strebt, umreißt, ändert, zerstört, und in der Erregung oft das eigene Leben hinwirft, halte ich nicht für größer, sondern für kleiner, da diese Dinge so gut nur Hervorbringungen einzelner und einseitiger Kräfte sind, wie Stürme feuerspeiende Berge Erdbeben. Wir wollen das sanfte Gesez zu erblicken suchen, wodurch das menschliche Geschlecht geleitet wird." "Vorrede (1852)," in *Bunte Steine*, ed. Helmut Bergner (= *Werke und Briefe. Historisch-kritische Gesamtausgabe*, vol. 2,2, ed. Alfred Doppler and Wolfgang Frühwald) (Stuttgart a.o.: Kohlhammer, 1982), 9–16, at 12.
34 In regard solely to the "poetic" component of German "poetic realism," Wolfgang Preisendanz employed the notion of "transfiguration" (*Verklärung*)—a term borrowed from Fontane. In a way, one can understand "transfiguration" as a precursor to Brecht's realist distancing effect [*Verfremdungseffekt*] because the idea is that German realism is "real" in making its own artfulness transparent. See Preisendanz' "Voraussetzungen des poetischen Realismus in der Erzählkunst des 19. Jahrhunderts," in *Formkräfte der deutschen Dichtung*, ed. Hans Steffen (Göttingen: Vandenhoeck & Ruprecht, 1963), 187–210, at 202: "Verklärung meint … eine Schreibweise, die den Unterschied zwischen dem vom Leben gestellten Bilde und dem dichterischen Gebilde nicht verwischt, sondern verbürgt."

of repressed aggression: Freud's *Civilization and Its Discontents*[35] presents the attempt to explain feelings of guilt as well as the institution of the super-ego as consequences of repressed aggression; Nietzsche conceptualizes resentment as caused by internalized aggression[36]—an idea that was formulated towards the end of the realist movement; and finally there is Hegel's critique, a generation earlier, of the passivity of "the beautiful soul."[37] Likewise, in the history of emotions, Norbert Elias's "'grand narrative' of incremental emotional control"[38] in the eighteenth and nineteenth centuries is still broadly accepted.

So why do we need literature? What literature accomplishes—that could not be accomplished otherwise—is that it presents scenes of crystallization that enable us to imagine how these otherwise abstract processes take place between strangers, lovers, or family members. "Dearest," writes Kafka in a letter to Felice Bauer, "but this I still have to tell you, you've read my Sunday letter only fleetingly, it's not possible otherwise, there was enough nasty stuff in the letter (I will explain it to you some time)."[39] The paradigmatic scenes of what I term "ambiguous aggression" show contradictory layers of affect and give cause for intense literary ambiguity—not, however, the pretty kind of ambiguity that has been the hobby-horse of scholars of literature since Empson and Jakobson, but a possibly perfidious kind of ambiguity.

This means, however, that we must turn the usual formalist argument about ambiguity on its head: in the readings that are collected in this book, ambiguity is not only an aesthetic virtue but also a conceptual one. Literary analysis, in turn, orients itself to intrinsically ambiguous phenomena, rather than viewing ambiguity as a defect to be remedied. Whereas scientific disciplines tend to work with preformatted concepts

---

35 Sigmund Freud, *Civilization and Its Discontents*, trans. James Strachey (New York/London: Norton, 1961 [1930]).
36 Friedrich Nietzsche, *On the Genealogy of Morals*, trans. Carol Diethe (Cambridge: Cambridge University Press, 2007 [1887]).
37 G. W. F. Hegel, *Phenomenology of Spirit*, trans. A. V. Miller (Oxford: Oxford University Press, 1977 [1807]), see "Conscience. The 'beautiful soul', evil and its forgiveness," VI. Spirit Cc, 399–400.
38 Norbert Elias, *The Civilizing Process: Sociogenetic and Psychogenetic Investigations*, trans. Edmund Jephcott (Oxford/Malden, MA: Blackwell, 1990 [1939]). The quote stems from Jan Plamper, *The History of Emotions: An Introduction* (Oxford: Oxford University Press, 2015), 68, see also 198.
39 Franz Kafka in a letter to Felice, February 17 to 18, 1913, *Briefe an Felice und andere Korrespondenz aus der Verlobungszeit*, ed. Erich Heller and Jürgen Born (Frankfurt/M.: Fischer, 1967), 303–305, at 304; in German: "Liebste, aber das muß ich Dir noch sagen, Du hast meinen Sonntagsbrief nur flüchtig gelesen, anders ist das nicht möglich, es war Widerliches in dem Brief genug (ich werde Dir das noch bei Gelegenheit erklären)."

that cannot accommodate phenomena that are themselves ambiguous, this limitation does not apply to literature, in which we can witness the emergence of ambiguity on the level of words and affects, and where the same ambiguity becomes an object of wonder, stupor, enjoyment, or terror like in Keller's *A Village Romeo and Juliet*, where both the event and aftermath of a father abusing his young daughter remain enigmatic on the epistemological level and ambivalent on the psychological: "and he slapped her in the face several times, without really knowing why, so that both children ran home in great sadness and crying, and neither did they really know why they were sad nor why they had been so merry before."[40]

Speaking of the epistemology of ambiguous aggression—what makes it so difficult, and thus fascinating, is its temporality of belatedness: for instance, whether there was a flirtation or not can only be answered belatedly with certainty, that is, after it has been consummated and thus in a sense negated. Or again, the beauty (yes, the beauty) of a passive aggressive statement is diminished once we have "decoded" the literal aggression it seems to hide. And finally, the decision to call something an act of "domestic violence," strictly speaking, throws the concept and ideal of family as such into crisis.

There are, admittedly, more common associations than realism when writing of German emotionality: *Sturm und Drang* (storm and stress) and its most famous novel *The Sorrows of Young Werther*, the age of *Empfindsamkeit* (or "sensibility"), Romanticism (and/or anti-Enlightenment thought) in the broad sense. But the second half of the nineteenth century and the beginning of the twentieth offer more untapped literary resources for thinking about emotionality and affect—the literary contemporaries of precisely Nietzsche and Freud, i.e., of those theorists who are still arguably the main influences for contemporary affect theory. In the last ten to fifteen years, a number of fascinating academic publications have come out in literary studies that engage in a critical manner with negative emotions and their historical (dys)functions in society: Sianne Ngai's *Ugly Feelings* (2005), Denise Riley's *Impersonal Passion: Language as Affect* (2005), Lauren Berlant's *The Female Complaint* (2008), followed by *Cruel Optimism* (2011), Jonathan Flatley's *Affective Mapping: Melancholia and the Politics of Modernism* (2008), Michael D. Snediker's *Queer Optimism* (2009), Elizabeth A. Povinelli's *Economies of Abandonment* (2011), Jörg Kreienbrock's *Malicious Objects, Anger Management, and the Question of Modern Literature* (2013), Eugenie Brinkema's *The Forms of the Affects* (2014), Claudia Rankine's *Citizen: An American Lyric*

---

40 Keller, *Romeo und Julia auf dem Dorfe*, 87.

(2015), and Anna Parkinson's *An Emotional State* (2015).[41] All of these books are situated at the intersection between literary studies, aesthetics, media and cultural studies, psychoanalysis, and queer and feminist theory. And all of them are testimonies to an effort still very much alive in the Anglo-American twenty-first century to capture destructive reality affect-effects.

In the echo-chambers of our everyday encounters negative affects call with special urgency for a reality principle: "Ordinary affects," Kathleen Stewart writes, "can be experienced as a pleasure and a shock, as an empty pause or a dragging undertow, as a sensibility that snaps into place or a profound disorientation. They can be funny perturbing, or traumatic."[42] Elizabeth A. Povinelli frames it as our ethical task to inquire into these ordinary, negative affects and to make them the object of study—"forms of suffering and dying, enduring and experiencing, that are ordinary, chronic, and cruddy rather than catastrophic, crisis-laden, and sublime."[43] Similarly, Claudia Rankine stages what she calls "microaggressions" as "the surprise of the intimate, or the surprise of the ordinary. So you're just moving along and suddenly you get this moment that breaks your ability to continue, and yet you continue."[44] Rankine's concept of "microaggressions," just like Povinelli's "quasi-events,"[45] breaks with idealist aesthetics and its hierarchizing of what is important or unimportant.

And this is what makes them "realist": novelistic realism is, in the words of Rancière, "first of all the reversal of the hierarchies of representation (the primacy of the narrative over the descriptive or the hierarchy of subject matter)."[46] "It's not catastrophes, murders, deaths, diseases, that age and kill us; it's the way people look and laugh, and run up the steps of omnibuses,"[47] writes Virginia Woolf, another hyper-realist modernist, in *Jacob's Room* (1922). It is these kinds of affective quasi-events

---

41 Anna M. Parkinson's *An Emotional State: The Politics of Emotion in Postwar West German Culture* (Ann Arbor, MI: University of Michigan Press, 2015) is in special proximity to my project insofar as it discusses "the complex coexistence of multiple emotive regimes and overlapping affective communities" in postwar West Germany by revisiting the concept of *ressentiment* (167).
42 Stewart, *Ordinary Affects*, 2.
43 Elizabeth A. Povinelli, "The Child in the Broom Closet," in *Economies of Abandonment: Social Belonging and Endurance in Late Liberalism* (Durham, NC/London: Duke University Press, 2011), 13.
44 Although Rankine's focus lies on latent *racial* aggression, i.e., on structural violence, her notion of "microaggressions" can help us to conceptualize other "surprise[s] of the intimate" in which aggression can only be acknowledged in the form of a belated representation, if at all. https://www.guernicamag.com/interviews/blackness-as-the-second-person/.
45 Povinelli, "The Child in the Broom Closet," 13.
46 Rancière, *The Politics of Aesthetics*, 24.
47 Virginia Woolf, *Jacob's Room* (Brooklyn, NY: Melville House, 2011 [1922]), 95.

that prompt us to write and read obsessively for little details—"the sideways gaze, the held breath, the mumbled phrase, or the strange piece of paper," as Berlant lists.[48] Where feelings have to be repressed because they are not noble or because they are socially impermissible (as in the case of female aggression[49]) the hidden detail multiplies and eventually becomes paramount. Strangely, in spite of its current ubiquity, the detail is often overlooked: "The turn to affect has corresponded with a disciplinary turn away from detail"[50] is how Eugenie Brinkema assesses the situation in the humanities. Which is to say that as readers we have to actively resist a naïve conception of "affect" as "the real" and instead (again) become critical realists who read closely for details. Even more so because the detail not only presents a primary feature of realism but also links realism to the feminine, a connection that prompted Naomi Schor to raise the hesitantly optimistic question: "Does the triumph of the detail dignify a triumph of the feminine with which it has so long been linked?"[51] This, at least, would explain why the scholarship in this field is almost exclusively authored by women-theorists. Where we talk about the ordinary, we invite the detail; where we invite the detail we invite the feminine, which has otherwise been excluded from the realm of literature for the longest time.

It is disciplinarily a bold move, for sure, to read German realism through twenty-first century US-American affect theory and to bring one archive to bear on another one in this manner, especially if the connectedness of these archives—which are separated by space and time—has not been perceived before. And yet, it is inscribed in the texts themselves. Take for instance Denise Riley's *Impersonal Passion: Language as Affect*—her list of theories of language, which pay the closest attention to affect, consists to a surprising degree of German-language writers: Kleist, Nietzsche, Marx, Freud, Heidegger, Benjamin, Adorno, and Wittgenstein. Just as Berlant writes in a certain spirit of critical theory, Sianne Ngai's *Ugly Feelings*—a book driven by an interest in "explicitly *a*moral and *non*cathartic"[52] feelings—starts with Adorno,

---

48 Lauren Berlant, *The Female Complaint: The Unfinished Business of Sentimentality in American Culture* (Durham, NC/London: Duke University Press, 2008), 15.
49 Frevert, *Emotions in History—Lost and Found*, 96: "A dominant way for women to express anger is, as present-day psychologists observe, to shed tears. Tears here stand for desperation, grief, and sadness, i.e. for emotions described as passive, self-referential and asthenic. They thus perfectly fit the nineteenth-century notion of women as weak, powerless human beings."
50 Brinkema, *The Forms of the Affects*, xvi.
51 Naomi Schor, *Reading in Detail: Aesthetics and the Feminine* (New York/London: Methuen, 1987), 6.
52 Sianne Ngai, *Ugly Feelings* (Cambridge, MA/London: Harvard University Press, 2005), 6.

continues with Freud, and is informed throughout by Nietzsche's concept of *ressentiment*. And this is not where the examples stop. But even though this tradition of theorizing about the emotions is largely German (with Nietzsche, psychoanalysis and critical theory), the linguistic underpinnings of these theories written in German and the literature that flourished alongside this body of theory has been neglected in critical affect theory. In fact, the literature in whose context these theories emerged—realism and early modernism—still remains something like "the un-thought" of affect theory.

Therefore, the decision to write a book on *Ambiguous Aggression* is also a decision for a narrower and less presentist historical focus, for a smaller corpus of texts, and for more focused attention to literary language. Together, these aspects bring something else to the discussion: a historically nuanced, formalist argument about German affects. The German tradition can help us think about these affects as such. Robert Walser, for instance, should be of as much general theoretical interest as Freud or Nietzsche, provided one learns how to read a statement like the following: "The rude ones are often also the most subtle. ... The subtle ones coat their rudeness with a layer of subtlety."[53]

The premise of the first chapter is that in critical theory, in an ambivalent continuation of Georg Simmel's reflections on *Koketterie*, we find a theory of flirtation: flirtation affords an experience of free play, not unlike the Kantian concept of aesthetic pleasure; at the same time, flirtation is described by Benjamin and Bloch as a war-like experience, albeit one that is the source of a particular terror (if not sublimity), in that women are in possession of the ammunition. With Simmel, one could suspect that the underlying cause of this terror in heterosexual scenes of flirtation is a "queer" inversion of gender-roles. Thus Simmel marvels: "In saying no and saying yes, in surrendering and refusing to surrender themselves, women are the masters." In a second step, I trace the literary-historical emergence of this constellation in realist German language writers, presenting three pairings between (proto-) critical theory and German realism—Simmel-Storm, Benjamin-Keller, Bloch-Fontane—in order to illuminate three aspects of the "terror" of flirtation.

Looking at flirtation from this angle makes it at times not seem entirely different from passive aggression. The object of inquiry for the chapter on passive aggression is therefore a series of letters, more

---

53 Robert Walser, *Der Räuber, Sämtliche Werke in Einzelausgaben*, ed. Jochen Greven, vol. 12 (Zurich/ Frankfurt/M.: Suhrkamp, 1986), 97; in German: "Die Gröbsten sind oft auch gerade die Feinsten. ... Die Feinen umhüllen ihre Grobheiten mit einer Schicht von Feinheit."

specifically Fontane and Kafka's respective love letters, in which Fontane becomes Kafka's epistolary alter ego. The seemingly trifling love correspondence turns into a battleground, characterized by a violence that is all the more insidious for its latency and belatedness. Emilie Fontane's letters, for instance, are treated as treacherous when they indulge in poetic ambiguity so that her husband admonishes her: "educated people express themselves in a way that their words cannot be misunderstood."[54] The battle between the lover or wife and the male author is therefore fought around the question of whether the literary belongs exclusively to the male author or to his love-interest as well, and whether it is to be associated with clear signification or with ambiguity.

"Home in Hiding" examines scenes of domestic violence from half a century of German prose. It aims to demonstrate how the domestic sphere (the space of the family) may work as a powerful force of ambiguity. I focus on one particular—and particularly enigmatic—mode of making violence appear ambiguous: the poetics of energy, which serves to displace subjective agency in favor of netlike structures and impersonal flows. I thus examine five short scenes of domestic violence—one each from Droste-Hülshoff, Stifter, Keller, Storm, Hauptmann, and Robert Walser—that frame domestic violence as a phenomenon of energetics. We are confronted with abstract patterns, with movements of beauty and terror, and of formation and deformation. The outcome of this interplay of rhetoric, syntax, and the reiterative imagery of beating is a decentralization of violence: a poetics of unaccountability.

While opening upon the afterlife of ambiguous aggression in modernism, the concluding analysis is a plea for an anti-idealistic reading of Robert Walser, an author commonly lauded for his alleged politeness, pacifism, and innocence. The essay in intimate dialogue with Walser's texts outlines the intensification and ultimate (self-)deconstruction of ambiguous aggression. Starting with an early letter from Walser to his sister Lisa and ending with passages from the posthumously published novel *The Robber*, I examine scenes in which a narrative voice gives instructions as to how to cope with aggressive affects. By the end of this chapter we have traversed a wide range of ambiguous aggression: starting off with an ambiguous plea for cursing, it discusses teasing, sublimation, dissimulation, and resentment, and closes the tour of ambiguous aggression with ambivalence. In Walser's œuvre, a general tendency of this endeavor becomes apparent: the three ambiguous

---

54 Theodor Fontane in a letter to Emilie Fontane, Berlin, August 15, 1876, *Der Ehebriefwechsel*, vol. 3: *Die Zuneigung ist etwas Rätselvolles. 1873–1898* (= Grosse Brandenburger Ausgabe, ed. Gotthard and Therese Erler) (Berlin: Aufbau-Verlag, 1998), 69–71.

aggressions constantly overlap and merge with one another; that means, ambiguity is no longer an occasional element of the text but is instead its essential characteristic.

The conclusion reflects on the relation of realist and modernist ambiguous aggressions to more spectacular forms of violence in German history, namely to National Socialism and the Shoah.

FLIRTATION

Two "Love Exploded on a Time Fuse": Flirtation and Critical Theory from Realism to #MeToo

"Ebba was a rocket"[1]—*Fontane*

Does anyone still flirt? This question makes a certain sense, given that apps such as Tinder and Grindr seem to have rendered flirtation superfluous, minimizing unexpected encounters. Thus says a student in a seminar devoted to the topic: "The only time that there might be something like flirtation is after you have hung out, and, well, then you decide whether you are going to see each other again." At the current moment, however, the question "do people still flirt?" is, of course, posed in view not of media-revolution but instead in respect to the power-relations that shape our society. In this light, the question sometimes takes on a speculative and even reproachful or self-pitying quality: "What ever happened to flirting?" Daphne Merkin asks in the *New York Times*, "what happened to women's agency?"[2] Then there is the infamous, ostensible defense of flirtation by French women declaring in *Le Monde* that "insistent or clumsy flirting is not a crime"[3]—a statement

---

1 "Ebba war eine Rakete," Theodor Fontane, *Unwiederbringlich* (= *Grosse Brandenburger Ausgabe*, vol. 13, ed. Christine Hehle) (Berlin: Aufbau-Verlag, 2003 [1892]), 159.
2 Daphne Merkin, "Publicly, We Say #MeToo. Privately, We Have Misgivings," *New York Times*, January 5, 2018, https://www.nytimes.com/2018/01/05/opinion/golden-globes-metoo.html (last retrieved on March 2, 2018).
3 "[L]a drague insistante ou maladroite n'est pas un délit," "Nous défendons une liberté d'importuner, indispensable à la liberté sexuelle," *Le Monde*, January 9, 2018, http://www.lemonde.fr/idees/article/2018/01/09/nous-defendons-une-liberte-d-importuner-indispensable-a-la-liberte-sexuelle_5239134_3282.html#b8PiSC1htUVLXFVG.99 (last retrieved March 1, 2018).

made as a reaction to ever more revelations by the #MeToo movement of sexual exploitation and abuse of power. The one who asks "can we still flirt?" has both understood and misunderstood the essence of flirtation. They have grasped that there is a necessary relation between flirtation and transgression, insofar as flirtation always flirts with the forbidden even as it does not cross the line. So the question itself, "can we still flirt?" I argue (against others) is not trivial because it is not evident where flirtation ends and harassment starts. Even the feminist historian Linda Gordon concedes that "the line between flirtation and harassment is not always obvious, and will vary for different people and in different circumstances" but quickly tries to disambiguate the situation: "Clearly, however, the thousands of complaints we are hearing today are not ambiguous."[4] The logical redundancy—"clearly … not ambiguous"—betokens a certain panic or anxiety. *Clearly*, ambiguity is frightening because it is messy. In this spirit, the notoriously provocative Laura Kipnis asked: "But how do you know an advance is 'unwanted' until you *try*?" And yet, even Kipnis, who likes to promote herself as a radical libertine, tries to formulate clear laws as to where flirtation ends: "Our bodies are zoned: there are public areas and private ones; parts you can touch without permission, such as my hand, and parts you're trespassing if you encroach on them without my permission."[5] While Kipnis' zoning makes a certain sense, it conflicts, for instance, with guidelines of sexual harassment training where, indeed, even the hand or the shoulder are listed among the forbidden zones. There is no flirtation without a risk-factor, but if we have to reckon with the loss of our job or social death then one will soon lose the fun in the game.

Now, the word "game" must not be misunderstood as if there were nothing to lose. Here I come to the common misconception of flirtation. What people who ask "can't we even flirt anymore?" have not yet understood is that flirtation is not where you take a break from more serious business; flirtation is not the more innocuous alternative to forcing someone to have sex with you. Do you really think anyone who is after abusing their power will try flirtation instead? Those who impose themselves aggressively upon the Other generally have a terror of flirtation. This is because the real risk in flirtation is not so much to accidentally harass somebody but in fact to crumble under the force of

---

4   Linda Gordon, "The Politics of Sexual Harassment (With a New Introduction)," in *Where Freedom Starts: Sex, Power, Violence, #MeToo* (New York: Verso, 2018), 102–126, at 104.
5   Laura Kipnis, "Has #MeToo Gone Too Far, Or Not Far Enough? The Answer Is Both," *The Guardian*, January 13, 2018, https://www.theguardian.com/commentisfree/2018/jan/13/has-me-too-catherine-deneuve-laura-kipnis (last retrieved on March 1, 2018).

the equalization that flirtation brings about—the real challenge consists in being able to endure the (precarious, volatile) balance of terror. When we flirt we trouble hierarchies, which again explains why anarchists may feel compelled to flirt in very hierarchical spaces. What those who pronounce shallow necrologies for flirtation miss is that flirtation has, according to its theory and practice, a far more radical effect than even the #MeToo movement could dream of: first, flirtation upsets gender dichotomies, which right now return through the back door in discussions around #MeToo that pitch "women" against "men," "brushing aside, as it were, a variegated vocabulary in common use for decades now: queer, trans, neutral, intersexed, intersectional, and so on."[6]

Second, flirtation is not just *not* harassment but rather its opposite because of the way it relates to power. The #MeToo debate is deepening in reflecting about the relation between sexuality and power. But reflection about the capitalist basis of these power structures is still scarce. In comparison, the discourse of flirtation makes us aware that even the way we relate to others is shaped by capitalist reasoning: hence, when we flirt, certain questions by which we normally live are out of place, like "Where is this going? What am I getting out of this? Am I wasting my time?" This is also why critical theorists have shown such an interest in the topic of flirtation—so much so that flirtation is theorized, for the first time ever, in the spirit of utopia. For Walter Benjamin and Ernst Bloch, to flirt means, in the best sense, nothing less than to call it off with capitalism and to encounter the Other in a way that is not directed at consumption; flirtation is about potentiality rather than actuality or actualization.

*

Let me begin now without any further ado and without any concealment—which is to say, in a decidedly unflirtatious manner—by introducing two literary-historical hypotheses on the history of flirtation. The first hypothesis is that for German literature and philosophy, the beginning of the twentieth century marks the highpoint in the theorization of flirtation. This climax is due first of all to critical theorists' interest in everyday life, in mass culture and the city, in encounters between strangers, and those rare moments, which resist commodification and the teleology aspired to by the discourse of seduction. Flirtation's radical openness allows for a mode of experience akin to Kant's famous aesthetic formula of "purposiveness without purpose,"[7] alluded to by

---

6 Emily Apter mourned this fact already in 2012, in the context of the Strauss-Kahn-case: "Transatlantic Feminism Post–DSK Affair," *Public Books*, November 13, 2012, http://www.publicbooks.org/transatlantic-feminismpost-dsk-affair/ (last retrieved March 13, 2018).

7 Georg Simmel, "Flirtation," in *On Women, Sexuality, and Love*, ed. and trans. Guy Oakes (New Haven, CN/London: Yale University Press, 1984), 133–152, at 144.

Georg Simmel—the famous precursor and antagonist *avant la lettre* of critical theory—and his seminal essay on "Flirtation" from 1909.[8]

The second hypothesis relativizes the first to a certain degree: Simmel's condensed theory of flirtation, and Bloch and Benjamin's thought-images on flirtation are the theoretical reverberations of an earlier, more intensely literary exploration of flirtation, which occurred in German realism. In this first chapter, I will trace the literary-historical emergence of flirtation in three constellations between critical theory and German realism: between Simmel and Storm, Benjamin and Keller, and Bloch and Fontane.

There is, finally, a third hypothesis lurking flirtatiously in these three constellations—namely, that flirtation appears in all of these texts, authored by men, as an ambiguous form of female aggression, if not an experience of terror.[9] Thus, Freud likens the man who has to decode a flirtation to a detective reading a crime scene.[10] This perception of flirtation is not limited to Germanic writers, as Richard A. Kaye made a similar observation for Victorian and Edwardian fiction:

> By the end of the nineteenth century, ... novelists increasingly represent the female flirt as a social menace, her strategies not only perniciously insincere, a threat to customary methods of unraveling identity, but unnatural as well. The coquette looms large as an individual whose connotations of danger—and admixture of theatricality and power—coupled with her status as a connoisseur of male beauty, shape her as an insurgent who wreaks havoc with nature's courtship plot and its aim of species procreation.[11]

What I would like to show in the following is that in German letters this terror is linked to a queer role-switch, with woman imagined as being in control of erotic potentiality. And although to some male characters (as well as, most likely, to many male authors) these role-switches can be quite unsettling, even aggressive, the realist texts make clear that they may also be erotically intriguing.

---

8 See also "'Almost Nothing; Almost Everything': An Introduction to the Discourse of Flirtation," in *Flirtations: Rhetoric and Aesthetics This Side of Seduction*, ed. Nagel, Barbara Natalie, Daniel Hoffman-Schwartz, and Lauren Shizuko Stone (New York: Fordham University Press, 2015), 1–12.
9 See my interlude "Three Terrors of Flirtation" in the aforementioned anthology *Flirtations*, 101–105.
10 Sigmund Freud, "Die Fehlleistungen," in *Vorlesungen zur Einführung in die Psychoanalyse* (= *Studienfassung*, vol. 1, ed. Alexander Mitscherlich) (Frankfurt/M.: Fischer, 2000), 41–98, at 51–52.
11 Richard A. Kaye, *The Flirt's Tragedy: Desire without End in Victorian and Edwardian Fiction* (Charlottesville VA: University of Virginia Press, 2002), 151.

Simmel and Storm: Coquettish Sovereigns

We started by challenging the belief that flirtation is something like *harassment light*, i.e., the safer alternative to sexual harassment. We objected that there is nothing *light* about flirtation because flirtation comes with its own risks, which might feel light to some but not to those infatuated with male domination. Thus, in his seminal essay "On Flirtation" ("Die Koketterie," 1909) the German sociologist Georg Simmel warns: "In saying no and saying yes, in surrendering and refusing to surrender themselves, women are the masters."[12] Simmel's object of study is European women at the beginning of the twentieth century, who in flirtation experience a rare "fascination with freedom and power," i.e., a fascination, of which they are normally deprived. According to Simmel, this female empowerment is the result of a role-switch occurring in heterosexually structured scenes of flirtation; though Simmel does not put it this way, there is something queer about the switching of gender roles that he outlines:[13] the woman "takes on his [the man's] decision, even if only in a symbolic and approximate fashion." For the woman of the time, this kind of power and freedom are rare:

> The power of the woman in relation to the man is exhibited in consent *or* refusal. It is precisely this antithesis—in which the conduct of the flirt alternates—that grounds the feeling of freedom, the independence of the self from the one as well as the other, the autonomous existence that lies beyond the dominated oppositions. ... And at least in a number of cases, it can be observed that women who are very domineering are also very flirtatious.[14]

---

12 Simmel, "Flirtation," 140. In the German original: "Im Neinsagen und im Jasagen, im Sich-hingeben und Sich-versagen sind die Frauen die Meister." Georg Simmel, "Die Koketterie," in *Philosophische Kultur. Über das Abenteuer, die Geschlechter und die Krise der Moderen. Gesammelte Essais* (Berlin: Klaus Wagenbach, 1983 [1929]), 81–98, at 88.

13 Simmel does not explicitly engage with the queer potential in flirtation but instead describes how, because we are not used to male flirtation, the latter might evoke the feeling of "disgust ...; a monstrosity, a human being with six fingers will be disgusting to most people, for all the money in the world they would not eat the meat of certain animals, that in itself have nothing disgusting about them but who we are not used to eating, etc." Georg Simmel, "Zur Psychologie der Frauen (1890)," in *Schriften zur Philosophie und Soziologie der Geschlechter*, ed. Heinz-Jürgen Dahme and Klaus Christian Köhnke (Frankfurt/M.: Suhrkamp, 1985), 27–59, at 57–58.

14 Simmel, "Flirtation," 141; Simmel, "Die Koketterie," 88–89: "Die Macht der Frau dem Manne gegenüber offenbart sich ja an dem Ja oder Nein, und eben diese Antithese, in der das Verhalten der Kokette schwingt, begründet das Freiheitsgefühl, die Nichtgebundenheit des Ich durch das eine wie das andere, das Fürsichsein jenseits der beherrschten Gegensätze. ... Und mindestens in einer Anzahl von Fällen hat sich beobachten lassen, daß sehr herrschsüchtige Frauen auch sehr kokett sind."

24   Ambiguous Aggression

From words such as "power" and "domineering" we can infer that Simmel's view of the increased "feeling of freedom" that women enjoy in flirtation is not without reservation; women's alleged libidinal liberation is perceived as a threat to established power relations. However, this destabilization comes with a certain thrill, and "On Flirtation" concentrates on the frisson emanating from these new, delicate power constellations. An essay authored by Simmel almost twenty years earlier, entitled "On the Psychology of Women" ("Zur Psychologie der Frauen"[15]), regards flirtation with far greater concern: although this essay only turns to the topic of *Koketterie* in its final pages, Simmel's voice exudes male hysteria (if by "hysteria" we understand a certain garrulousness). Similar to the discourses of irony or mimesis, that of flirtation too persists in its absence; there is in fact no opposition to flirtation, no outside of it—or, in Simmel's words, "there are women who even flirt with their flirtatiousness, just like there are others who flirt with their non-flirtatiousness."[16] In conclusion, women are simultaneously over-sexualized (women are always flirting—especially when they are not) *and* deprived of any erotic agency. This is because Simmel assumes a lack of sexual self-consciousness in women, even in militant flirts:

> By far in most cases even the most flirtatious women have no thought whatsoever as to a sexual unity with the man, with whom they are flirting; this is so utterly far from their thoughts that if one would make an imposition of this kind to them, based on this type of behavior, they would reject it with outrage and in the consciousness that their flirtatiousness in no way was supposed to contain any concession in this direction.[17]

"Relax, brothers!" Simmel seems to cry out to his fellow males, "I know I wrote a moment ago that the female flirt 'holds power over the man'[18] but really she has no clue what to do with it!" This, again, puts men in a strategically advantageous position:

---

15   Simmel, "Zur Psychologie der Frauen," 27–59.
16   Ibid., 57: "[E]s gibt Frauen, die sogar mit ihrer Koketterie kokettieren, wie es solche gibt, die es mir ihrer Nicht-Koketterie tun."
17   Ibid., 53: "[S]o liegt in den weitaus meisten Fällen auch den kokettesten Frauen der Gedanke einer sexuellen Gemeinschaft mit dem Mann, dem gegenüber sie kokettieren, völlig fern und sie würden eine auf ihr derartiges Benehmen sich stützende Zumutung mit Entrüstung und dem Bewußtsein zurückweisen, daß ihre Koketterie durchaus kein Entgegenkommen nach dieser Richtung hin enthalten sollte."
18   Ibid., 55.

Knowing that the flirtatious woman is not serious gives us a certain security, with the consequence that for the most part we abandon ourselves more to her allure than if we knew that the path, once we have begun on it, would now also lead to its endpoint; then again, it is precisely the enticement to triumph over the flirt's inner cool, to take away all obstacles to which she leads us in order then to let her rise all the higher in front of us, to turn the semi-concession into a whole through the impression of one's own personality—one of her most powerful weapons and, what's more, a terrible danger for vain natures.[19]

According to Simmel, the female flirt never knows where she is going with her flirtation, which is why man has to be careful not to go there—not out of consideration for the woman but because men are in "terrible danger" of being seduced into doing something that the woman does not actually want or does not know that she wants, that is: "to turn the semi-concession into a whole through the impression of one's own personality—one of her most powerful weapons." Like in Kleist's *The Marquise of O ...*, the dash marks the event of coitus by way of a sublime caesura, even as it at the same time resembles obscene bathroom graffiti (with the caveat that in Simmel's sketch the penetrating dash belongs to the female flirt, a kind of typographic strap-on). But this typo-graffiti only obscures the real problem: Simmel's initial definition of women as "lacking in differentiation"[20] (in more positive terms: "the unity and totality in the essence of women"[21]) is now creeping up on his own theory insofar as the underlying question of whether a subject that has no agency, i.e., a woman, can will anything at all brings up the serious problem of consent. As far as Simmel is concerned, consent is not a problem for women (who might be raped, after all) but for men who are in danger of getting confused enough to end up having sex with a person lacking in will and then having to deal with the messy consequences.

---

19 Simmel, "Zur Psychologie der Frauen (1890)," 55: "Daß wir wissen, es ist der Kokette nicht Ernst, gibt uns ihr gegenüber eine gewisse Sicherheit, infolge deren wir uns ihrem Reiz weitergehend überlassen, als wo wir wüßten, daß der einmal begonnene Weg nun auch zum Endpunkt führt; andererseits ist gerade der Anreiz, über die innere Kühle der Kokette zu triumphieren, die Hindernisse zu nehmen, an die sie uns nur heranführt, um sie dann um so höher vor uns aufsteigen zu lassen, das halbe Entgegenkommen durch den Eindruck der eigenen Persönlichkeit in ein ganzes zu verwandeln—eine ihrer mächtigsten Waffen und namentlich für eitle Naturen eine furchtbare Gefahr."
20 Simmel, "Zur Psychologie der Frauen (1890)," 29; in German: "Mangel an Differenziertheit" or also "Undifferenziertheit" (33).
21 Ibid.; in German: "Die Einheitlichkeit und Ganzheit im Wesen der Frauen," 44.

What do we do with this twisted and convoluted misogynist argument? It is as if the non-mastery characterizing flirtation as such inverts or upsets Simmel's own argument; that is, as if the basic irrationality and lack of consciousness that Simmel imputes on woman ricochets back upon himself.[22] In effect, Simmel becomes the male victim of flirtation, a symptomatic hysterical voice. Interestingly, Simon Morgan Wortham describes flirtation as a form of hysteria that is contagious because it invites mimesis by others, in this case by the theorist of flirtation himself:

> The flirt ... courts the 'other' neither through conflict nor identification alone, but through a sort of mutation of hysterical behaviour. The flirt sets his or her mark, so to speak, on the other's desire; but that mark itself shudders with the frisson of destinerrance reverberating through the possibility of (postal) return. We flirt not just in uncertainty of others, but through uncertainty of ourselves.[23]

With this, we have come from coquettish sovereigns to male hysterics, and thus have gotten a first taste of the queerness that makes flirtation so terrifying from the standpoint of the patriarchy. But why would the male ego be more likely to crumble? Like Kaja Silverman, one could speculate that "the normative male ego" is too fortified to gracefully engage in flirtation because of its "ideological alignment with mastery," which makes masculinity "particularly vulnerable to the unbinding effects of the death drive."[24]

As compelling as these theoretical reflections are they do not address the representational problem, which is that of imagining the female flirt's constant oscillation between active and passive positions, as described by Simmel. How can woman be imagined as threateningly powerful *and* powerless at the same time, flirtatious and not flirtatious, inciting sex and being oblivious to it? Within German literature one hardly finds a better poetic answer to this question than in the writings of the northern realist Theodor Storm. This is because the role switches

---

22 "Simmel was a man of the previous fin-de-siècle, and there is much that calls for critique or outright rejection—notably, his views on gender and his attitude toward racial others. What is ultimately at stake in returning to him is the relationship between our thinking and that particular past: a historical and theoretical genealogical relationship that calls for reflection." Elizabeth S. Goodstein, *Georg Simmel and the Disciplinary Imaginary* (Stanford, CA: Stanford University Press, 2017), 235.
23 Simon Morgan Wortham, "*Flirtations: Rhetoric and Aesthetics This Side of Seduction* (review)," *Oxford Literary Review* 39, no. 1 (June, 2017): 141–145, at 144.
24 Kaja Silverman, *Male Subjectivity at the Margins* (New York/London: Routledge, 1992), 61.

within classical gender dichotomies are already at the center of Storm's scenes of flirtation. It is Storm's *Renate* (1878) to which flirtation is most central—an early novella where "a future man of the pulpit [is] seen losing his text in front of a little Hofbauer's girl."[25] Similarly, in Storm's most famous novella *The White Horse Rider* (*Der Schimmelreiter*, 1888), the protagonist, when asked to dance by the young Elke, responds in a panic: "I don't understand this well enough."[26] What makes Storm's young girls so terrifying is that they may, at any given moment, metamorphose from small to big, from weak to powerful, from a sublime coquettish sovereign to a small girl, and vice versa.

The character Renate, for instance, is frequently identified with smallness by the use of diminutives, such as "two small brown arms" (135), "the small face" (136), or "little Hofbauer-girl" (154) as well as by way of *partes pro toto*; the narrator mentions her "small, brave voice" (135), "her small elbow" (141); but it is the mention of Renate's "little fist [*Faust*]"[27] that lets one divine that her smallness might be the flipside of an exceptional greatness—after all, "Faust" evokes the mightiest German literary precursor for any German text and one that intensifies superstition about Renate's link to the devil. In his reflections on the beautiful, Edmund Burke writes that the things we find beautiful "excite in us the passion of love, or some correspondent affection."[28] More specifically, Burke purports that "the objects of love are spoken of under diminutive epithets."[29] One could take Burke's statement about the link between the beautiful and the small to say that we have proceeded from flirtation as a *social* phenomenon to an *aesthetic* problem. But this would not be quite right, because Burke's theory of the beautiful and the sublime is just as much a theory of social relations; Burke assumes that the ideas of the beautiful and the sublime can exist in us only separately but not simultaneously—for the beautiful and the sublime not only function differently but also elicit different effects: "[W]e submit to what we

---

25 Theodor Storm, *Paul the Puppeteer with The Village on the Moor and Renate*, trans. Denis Jackson (London: Angel Books, 2004), 154; "den Text verlieret," *Renate* (= *Sämtliche Werke: Novellen 1867–1880*, vol. 2), 523–587, at 550.
26 "Ich verstehe das nicht gut genug." Theodor Storm, *Der Schimmelreiter* (= *Sämtliche Werke: Novellen 1881–1888*, vol. 3, ed. Karl Ernst Laage) (Frankfurt/M.: Deutscher Klassiker Verlag, 1987), 634–756, at 672; Stella Humphries translates more freely "I don't know much about dancing" (206) but the admittance of not-knowing is more open, and thus radical, in the original.
27 In German: "zwei braune Ärmchen" (530); "das Köpfchen" (537); "kleine tapfere Stimme" (530); "de(n) kleinen Ellenbogen" (537); "kleine(r) Faust" (562).
28 Edmund Burke, *A Philosophical Enquiry into the Origins of our Ideas of the Sublime and Beautiful*, ed. Adam Phillips (Oxford: Oxford University Press, 1990), part 2.XII, 102.
29 Ibid. See also section XVI on delicacy (106): "The beauty of women is considerably owing to their weakness, or delicacy, and is even enhanced by their timidity, a quality of mind analogous to it."

admire, but we love what submits to us; in one case we are forced, in the other we are flattered into compliance."[30] If Storm's narrator depicts Renate as "small" then one might with Burke deduce that the attraction of the young priest to Renate would be the result of her submission to him. But this is only half the truth: Renate—as young or small as she is— is also capable of eliciting his terror. What makes the sovereign coquette terrifying is that she is as close to the sublime as she is to the beautiful:[31] she herself submits, just as we feel compelled to submit ourselves to her.

In Storm's texts desire often follows a pattern whereby a man experiences terror due to the flirtation of a young girl on the threshold of puberty. Renate, for instance, is said to have "not long left her childhood behind, for her tanned cheeks were still covered with soft peachy down" (Storm, *Renate*, 141). Given this erotic script, in the scholarship on Storm, whether oriented towards his poetics or his biography, pedophilia has become a prominent topic.[32] As soon as a suspicion such as pedophilia is raised of an author, the reader is pulled into a psychoanalytic frenzy, in which all literary characters equally are drawn into the spiral of biographical humanism. Even if one is generally critical of such identificatory interpretations, one also might be inclined to resist simply perpetuating Freud's later narrative of "the seductive child,"[33] the story in which the harasser claims to feel harassed by the

---

30 Ibid., part 2.XII, 102.
31 Jean Paul Richter is a rare exception in refuting Kant's identification of the great with the (mathematical) sublime when proposing "nur das Kleinste ist das erhabenste." *Vorschule der Aesthetik: Nebst einigen Vorlesungen in Leipzig über die Parteien der Zeit*, vol. 1 (Stuttgart/Tübingen: Cotta, 1813), 187–189, at 189.
32 Mareike Börner, *Mädchenknospe—Spiegelkindlein. Die Kindfrau im Werk Theodor Storms* (Würzburg: Königshausen & Neumann, 2009); Heinrich Detering, *Kindheitsspuren. Theodor Storm und das Ende der Romantik* (Heide: Boyens, 2011); Gerhard Neumann, "Theodor Storms 'Psyche'. Ein Wahrnehmungsmodell des Realismus," in *Wirklichkeit und Wahrnehmung. Neue Perspektiven auf Theodor Storm*, ed. Elisabeth Strowick and Ulrike Vedder (Bern a.o.: Peter Lang, 2013), 131–148; Ernst Osterkamp, "Dämonisierender Realismus. Bemerkungen zu Theodor Storms Erzählkunst," in *Wirklichkeit und Wahrnehmung*, 39–54.
33 In the writing of pedophiliac desire, the border between flirtation and seduction becomes blurry. In this sense, in Storm's œuvre we face the same pitfalls as in Freud's theory of seduction; every moment of reading brings up the question: "Is the young girl described as seductive in order to present her as an agent and consequently as responsible for the feelings she elicits?" For the Freud of and after "Dora" (1901), the seduced child is also the seductive child. Famously, whereas still in "Zur Ätiologie der Hysterie" (1896), *Studienausgabe*, vol. 6, ed. Alexander Mitscherlich, Angela Richards, and James Strachey (Frankfurt/M.: Fischer, 2000), 53–81, Freud considered sexual abuse of children as the source of hysteria, he later on in introducing the concept of psychic reality revised this theory in *Drei Abhandlungen zur Sexualtheorie, Studienausgabe*, vol. 5, ed. Alexander Mitscherlich, Angela Richards, and James Strachey (Frankfurt/M.: Fischer, 2000) and "Meine Ansichten über die Rolle der Sexualität in der Ätiologie der Neurosen," *Studienausgabe*, 147–157 (both 1905).

(young) victim of his harassment (in our current discourse this rhetoric is described as *blaming the victim*). How *not* to wonder whether we owe Storm's riveting literary terrors of flirtation to a more disturbing terror of the one who sexually desires a child? Storm's terrifying(ly) little coquettish sovereigns would then be the brutal literalization of "the flirtation of childhood," by which the child-psychotherapist and essayist Adam Phillips circumscribes the phenomenon that the flirtatious child does not know the object of its flirtation; according to Phillips, this very uncertainty becomes a structural characteristic and motivation for every later flirtation.[34]

Storm depicts his young coquettes as being in power—in a problematic way—and the way they demonstrate such power is by having mastery to flirt with *whatever* (also for Storm a deciding quality of the flirt).[35] In *The White Horse Rider* Storm depicts another young female character, who flirts with three older men at the same time while turning, of all things, *the law* into the object of a flirtation. Whereas age, in this novella, is less of an issue, the real taboo that must not be transgressed—and that thus provokes flirtation—is social class, determined by property and property law: Hauke works as an aid on the estate of Elke's father, the old dike master, and hence does not dare to pursue Elke. The flirtation between the two young people remains beautifully restrained, melancholic, almost muted. Thus, the most flirtatious scene occurs in the absence of one party. Instead of Hauke, Elke is talking to three older men whom she indirectly persuades to support her plan to marry Hauke. Paradoxically, the way in which Elke enforces her will is by abdicating her very agency—another variation on our theme of the coquette being able to switch from big to small and from sublime to beautiful.

And this is how it goes: when Elke's father dies, the community has to appoint a new dike-master. The three men covering the highest administrative bodies in the region agree that Hauke is best suited for the position of the dike-master. Yet, Hauke does not own enough land to be electable. Being the daughter as well as the only heir of the

---

34 Adam Phillips, "On Flirtation: An Introduction," in *On Flirtation* (Cambridge, MA: Harvard University Press, 1996), xvii–xxv, at xxiv, see also the essay on "Perversion" in the same book, which deals in more detail with Freud's theory of seduction (100–108) and Sándor Ferenczi, "Confusion of Tongues Between the Adults and the Child: The Language of Tenderness and the Language of Passion (1933)," trans. Michael Balint, *International Journal of Psychoanalysis* 30 (1949): 225–230, at 227: "[T]he hidden play of taking the place of the parent of the same sex in order to be married to the other parent … is merely a phantasy. … If *more love* or *love of a different kind from that which they need*, is forced upon the children in the stage of tenderness, it may lead to pathological consequences."
35 Simmel, "Flirtation," 133–152.

deceased dike-master, Elke is invited to join the meeting of the men. As the conversation turns to Hauke's lack of means, Elke informs the three high officials that Hauke's property will be increased by the amount of her father's land. Elke intends to marry Hauke and, once she does so, Hauke will be able to become the new dike-master. The elders react with amusement to Elke's plan, though they are still worried that it might be difficult to merge property *after* the wedding:

> And how do the marriage laws on property run in this part of the world, my dear? I confess I am not well versed in these complicated legalities.
> "Nor do you need to be," answered the reeve's daughter. "I shall have the title deeds transferred to my future husband before the marriage ceremony. After all, I too have my pride," she added mischievously. "I want to marry the richest man in the village." (*The White Horse Rider*, 218)[36]

The "young maiden" sketches out a legal solution: she will gift her property to Hauke *before* the wedding in order *then* to be able "to marry the richest man in the village." The three men are nothing short of perplexed by Elke's masterplan:

> But the truly remarkable feature of today's business is that such a very young lady has been responsible for the creation of a new dike reeve.
> "Well, sir," replied the girl, and she looked at the kindhearted dignitary with those grave eyes of hers, "surely a woman may be allowed to help a real man." (*The White Horse Rider*, 218)[37]

We can read this legal-erotic negotiation alternatively as a gesture of female empowerment or of female submissiveness: either Elke "buys"

---

36 Theodor Storm, *The White Horse Rider*, trans. Stella Humpries, *German Novellas of Realism*, vol. 2, ed. Jeffrey L. Sammons (New York: Continuum, 1989); *Der Schimmelreiter*, 687: "'Ja, liebe Jungfer', sagte [der Oberdeichgraf] endlich, 'aber wie steht es denn hier im Kooge mit den ehelichen Güterrechten? Ich muß gestehen, ich bin augenblicklich nicht recht kapitelfest in diesem Wirrsal!'—'Das brauchen Euer Gnaden auch nicht', entgegnete des Deichgrafen Tochter, 'ich werde vor der Hochzeit meinem Bräutigam die Güter übertragen. Ich habe auch meinen kleinen Stolz', setzte sie lächelnd hinzu, 'ich will den reichsten Mann im Dorfe heiraten!'"
37 Storm, *Der Schimmelreiter*, 687: "'[A]ber—daß ein Deichgraf von solch junger Jungfer gemacht wurde, das ist das Wunderbare an der Sache!'—'Euer Gnaden', erwiderte Elke und sah den gütigen Oberbeamten noch einmal mit ihren ernsten Augen an, 'einem rechten Manne wird auch die Frau wohl helfen dürfen!'"

herself a husband or the "young maiden" signs over her entire property to a man, even before the wedding. In any case, Elke's erotic trajectory is by no means a direct one. Simmel writes that flirtation presents a form of *Mit-Sein* (being-with), in which the *with* takes on an instrumental character: we play with people, with cute dogs, or with children in order to attract someone else's attention qua triangulation. This is because flirtation is all about mediation: *anything* can be used as a means for flirtation. Young Elke's flirtatious discourse involves three prestigious, older men—but the instrument through which she really proves her sovereignty is the law. Having been a lawyer himself, Storm took care in developing the relation between flirtation and the law in this scene. One of the more apparent points of contact between flirtation and the law is that, first, every flirtation is a contractual relation—or more precisely, a relation, in which we are never sure whether we are entering into a contract or not. But the minute we make the rules explicit, we make the flirtation explicit and thereby normalize the relation. Elke's flirtatious discourse presents flirtation as the best kind of relation: a relation of absolute pragmatism in the face of absolute uncertainty. A second point of contact between flirtation and the law is their shared fictionality: Elke wishes for Hauke to become the new dike-master and she has the ambition to marry the wealthiest man in the village. Given that Hauke has the social status to become neither the dike-master nor her husband, Elke is in need of a legal fiction that allows her to extend the concept of social status. She preempts the law insofar as she *first* gives her property to Hauke so that she can *then* marry him. Because the precedent for a legal consequence to become effective is not *yet* given—Hauke is still poor—Elke retrospectively fulfills this condition by making him rich so that the legal consequence (the marriage as well as the job) may become possible. Ernst Kantorowicz used the legal fiction to compare the "sovereignty of the artist" to that of the lawyer:[38] if the artist uses the mode of *as if* with the goal of creating a fiction, then the legal fiction makes use of fictionality by acting *as if* the old law applied to the new case. Similarly, flirtation makes use of fictionality; no flirt without a fiction, no flirt without an *as if*. The effect of this hypothetical character of flirtation is that we never know what our relation to the Other is; we cannot even know for sure whether we are flirting at all and from this an epistemological terror arises.

---

38 Ernst H. Kantorowicz, "The Sovereignty of the Artist: A Note on Legal Maxims and Renaissance Theories of Art," in *Selected Studies* (New York: J. J. Augustin, 1965), 352–365, at 354.

Benjamin and Keller: Rivalry and Deferral

More so than for Simmel and Bloch, for Benjamin flirtation arouses intense anxiety. The topic but also the tone of flirtation permeate his autobiographic writings in *Berlin Childhood* and *One-Way-Street* as well as the diary entries during his stays on Capri, where Benjamin had an affair with the Dutch painter Anna Maria Blaupot ten Cate, and in Moscow where he visited Asja Lacis. Whereas most of these passages celebrate the terrors of flirtation, there is one thought-image, "Betting Shop," which demands to put an end to flirtation altogether and to stage the pursuit in public; this is because flirtation, so goes the reasoning, is complicit with the privatization of desire:

> Philistines proclaim the complete privatization of love life. For them, wooing becomes a silent, dead-serious transaction conducted in total privacy, and this thoroughly private wooing, severed from all responsibility, is what is really new in "flirting." In contrast, the proletarian and the feudal type of men resemble each other in that in wooing it is much less the woman than their competitors that they overcome. However, in this they respect the woman far more deeply than in her "freedom," it means doing her bidding without consulting her.[39]

Obviously, it is not only the privatization of desire that unsettles the narrator but also the master-role that woman inhabits in flirtation. Benjamin alludes to this female "freedom," but only in quotation marks—a clear side-blow at Simmel—and then counters the very change in erotic power dynamics, which Simmel diagnosed, by promoting the exclusion of women from flirtation in order to return to the courtship model: i.e., to a form of homoerotic rivalry, in which the woman, the passive object of idealization, observes the men's battle from the sidelines.[40]

---

39 Walter Benjamin, "Betting Office," in *One-Way Street and Other Writings*, ed. Michael W. Jennings, trans. Edmund Jephcott (Cambridge, MA: The Belknap Press of Harvard University Press, 2016), 90–91; Benjamin, "Wettannahme," *Einbahnstrasse* (= *Gesammelte Schriften*, ed. Rolf Tiedemann and Hermann Schweppenhäuser, vol. IV.1) (Frankfurt/M.: Suhrkamp, 1991), 83–148, at 144: "Das Philisterium proklamiert restlose Privatisierung des Liebeslebens. So ist ihm Werbung zu einem stummen, verbissenenen Vorgang unter vier Augen geworden, und diese durch und durch private, aller Verantwortung entbundene Werbung ist das eigentlich Neue am 'Flirt'. Dagegen sind der proletarische und der feudale Typ sich darin gleich, dass in der Werbung sie viel weniger die Frau als ihre Konkurrenten überwinden. Das aber heißt die Frau viel tiefer respektieren als in ihrer 'Freiheit', heißt ihr zu Willen sein, ohne sie zu befragen."
40 If one were to look out for comparable constellations within the literature of flirtation, figures like Turgenev's Zanayda in *First Love* (1860) or James' *Daisy Miller* (1879) come to mind: self-proclaimed female flirts who encourage male rivalry, even in public.

There is one text in Swiss literature that perfectly illustrates Benjamin's horror of female coquettes, and it was authored by Gottfried Keller—not by coincidence also one of Benjamin's favorite writers. Keller's novella *The Three Decent Combmakers* tells the story of a deadly courtship. Three German pennywise combmakers compete to win the interest—and the small fortune—of a precocious young laundry woman with the name Züs Bünzlin who previously had been (almost) engaged no fewer than three times. At one point in the novella it becomes explicit that it is the rivalry between the three men that make Züs appear so sweet (*süss*). Finally, Züs has to announce a competition between the three rivals; but the one who "wins" her at the end no longer finds joy in life, the other one hangs himself, and the last one goes mad. If the outcome of the pursuit is catastrophic, then it is flirtation's temporality of anticipation that serves as the source of pleasure. While the men seem to be energized by the rivalry, the woman for her part revels in the attention she gets while being pursued by three men simultaneously:

> She therefore saw herself surrounded by a whole court of decent and respectable combmakers. That she relished greatly; never before had she had a number of admirers at one time. It became a novel entertainment for her shrewd mind to handle these three with the greatest impartiality and skill, to keep them at all times within bounds and cool reason, and to thus influence them by frequent speeches in favor of the beauties of resignation and unselfishness until Heaven itself should by some act of intervention decide matters irrevocably.[41]

If Benjamin's courtly contract stipulates that the "bidding" must take place "without consulting" the woman, Keller's novella imagines what would happen if the courtship were left up to her: she would extend the process for as long as possible. With this, the moment of gender terror—in Simmel's words "the power of the woman over yes and

---

41 Gottfried Keller, "The Three Decent Combmakers," in *Seldwyla Folks: Three Singular Tales*, trans. Wolf von Schierbard (New York: Brentano's Publishers, 1919), 1–79, at 34–35. Gottfried Keller, "Die drei gerechten Kammacher," in *Die Leute von Seldwyla*, vol. 1 (= *Sämtliche Werke. Historisch-Kritische Ausgabe*, vol. 4, ed. Walter Morgenthaler) (Zürich: Stroemfeld, 2000 [1856]), 215–265, at 237: "Das gefiel ihr ausnehmend wohl; noch nie hatte sie mehrere Verehrer auf einmal besessen, weshalb es eine neue Geistesübung für sie ward, diese drei mit der größten Klugheit und Unparteilichkeit zu behandeln und im Zaume zu halten und sie so lange mit wunderbaren Reden zur Entsagung und Uneigennützigkeit aufzumuntern, bis der Himmel über das Unabänderliche etwas entschiede."

no"[42]—finds its way into Keller's novella; Simmel emphasizes that "the power of the woman over consent and refusal is *prior* to the decision. Once she has decided, in either direction, her power is ended. Flirtation is a means of enjoying this power in an enduring form."[43] Likewise, while the three combmakers obsessively save up money for the future, the much-courted woman saves up time. Keller hence implicitly compares flirtation with parsimony in that both are about deferring pleasure. In another thought-image of Benjamin's, the danger of the female flirt becomes even more pronounced, explosive. In the thought-image "Arms and Ammunition" from *One-Way-Street* (devoted to the Bolshevik actress and theater director Asja Lacis) the narrator imagines running into the woman he adores without defense:

> From every gate a flame darted; each cornerstone sprayed sparks, and every streetcar came toward me like a fire engine. For she might have stepped out of the gateway, around the corner, been sitting in the streetcar. But of the two of us, I had to be, at any price, the first to see the other. For had she touched me with the match of her eyes—I, without fail, would have gone up like a powder keg.[44]

Flirtation becomes a fantasy of male castration and female-empowerment, of a state of exception in which women are in possession of the ammunition.

Bloch and Fontane: War

In Ernst Bloch's lyrical thought-image "Pippa Passes,"[45] flirtation equally evokes war-like scenarios. Bloch's narrator first describes flirtation as

---

42 Ibid., 141. I prefer a more literal translation here than Oakes, who speaks of "consent and refusal"; "Die Koketterie," 88.
43 Simmel, "Flirtation," 141; Simmel, "Die Koketterie," 88–89: "Die Macht der Frau über Ja und Nein liegt *vor* der Entscheidung; hat sie entschieden, so ist, in beiden Fällen, ihre so gefärbte Macht zu Ende."
44 Walter Benjamin, "Ordnance," *One-Way Street and Other Writings*, 52; "Waffen und Munition," *Einbahnstrasse*, 110: "Aus jedem Haustor schlug eine Stichflamme, jeder Eckstein stob Funken und jede Tram kam wie die Feuerwehr dahergefahren. Sie konnte ja aus dem Tore treten, um die Ecke biegen und in der Tram sitzen. Von beiden aber musste ich, um jeden Preis, der erste werden, der den andern sieht. Denn hatte sie die Lunte ihres Blicks an mich gelegt—ich hätte wie ein Munitionslager auffliegen müssen."
45 Ernst Bloch's thought-image *Pippa geht vorüber*, written between 1910 and 1929, was most likely inspired by Robert Browning's scandal-provoking Victorian verse drama *Pippa Passes* (1841), which D. W. Griffith translated into a silent movie (1909).

no more than "a twinkling ..., short and sharp, that wounds."[46] But when he goes on to report how a friend, after a brief, involuntary flirtation with a pale blue-eyed girl on a public bus in Paris, suddenly loses control over the after-effects of the seemingly harmless flirtation, the initial "twinkling" leads to "a crash that almost buried him: love exploded on a time-fuse."[47] Already the etymology of the word "flirt" captures this sudden, physical violence; the Oxford English Dictionary records that the first uses of the word *flirt* were "a smart tap or blow, a rap, a fillip" and "a sudden jerk or movement, a quick throw or cast" (as in the phrase "I'll give you a good flurt on the Ear"). Thus, flirtation seems to have always been associated with an ambiguous aggression, if not violence.

I invite you now to mentally travel from the Paris bus that explodes under a pair of blue eyes, to a dinner party that will turn into the Battle at the Nile under the command of a young woman. We are coming to our last realist text: Theodor Fontane's early novel *Jenny Treibel* (*Frau Jenny Treibel—Wo sich Herz zum Herzen find't*, 1892). The female flirt is a rare species in Fontane—in fact, I only count three: the actress Franziska Franz in *Graf Petöfy* (1884), the lady-in-waiting Ebba von Rosenberg in *Irretrievable* (1892), and a witty, single, young woman from the middle class, named Corinna. Each of these women is put back in her place at the end of the novel in which she appears (thus, goes the international script for the female flirt; see also Henry James' *Daisy Miller* or Turgenev's Zanayda in *First Love*). But before this happens, these characters and everybody around them may enjoy their flirtatious escapades for a precious moment. Imagine now a fancy nineteenth-century dinner party. Among those invited, there is an unlikely guest: the above-mentioned precocious young woman from the middle class, Corinna. Corinna—already through his name of choice Fontane affirms the link between flirtation, aggression, and femininity: the name Corinna goes back to *kore* (Greek for "maiden"), i.e., the archetypal young girl as

---

46 Ernst Bloch, "Pippa Passes," in *Traces*, trans. Anthony A. Nassar (Stanford, CA: Stanford University Press, 2006), 59–61, at 59; "[E]in Glitzern, ein kurzes und spitzes, das verwundet." "Pippa geht vorüber," in *Spuren* (Frankfurt/M.: Suhrkamp, 1985 [1910–1929]), 82–84, at 82.
47 Ibid., 60; "[E]in Einschlag, der fast verschüttete; Liebe explodierte mit Zeitzündung. Der Schein begann zu arbeiten und das Mädchen, das darin stand, wurde zur Geliebten, zur eben vorübergegangenen, auch versäumten, hoffnungslos vergangenen, mit der ein ganzes Leben versank." "Pippa geht vorüber," 83. Note Bloch's allusion to Baudelaire's poem "Une passante," which Stefan George translated as "Einer Vorübergehenden."

well as the name of the female lover of Ovid's *Ars Amatoria* (20 BCE).[48] "[E]very lover is a soldier" ("Militat omnis amans" I.9 line 1) goes the famous line from Ovid's lyrical exploration of erotic topoi: a *sententia*, with which Ovid takes flirtation hostage and turns it into scenes of seduction or rape. We have grown accustomed to this shift from flirtation to seduction by way of Ovid's own writing but also that of his disciples, among them the military strategist and literary seducer Pierre Choderlos de Laclos and his *Liaisons Dangereuses*. Fontane's Corinna may approach the erotic discourse equally strategically, or even militaristically, but she is still less seductive and more playful than Ovid or Laclos, more flirtatious. First, however, Corinna seizes her good fortune like a military *occasio*: at the dinner party she entangles no less than three men in one flirtation;[49] while engaging in ostentatious flirtation with the evening's guest of honor, a British gentleman named Mr. Nelson, she elicits not only the jealousy of her cousin Marcell, but, more significantly, the interest of her primary prey—Leopold Treibel, the offspring of the wealthy hosts. As in Storm's *The Rider on the White Horse* and Keller's *The Three Decent Combmakers*, here too three men try to hold their ground against one young woman in flirtation—and surrender.

How do you start a flirtation? Corinna chooses to talk war. She picks up on the fact that the British guest shares his name with the war hero Lord Nelson, who led the British navy in the Battle of the Nile in 1798. Corinna initiates her own attack by extravagantly praising British men: aren't they the most virtuous of all men? Her flattery of the British does not fail to provoke the jealousy of the German men present. One such German man, her cousin Marcell, reprimands Corinna that when talking to a representative of another nation "it is more or less her duty to set a good example of German womanhood."[50] The British gentleman defends Corinna, objecting that nobody expects German women to be feminine: "Oh, no, no, … nothing about womanhood; always quick and clever … that's what we love in German women. Nothing about womanhood" (Fontane, *Jenny Treibel*, 162). To which Corinna replies:

---

48 It would not be the only time that Fontane makes reference to Ovid: see his allusions to Melusinas and Undinas in *Der Stechlin* as analyzed by Walter Müller-Seidel in "Fontane—*Der Stechlin*," in *Der deutsche Roman vom Barock bis zur Gegenwart: Struktur und Geschichte*, ed. Benno von Wiese (Düsseldorf: Bagel, 1965), 146–189, at 172.

49 Christian Grawe has a closer look at how this triangulation works in "Lieutenant Vogelsang a.D. und Mr. Nelson aus Liverpool. Treibels politische und Corinnas private Verirrungen in 'Frau Jenny Treibel'," *Fontane-Blätter* 38 (1984): 588–606, at 596–598.

50 Fontane, *Jenny Treibel*, 162; *Frau Jenny Treibel oder ‚Wo sich Herz zum Herzen findt'*, 39.

"There you have it, Marcell ... Mr. Nelson is leaving you in the lurch, and Frau Treibel, I imagine, will leave you in the lurch too and Herr Enghans too and my friend Leopold too." (Fontane, *Jenny Treibel*, 162)

If Bloch and Benjamin in their twentieth-century thought-images picture flirtatious women as being able to command a whole arsenal of ammunition, then it is striking that Fontane already weaponizes Corinna—but more subtly so, by repeatedly referencing the morpheme "Stich" ("Mr. Nelson läßt dich im *Stich*, und Frau Treibel, denk ich, läßt dich auch im *Stich*";[51] *im Stich lassen*—"to desert"; "to leave in the lurch"). What is a *Stich*? We could answer this question with Bloch's poetic depiction of flirtation as something "short and sharp, that wounds."[52] Fontane employs the *Stich* in its whole polysemic range: from the production of affect to that of texture. In total, there are no less than three meanings of *Stich* interacting in the scene:

- Stich I. The tone of the scene is a teasing one, in German: *sticheln* ("to tease").
- Stich II. Corinna teases Marcell that the other guests bailed on him (*im Stich gelassen*) after he had criticized her lack of femininity. This turn of phrase continues the semantic field of combat insofar as *jemanden im Stich lassen* means to give somebody to the sword of his opponent.[53]
- Stich III. Relates to the craft of *stitching*, a technique that becomes crucial for the scene as it begins to unfold from hereon.

Stitching then becomes a concrete topic in the conversation insofar as Corinna seems to give in to Marcell's reprimand: she assures Marcell that she is "after all of female nature and a real German" as shown by her ability to cook, sew, iron, and darn. Then Corinna, in a very ladylike *and* most unladylike manner, challenges Lord Nelson to a bet:

"You see, here is my friend Leopold Treibel and he's wearing, as you see, a faultless coat with a double row of buttons, and really buttoned up too, as is proper for a gentleman and a son of a Berlin

---

51 "Da hast du's, Marcell ... Mr. Nelson läßt dich im Stich, und Frau Treibel, denk ich, läßt dich auch im Stich und Herr Enghaus auch und mein Freund Leopold auch." *Frau Jenny Treibel*, 39.
52 "[E]in Glitzern, ein kurzes und spitzes, das verwundet."
53 If, in a medieval tournament, a knight fell of his horse, due to his heavy armor he was dependent on this knave to pick him up—if his knave bailed on him (*liess ihn im Stich*), the knight was thereby given to the *Stich* of his opponent's sword.

Kommerzienrat. And I would estimate [*taxiere*] that the coat cost at least a hundred marks. ... In any case, it's a fine coat, first-class. And now when we get up, Mr. Nelson, and the cigars are passed around—I imagine you do smoke—I'll ask you for your cigar and I'll burn a whole into my friend Leopold Treibel's coat, right here, where his heart is, and then I'll take the coat home in a cab, and tomorrow at the same time we'll all gather again in the garden and we'll place chairs around the basin of the fountain, as for a performance. And the cockatoo can be there, too. And I'll make my entrance like an artist—which indeed I am—and I will let the coat make the rounds, and if you, dear Mr. Nelson, are still able to find the spot where the hole was, then I'll give you a kiss and will follow you to Liverpool as your slave. But it won't come to that. Should I say, unfortunately?" (Fontane, *Jenny Treibel*, 164)[54]

Note the contrast between the bet's convoluted but logical *if ... then* pattern and its highly-sexually charged vocabulary. First, the young woman appraises the coat of the wealthy heir by "looking it up and down" (the German is *taxieren*, derivative from the Latin *tangere*—"to touch," and from middle Latin *taxitare* "to feel for"). Then, like a dominatrix, Corinna lies out the rules of the flirtatiously masochistic contract:[55] she demands that he undress himself; there is a cigar (Freud!), the penetrating of the dress, a hole, a cab (Emma Bovary! Effi Briest!), a

---

54 "'Sehen Sie, hier ist mein Freund Leopold Treibel und trägt, wie Sie sehen, einen untadeligen Rock mit einer doppelten Knopfreihe, und auch wirklich zugeknöpft, ganz wie es sich für einen Gentleman und einen Berliner Kommerzienratssohn geziemt. Und ich taxiere den Rock auf wenigstens hundert Mark. ... Jedenfalls ein feiner Rock, prima. Und nun, wenn wir aufstehen, Mr. Nelson, und die Zigarren herumgereicht werden—ich denke, Sie rauchen doch—werde ich Sie um Ihre Zigarre bitte und meinem Freunde Leopold Treibel ein Loch in den Rock brennen, hier gerade, wo sein Herz sitzt, und dann werde ich den Rock in einer Droschke mit nach Hause nehmen, und morgen um dieselbe Zeit wollen wir uns hier im Garten wieder versammeln und um das Bassin herum Stühle stellen wie bei einer Aufführung. Und der Kakadu kann auch dabeisein. Und dann werde ich auftreten wie eine Künstlerin, die ich in der Tat auch bin, und werde den Rock herumgehen lassen, und wenn Sie, dear Mr. Nelson, dann noch imstande sind, die Stelle zu finden, wo das Loch war, so will ich Ihnen einen Kuß geben und Ihnen als Sklavin nach Liverpool hin folgen. Aber es wird nicht dazu kommen. Soll ich sagen leider?'" *Frau Jenny Treibel oder ‚Wo sich Herz zum Herzen findt'*, 40–41.
55 "Like masochism, flirtation is a 'game' with certain rules that actually constrain the forms of power with which it seems to play," Wortham, "*Flirtations: Rhetoric and Aesthetics This Side of Seduction* (review)": 142. For a reflection on the comedy of this position see Barbara N. Nagel, "Flirt als semiotische Krise bei Henry James, Thomas Mann, Jean Genet," *Figurationen* 2 (2018): 25–42.

garden, and at the end a cockatoo, of all beasts, which like other exotic birds in seventeenth- and eighteenth-century Dutch and French painting symbolizes seduction and lost virginity.[56] We somehow have to find our way out of this cabinet of obscene props[57] if we want to identify the bet's content: like in Benjamin's "Betting Office" and like the bet in Keller's novella, this bet, too, implies a contract between two parties that determines the distribution of a risk on the basis of the outcome of a future event. So here is Fontane's bet once more in all its contractual beauty: Corinna intends to burn a hole into Leopold Treibel's dress at the height of his heart (*ein Stich ins Herz*—"a stitch into the heart," so to speak); she then wants to take his jacket home and stitch the hole. If Mr. Nelson is able to find the hole the next day then he can have her. Those are the terms of the bet, the contract.

In her book *The Subversive Stitch. Embroidery and the Making of the Feminine*, the art-historian Rozsika Parker claims that the craft of stitching has reliably intensified gender dichotomies by linking women to the household. But Parker also purports that stitching, especially in Victorian novels, had the potential to subvert (and, one should add, at the same time to *intensify*) these gender roles: "The silent embroiderer has ... become a part of a stereotype of femininity in which the self-containment of the woman sewing is interpreted as seductiveness."[58] Corinna seems to weaponize and ironize the seductiveness of the embroiderer: stitching, like flirtation, is all about mediation—for it simultaneously seals and invites desire; the stitching of the hole brings

---

56 See Emma Barker, "Reading the Greuze Girl—The Daughter's Seduction," *Representations* 117 (2012): 86–119, at 90; Barbara Vinken, who concentrates on the phallic-erotic connotations of the parrot in her essay "L'abandon de Félicité—*Un cœur simple* de Flaubert," in *Le Flaubert Réel*, ed. ibid. and Peter Fröhlicher (Tübingen: Max Niemeyer, 2009), 141–164, at 153–154.
57 This obscene series contradicts Norbert Mecklenburg's assessment "that erotic allusions and jokes" in Fontane "belong to the men's domain," and that if women say something of erotic content, this happens involuntarily or is used as a social marker for a lower class: *Theodor Fontane. Realismus, Redevielfalt, Ressentiment* (Stuttgart: Metzler, 2018), at 117–121.
58 Rozsika Parker, *The Subversive Stitch. Embroidery and the Making of the Feminine* (London: I.B. Tauris, 1984), 10, see also 167. Obviously, Corinna ironizes the idea of "[t]he silent embroiderer." Theodor Storm's early novella *Renate*, on the other hand, offers the perfect example for Parker's claim on the seductiveness of "the silent embroiderer," as seen by a young priest: "I looked at Renate who sat by the window embroidering a small sampler. Kept thinking she should turn her large eyes towards me, but she only looked at her work." Storm, *Paul the Puppeteer with The Village on the Moor and Renate*, 150–151; in German: "Ich sahe auf Renaten, die am Fenster saß und an einem Namentüchlein stichelte. Dachte immer, sie solle einmal wieder die großen Augen auf mich wenden; aber sie schaute nur auf ihre Arbeit." *Renate*, 547.

about both an event *and* the erasure of the event. This is because Corinna's stitching is supposed to be so perfect that Mr. Nelson will no longer be able to tell whether there was a hole in the first place. Flirtation is just that: the event *and* the erasure of the event (and the event of the erasure of the event). If Fontane, by giving the flirtatious girl the name *Corinna*, invited Ovid into his novel, then let us also remember that for Ovid rhetoric is the art that conceals art (*ars adeo latet arte sua*).[59] In Fontane this thought is exponentiated: flirtation as rhetoric is the *visible* concealing of the art that conceals art. Likewise, the contractual manner in which Corinna's bet is formulated (like that of Elke in *The Rider on the White Horse*) approaches a zero-point of rhetoricity in the sense that her words are strictly paratactic:

> "You see, here is my friend Leopold Treibel and ..., and .... And I would .... And now, ... and I'll ..., and I'll ..., and then I'll ..., and tomorrow ... and we'll .... And the cockatoo .... And I'll ..., and I will let the coat make the rounds, and if you, dear Mr. Nelson, are still able to find the spot where the hole was, then I'll give you a kiss and will follow you to Liverpool as your slave." (Fontane, *Jenny Treibel*, 164)

The paratactic order of *and*-sentences resembles a line of stitches that only concludes after the thirteenth *and* with the phrase "I'll give you a kiss." One might object that this is bad stitching insofar as we still see the grammar or *techne* of the sentence laid out in front of us. If we think about the bet in these terms, then Corinna's implicit claim that the bet is about discretion—i.e., about hiding the hole[60]—is not to be trusted because her bet is just as much about ostentation as it is about

---

59 Renate Böschenstein doubts that Fontane is alluding to Ovid's lover, but does, however, not substantiate her disbelief (229, footnote 9) but instead remarks on Fontane's great interest in antiquity: "Das Rätsel der Corinna. Beobachtungen zur Physiognomie einer 'realistischen' Figur aus komparatistischer Perspektive," in *Verborgene Facetten. Studien zu Fontane* (Würzburg: Königshausen & Neumann, 2005), 224–246.
60 It is hard when Corinna talks about a "hole" *not* to think of "a narrow thing within one word," i.e., the vagina. In the famous tragicomic early-modern novel *La Celestina* (1499) by Fernando de Roja, the protagonist Celestina is a prostitute who performs abortions but also restores ripped hymens through stitching. Virginity, which in a certain sense founds the tropological system, turns out to be itself a catachresis in de Roja. Finally, note the way in which stitching hence is linked to an increase in female agency, whereas weaving remains associated with the trauma of being raped, as in Ovid's myth of Philomela.

concealment.[61] The same goes for flirtation: to engage in flirtation requires the same amounts of discretion and indiscretion; one has to hide or forget about the obvious—"the hole"—for the sake of the fiction ("we are only talking"), that is, for the sake of the artificiality of the game, the artifice of the *techne*. But if we *only* play it is not flirtation either: there must be the potentiality for something more to happen. By definition, the "as if" of flirtation is never pure, never absolutely divided from actuality.

"The Mind's Capacity for Reverie"

Isn't it frivolous or counter-productive to write on flirtation at the current historical moment, when all critical attention is finally directed toward sexual harassment and sexual violence? Jacqueline Rose makes it clear why we need to talk about flirtation *right now*. "The aim of harassment," Rose writes, "isn't just to control women's bodies but also to invade their minds. … Harassment brings mental life to a standstill. It destroys the mind's capacity for reverie."[62] "The mind's capacity for reverie"—this is why flirtation is so important, especially right now. The examples from early theories and literature of flirtation demonstrate how the patriarchy experiences any increase of female freedom hysterically, as a moment of terror. As a consequence, the effect of flirtation is twofold: on the one hand, male theorists and male realist authors react to the topic of flirtation by increasing the divide between "male" vs. "female." On the other hand, the queerness of the constellation cannot simply be repressed, its erotic energy is not to be taken back. If Rose cautions us that a "feminism that takes harassment as the unadulterated expression of male power and authority is in danger of colluding with the image of masculinity it is protesting against,"[63] then flirtation helps us to imagine other forms of masculinity—those that can bear being terrorized out of mastery—as well as other forms of femininity, including those that are comfortable with power. Novels are therefore not just a welcome distraction from "all the violence"; they model and

---

61 Ulrike Vedder offers two further associations concerning the hole: the socially imposed self-erasure of female existence as well as the the aporia of the "realist novel [as] an art form, that has to make everything artful disappear in order to be regarded realist": "'in den Ton ausgesprochenster Wirklichkeit verfallend' Poesie und Prosa in Fontanes *Frau Jenny Treibel*", *Herausforderungen des Realismus. Theodor Fontanes Gesellschaftsromane*, 189–202, at 195.
62 Jacqueline Rose, "I Am a Knife," *The London Review of Books* 40, no. 4 (February 22, 2018): 3–11.
63 Ibid., 3.

incite desire and fantasy. Jordy Rosenberg, in a recent *Los Angeles Review of Books* article, puts it as follows:

> Because without this language shadow? Without our sensuous forms of thought? It would be brutal. The putrid heart of capitalism is there in the room with you every night in the form of the demand to enjoy. Indeed, in the 21st century, it's not about being an upstanding community member. Now, all that matters is whether or not you, as a person, have reached your full potential by enjoying your life enough, at whatever cost to yourself and others. And if you can't consume enough, enjoy yourself enough, experience your desire enough, what a failure you are.[64]

In this sense, flirtation stands as a form of resistance to the permanent imperative to consume, to enjoy, to consummate; it not only makes a space for failure, but opens a critical interval from the norm itself.

---

64 Jordy Rosenberg, "The Daddy Dialectic," *The Los Angeles Review of Books*, March 11, 2018, https://lareviewofbooks.org/article/the-daddy-dialectic/ (last retrieved March 19, 2018).

PASSIVE AGGRESSION

Three Twice-Read Love Letters: The Ambiguities of Epistolary Violence

"Peace doesn't need letters."[1]—*Kafka*

People are happy to sing the praises of flirtation and its beauty (less so, its terror), but what of odes to the beauty of passive aggression? This is was the following chapter is about: celebrating the beauty of passive aggressive remarks and thus approaching as an aesthetic object something that is commonly considered an everyday annoyance. The rationale for such an aesthetic rehabilitation of passive aggression is that if certain statements have the ability to stick with us and, only belatedly, release their poisonous content like a leaking battery, then this ability is "poetic"—in the sense that we have received the gift of a well-crafted ambiguity, an ambiguity that arises, *nota bene*, from considerable linguistic labor. Ambiguity, it should be noted, is also a crucial ingredient in jokes. Websites like *PassiveAggressiveNotes.com* that collect "painfully polite and hilariously hostile notes from shared spaces" are testimony to the curious fact that a well-crafted passive aggressive statement—as hurtful as it may be—functions like a joke; it makes use of a riddle-structure, which explains why many times we find ourselves

---

1 Franz Kafka in a letter to Felice from August 14, 1913, *Briefe an Felice und andere Korrespondenz aus der Verlobungszeit*, ed. Erich Heller and Jürgen Born (Frankfurt/M.: Fischer, 1967), 445–446, at 446. An earlier version of this chapter was published under the title "'Ich weiss nicht, was soll es bedeuten …' Bitten um Deutung in Kafkas und Fontanes Liebesbriefen," in *Was heißt Deutung? Verhandlungen zwischen Recht, Literaturwissenschaft und Psychoanalyse*, ed. Susanne Lüdemann and Thomas Vesting (Munich: Wilhelm Fink, 2017), 227–244.

laughing out loud in the midst of a recognition: "Oh no, that was mean! Or, was it?"

The word "mean" calls forth Nietzsche, the philosopher of *ressentiment*—Nietzsche who knew better than any other *how to aggress well*. In *On the Genealogy of Morals*, published toward the end of the realist movement, Nietzsche points out the shared etymology of the words *schlicht* (mean; common) and *schlecht* (mean; bad) in order to bring home the point that our system of moral values is built upon a bias against "the strong, healthy, brutal."[2] While Nietzsche dismisses the ascetic ideal and the wish to control one's affects, especially aggressive ones, as Judeo-Christian "slave morality,"[3] he nonetheless makes ample use of irony and performs intricate maneuvers of critique in his own writing; even, or perhaps *especially*, the theorist and critic of *ressentiment* knows how to make effective rhetorical use of passive aggression. In this regard, the most famous maneuver in the *Genealogy* is probably Nietzsche's oscillating position towards anti-Semitism: after his initial identification of Judaism with resentment (which bodes well for every anti-Semite), he then uses the terms "Judaized, Christianized" synonymously, and finally ridicules all anti-Semites, having thus lured them into an unforeseeable conceptual trap.[4]

Of course, resentment is not exactly passive aggression and vice versa. To begin with, the two concepts have vastly different histories: whereas Nietzsche focuses on the history of religion and philosophy (causing us to wonder *Is Socratic-dialogue passive-aggressive?*), the notion of passive-aggression was invented in the military during the Second World War where "passive aggressive" became "shorthand for a person with hostility issues";[5] a passive-aggressive soldier was hence one who displayed gestures of passive resistance towards superiors, "such as pouting, stubbornness, procrastination, inefficiency, and passive obstructionism."[6] A diagnosis that made punishable what before had

---

2 Friedrich Nietzsche, *On the Genealogy of Morals*, trans. Carol Diethe (Cambridge a.o.: Cambridge University Press, 2007 [1887]), 17.
3 Ibid., 154.
4 Ibid., 19.
5 Christopher Lane, "The Surprising History of Passive-Aggressive Personality Disorder," *Theory & Psychology* 19, no. 1 (2009): 55–70, at 58.
6 Ibid. Lane informs us that the first official document about passive aggression as a disorder is a single Technical Bulletin issued by the US War Department towards the end of the Second World War: "In 1945, Colonel William Menninger voiced concern about soldiers who were shirking duty by willful incompetence. They were not openly defiant, he conceded, but expressed their aggressiveness 'by passive measures, such as pouting, stubbornness, procrastination, inefficiency, and passive obstructionism.'" Menninger quoted after "Bulletin TB M.D. 203," dated October 19, 1945, as cited in K. L. Malinow, "Passive-Aggressive Personality," in *Personality Disorders: Diagnosis and Management*, ed. J. R. Lion (Baltimore, MD: Williams & Wilkins, 1981), 121–132: 123.

simply slipped through the disciplinary apparatus. Perhaps this background is why Slavoj Žižek goes so far to rehabilitate passive aggression as a timely mode of resistance:

> We all know the pop-psychological notion of "passive-aggressive behavior," usually applied to a housewife who, instead of actively opposing her husband, passively sabotages him. ... [P]erhaps, we should assert this attitude of passive aggression as a proper radical political gesture, in contrast to aggressive passivity, the standard "interpassive" mode of our participation in socio-ideological life in which we are active all the time in order to make sure that nothing will happen, that nothing will really change. In such a constellation, the first truly critical ("aggressive," violent) step is to withdraw into passivity, to refuse to participate.[7]

The image that Žižek evokes of the "housewife who, instead of actively opposing her husband, passively sabotages him" is, consciously or not, superimposed upon a similarly gendered thought-image from Adorno's *Minima Moralia*:

> *Philemon and Baucis*—The domestic tyrant has his wife help him on with his coat. She eagerly performs this service of love, following him with a look that says: what else should I do, let him have his little pleasure, that's how he is, only a man. The patriarchal marriage takes its revenge on the master in the wife's indulgent considerateness, which in its ironic laments over masculine self-pity and inadequacy has become a formula.[8]

According to Adorno, passive aggression still forms part of the bigger, Hegelian master-slave dialectic, in which again the slave attempts to rebel (note the centrality of the slave-position for Adorno's anti-idyll as well as for Nietzsche's *ressentiment*), however timidly or indirectly. Yet in his thought-image Adorno has transposed the phenomenon of resentment or passive aggression into the intimate sphere: into the realm of "love."

But why on earth would passive aggression especially proliferate between lovers and loved ones? Because there is no other demand than that of love ("love!") that would prove us less deserving and more deficient, even and especially if the Other is a "loved one" or "my true Love." This is most pertinent for our modern understanding of love,

---

7 Slavoj Žižek, *The Parallax View* (Cambridge, MA: MIT Press, 2006), 342.
8 Theodor W. Adorno, *Minima Moralia: Reflections of Damaged Life*, trans. E. F. N. Jephcott (London/New York: Verso, 2005), 111.

which, following Niklas Luhmann, constantly overtaxes the individual: "modern lovers" are expected to see the world at large through the eyes of "the other person in my environment who bestows meaning upon my world, but can only do so if I accept him and his environment as my own." As if this were not challenging enough, this acceptance has to be joyous: "No love can be satisfied with an 'oh, all right.'"[9] This is why we drive slowly around the corners (because that is the way *he* likes it), or cook quinoa instead of rice (because *she* is concerned about her protein intake). Feelings of disappointment in the Other who can never love me adequately and, conversely, aggressive affects toward the Other who makes me feel constantly insufficient are both unavoidable. Luhmann calls this impossible love-concept, from which we have suffered ever since the Romantic concept of love lost its validity, "a concept of interpersonal interpenetration."[10] For our analysis of passive-aggressive love letters it will be crucial that "interpenetration" is highly verbal, i.e., that it leads to an intensification of communication because "what one regards as relevant almost always is also held relevant by the other. Communicative relationships accordingly become more dense."[11]

Because of their beauty, let me give you two examples of such passive aggressive love-discourses from "real life" before I turn to literature. Passive aggression has a strong relation to triviality—not because we could only be passive aggressive about trivial things like office-refrigerators—but because the disjunction between the intensity of the affect and the triviality of the object makes us aware of the form; more precisely, it makes us aware that passive aggression *is* a social form. Those of you who have not yet had a taste of chilling, German passive aggression (according to Nietzsche a result of the Reformation's turn to reaction and inwardness) will at least be acquainted with the stereotype of passive-aggressive Canadians. Of course, comparing Canadians to Germans is like comparing apples and oranges insofar as few German have raised suspicion on account of their friendliness. But once I sat on a bench in Vancouver, enjoying the view of the sun kissing the water as it was setting, when my partner drew my attention to the inscription on our bench:

FOR ALLAN (2000) & THEO HILL (1995); JANE CHOI (1988), MOM (2003); DAD (1977) & JOHN WONG (2007). I LOVE YOU WITH MY LIFE & SOUL. YOU HAVE ENRICHED MY LIFE BEYOND MEASURE THRU YOUR STRUGGLES & UNSPOKEN LOVE FOR ME.

---

9 Niklas Luhmann, *Love as Passion: The Codification of Intimacy*, trans. Jeremy Gaines and Doris L. Jones (Stanford, CA: Stanford University Press, 1998 [1982]), 174–175.
10 Ibid., 174.
11 Ibid., 158.

I have a soft spot for those bench inscriptions; one of my favorite ones is in Central Park on a bench gifted by Leelee Brown Jaffe to her husband as a wedding present: "I LOVE YOU VERY MUCH AND LOOK FORWARD TO MARRYING YOU ... BUT IF WE HAVE A FIGHT YOU CAN ALWAYS SLEEP HERE." The Canadian bench, however, felt more unsettling than the one in Central Park. The idea of enriching someone else's life through my own struggles did not sound appealing to me—and what was meant by "unspoken love"? A silent gift, an understanding of the fact that love does not need words? Or was it rather a silent reproach and "unspoken love" is another way of saying *Thanks for nothing*. My mind had not yet stopped spinning when *Slate* magazine's advice-column "Dear Prudence" featured the letter of a soon-to-be husband who asked for help in interpreting his fiancée's recent behavior:

> QUESTION. *Forever Till Divorce?* In order to protect my assets, I have asked my fiancée for a prenup. It was awkward to bring it up but fortunately she agreed. I encouraged her to review it with her own attorney before signing. She came back to me with an odd proposal. She has no problems with the prenup itself, but she wants to alter our wedding vows. Specifically, instead of better or worse, she wants to say something like "I take you as my husband/wife for the foreseeable future unless otherwise arranged." She wants to include similar phrases throughout the vows—"I forsake all others, until death or divorce parts us." "This ring symbolizes my current love for you." She says using words like "eternal" or "till death" are contradictory to prenups, which prepare for a potential divorce. I wonder if she is just being passive aggressive, but she insists it's necessary to avoid contradictions in our wedding vows and prenup. What should I do?[12]

The clueless man was subjected to a triple humiliation by having first been the potential victim of passive aggression, by then disclosing the incident in public, and finally having "Prudence," aka Emily Joffe, poke fun at him: "How nice of you to 'encourage' your fiancée to review this contract with a lawyer. ... But it sounds as if you're not a sophisticated enough partner to recognize sarcasm and dripping resentment when you hear it." But really, the climate in which passive aggression flourishes is always more ambiguous—for who knows, maybe the man's fiancée was just an obsessive compulsive, worried about contradiction. Although passive aggression presupposes a psyche, it can also simply

---

12 Emily Joffe, "Dear Prudence," *Slate*, October 16, 2012, http://www.slate.com/articles/life/dear_prudence/2012/10/dear_prudence_my_girlfriend. (last retrieved October 20, 2012).

48   Ambiguous Aggression

be mechanics, an automatism. That is what makes passive aggression hermeneutically so interesting: it appeals to rationality but there is an infinity of readings built into it because it performs an operation on a prior discourse.

*

Let us now turn to realist literature and its condensed scenes of social interaction in order to develop a more nuanced analytical vocabulary for how passive aggression actually works. We will begin with a scene from Theodor Fontane's "woman's novel" *Frau Jenny Treibel* (1892). On an outing in the countryside, two elderly gentlemen, Krola and Treibel, walk behind the latter's son and his wife. The tableau of the young couple prompts the following reflection:

> "There just isn't anything better than a real marriage," Krola said to Treibel and pointed to the young couple in front of them. "You must be sincerely pleased when you see your eldest walking so happily and so tenderly beside this pretty and spic and span woman. Up above they were already sitting close together, and now they're walking arm in arm. I almost think they're quietly squeezing one another."
>
> "Sure proof to me that they had a quarrel this morning. Otto, the poor fellow, now has to pay forfeit money. ... And the worst marriages are those, my dear Krola, where they argue in a dreadfully 'cultured' way, where, if you'll permit the expression, war is carried on with velvet gloves, or more correctly, where they throw confetti into one another's faces as they do during the Roman carnival. It looks pretty, but it still wounds. And at this pleasant-looking confetti-throwing my daughter-in-law is a master. ..."
>
> "Well, all right. But if that's the way it is, how can there be quarrels?"
>
> "There still are. They just show up differently, differently but not better. No thunderstorms, just little words with the poison content of half a mosquito bite, or instead silence, muteness, sulking—the inner window of marriage—while on the outside the face doesn't show a single crease. Those are the forms. And I'm afraid all the tenderness we see parading in front of us, and that appears so very one-sided, is nothing but penance .... Just look at the poor fellow; he is constantly turning his head to the right and Helene doesn't stir and doesn't get out of that straight Hamburg line ... But now we have to be quiet. Your quartet is just beginning. What is it?"
>
> "It's the famous: 'I know not what it should mean.' [*Ich weiss nicht, was soll es bedeuten?*]"

"Oh, that's right. A good question to ask anytime, especially on country outings."¹³

The scene is taken from Theodor Fontane's novel *Frau Jenny Treibel* (1892)—a literary scene of interpretation, no doubt: one gentleman perceives the young couple as a happy couple, the second one takes them to be an unhappy one. For German realism, scenes of rereading are quite typical. After all, Roland Barthes writes that Realism is based upon repetition—more specifically on the repetition of the "real"; this repetition has realizing as well as derealizing effects.¹⁴ And we detect, in this regard, still in Kafka—who was most heavily influenced by two realist writers, Flaubert and Dickens—a late fascination for realism because we find many scenes of such revision in his work.¹⁵ The

---

13 Theodor Fontane, *Frau Jenny Treibel, Short Novels and Other Writings*, ed. Peter Demetz, trans. Ulf Zimmermann (New York: Continuum, 1982), 236–238; in German: "'Es geht doch nichts über eine richtige Ehe', sagte Krola zu Treibel und wies auf das junge Paar vor ihnen. ‚Sie müssen sich doch aufrichtig freuen, Kommerzienrat, wenn Sie Ihren Ältesten so glücklich und so zärtlich neben dieser hübschen und blink und blanken Frau einherschreiten sehen. Schon oben saßen sie dicht beisammen, und nun gehen sie Arm in Arm. Ich glaube, sie drücken sich leise.'—‚Mir ein sichrer Beweis, daß sie sich vormittags gezankt haben. Otto, der arme Kerl, muß nun Reugeld zahlen. ... [D]ie schlimmsten Ehen sind die, lieber Krola, wo furchtbar 'gebildet' gestritten wird, wo, wenn Sie mir den Ausdruck gestatten wollen, eine Kriegsführung mit Sammethandschuhen stattfindet oder, richtiger noch, wo man sich, wie beim römischen Karneval, Konfetti ins Gesicht wirft. Es sieht hübsch aus, aber verwundet doch. Und in dieser Kunst anscheinend gefälligen Konfettiwerfens ist meine Schwiegertochter eine Meisterin.'—'Nu'n meinetwegen. Aber wenn es so ist, wo kommt dann der Zank her?'—‚Der kommt doch. Er tritt nur anders auf, anders, aber nicht besser. Kein Donnerwetter, nur kleine Worte mit dem Giftgehalt eines halben Mückenstichs, oder aber Schweigen, Stummheit, Muffeln, das innere Düppel der Ehe, während nach außen hin das Gesicht keine Falte schlägt. Das sind so die Formen. Und ich fürchte, die ganze Zärtlichkeit, die wir da vor uns wandeln sehen und die sich augenscheinlich sehr einseitig gibt, ist nichts als ein Bußetun .... Sehen Sie nun den armen Kerl; er biegt den Kopf in einem fort nach rechts, und Helene rührt sich nicht und kommt aus der graden Hamburger Linie nicht heraus. ... Aber jetzt müssen wir schweigen. Ihr Quartett hebt eben an. Was ist es denn?'—'Es ist das bekannte: Ich weiß nicht, was soll es bedeuten?'—‚Ah, das ist recht. Eine jederzeit wohl aufzuwerfende Frage, besonders auf Landpartien.' *Frau Jenny Treibel oder Wo sich Herz zum Herzen findt*, 153–156.
14 Barthes' hypothesis forms the conceptual starting point for Eric Downing's *Double Exposures: Repetition and Realism in Nineteenth-Century German Fiction* (Stanford, CA: Stanford University Press, 2000), 2–3.
15 Maurice Blanchot writes on the problem of interpreting modern works that present their own commentary in the context of Kafka's *Schloß*: "Wiederholung und Verdoppelung. Notiz über Literatur und Interpretation," trans. Elsbeth Dangel, *Neue Rundschau* 99 (1988): 121–130, at 125.

successive depiction of the same scene from different perspectives functions like a reversible figure, a picture puzzle. One can see only one image at a time. This "Kipp phenomenon" is comical because the sudden change, as Wolfgang Iser points out, "undoes the reliability that results from the oppositional set up of the positions."[16] By virtue of this *Kipp*-mechanism the recipient is "absorbed" into the comical constellation; at the same time, the recipient is overwhelmed because the two depictions contradict one another.

In the case of Fontane's *Kippfigur*, the object of interpretation is trivial; it is the question: *How happy is the marriage?* With this question, emotional life is treated as an object of fascination that requires interpretation—to the degree that in the final sentence of the chapter the interpretation of the scene is declared to be undecidable: "I know not what it should mean." And yet, Heine's poem that is quoted here—a song that sets in with the loneliness of the lyrical I trapped in interpretation—continues: "I know not what should it mean *that I am so sad* ..."[17] Female aggression, which was the topic in the conversation between the two gentlemen, is accompanied by sadness. However, we do not know if aggression is the pretense for sadness or if sadness serves as the pretense for aggression. After all, Heine's song is devoted to none other than the man-murdering Loreley: "and this is what with her singing/the Loreley has done."[18] Interpretation ends with death; death is the gravestone of interpretation. The intertextual reference offers an interpretation that threatens to level all ambiguity. This is because Heine's poem not only implicitly affirms Treibel's pessimistic view of the condition of the marriage, it also supports Treibel's claim that it is the woman's fault that the young couple falls short of domestic bliss. What is paradoxical about this interpretation is, of course, that the father-in-law thereby repeats performatively what he has just criticized about his daughter-in-law: namely, he beats around the bush, hedging his criticism with linguistic subtleties.

Twice-Read Love Letters

With this, we go from Heine's lyrical address to the epistolary one, i.e., we proceed from one genre that creates the fiction of overhearing interpersonal exchange to another one. This is because Fontane puts the same *Kipp*-mechanism to work in his 1892 novel *Irretrievable* (*Unwiederbringlich*) in a proper scene of reading: a husband, far away from home,

---

16 Wolfgang Iser, "Das Komische: Ein Kipp-Phänomen," in *Das Komische*, ed. Wolfgang Preisendanz and Rainer Warning (Munich: Wilhelm Fink, 1976), 398–402, at 400.
17 "Ich weiss nicht, was soll es bedeuten/Daß ich so traurig bin."
18 "... und das hat mit ihrem Singen,/die Loreley gethan."

rejoices when receiving a letter from his wife but is then disappointed by her nagging tone. When the next letter arrives, he curbs his expectations—only to be pleasantly surprised:

> After finishing reading, Holk felt somewhat given to emotion. There was so much kindness in the letter that he felt old times and old happiness coming up again. She was the best, after all. ... And given to this feeling, he skimmed the letter once more. But there it waned again, all friendly impressions were gone, and what he picked out was only, or mostly, the tone of cantankerousness.[19]

The first reading brings a positive surprise ("She was the best, after all.") but the second reading causes disenchantment due to a "tone of cantankerousness." But how do you read tone? Fontane appears to be aware of the difficulty of such a hermeneutic endeavor: in the moment the husband perceives his wife switching, he switches too, as in a mirror image. His wife's ambiguous aggression proves to be contagious because a little later the husband has the same derealizing experience when he reads the letter he himself wrote in his own defense: "As if mesmerized his eye lingered on this, until eventually his satisfaction dwindled and nothing else looked at him from there but the confession of his guilt."[20]

Since William Empson's famous declaration "The machinations of ambiguity are among the very roots of poetry"[21] (a phrase also picked up by Roman Jakobson[22]) verbal ambiguity has been the hobby-horse of poetics and literary theory. Literary scholars tend to think of ambiguity as something beautiful, a generous opening for thought and feeling. But, of course, ambiguity can just as well be used for more perfidious purposes like dissimulation. While Empson perceives ambiguity solely in aesthetic terms, Quintilian judged ambiguity ethically

---

19 Theodor Fontane, *Unwiederbringlich* (= *Grosse Brandenburger Ausgabe*, vol. 13, ed. Christine Hehle) (Berlin: Aufbau-Verlag, 2003 [1892]), 159–160: "Holk fühlte sich, als er gelesen, einer gewissen Rührseligkeit hingegeben. Es war so viel Liebe in dem Briefe, daß er alte Zeiten und altes Glück wieder heraufsteigen fühlte. Sie war doch die Beste. ... Und diesem Gefühle hingegeben, überflog er den Brief noch einmal. Aber da schwand es wieder, alle freundlichen Eindrücke waren wieder hin, und was er heraushörte, war nur noch, oder sehr vorwiegend, der Ton der Rechthaberei."
20 Ibid., 214–215.
21 William Empson, *Seven Types of Ambiguity* (New York: New Directions, 1966 [1930]), 3.
22 Roman Jakobson, "Linguistics and Poetics," *Language in Literature*, ed. Krystyna Pomorska and Stephen Rudy (Cambridge, MA: Havard University Press, 1997), 62–94, at 85.

when he pointed out that for dissimulation "ambiguity doubtless affords the most frequent opportunity."[23] Now, in Fontane's country outing, the real act of dissimulation is withdrawn from representation; we only hear the father-in-law's complaints, and even those only in an indirect manner. If one wants to know how the emotional enigma of interpretation functions technically, one finds more concrete examples in the marital dialogues from Fontane's novels, and even better, or more troubling, those in Fontane's correspondence with his wife.

Interpreting letters, however, poses a special challenge to its readers. The most pointed discussion in this regard is probably the one circling around Edgar Allen Poe's *The Purloined Letter*. The competing readings by Lacan, Derrida, and Barbara Johnson of Poe's short story have one thing in common: the letter becomes an allegory of the conditions of language as such, which is condensed in the polysemy of the word *letter/lettre*. For Lacan, both letters are symbols of an absence: the letter is there and isn't there. Derrida criticizes Lacan's definition of the letter, and/or of language because Lacan's privileging of the lack would come close to an ontologization. Johnson, on the other hand, remarks that one could accuse Derrida of the same: although the epistolary letter as well as the alphabetic letter for Derrida are not topoi of lack, they become figures of dissemination. For Derrida, the letter presents the idea of a free movement of signification, a movement that crosses itself out and thus resembles the ruin of signification as such. What remains is that for Lacan, Derrida, and Johnson the letter is exemplary in that every utterance is severed from the intention of its referent. In Derrida's words: "The letter is held but never possessed. Never, neither by its sender nor its addressee .... It has no proper meaning .... Or: there is more than one sense and this multiple possibility is responsible for the movement."[24] This being-nowhere of the letter, as Lacan calls it, expresses itself in a very concrete manner in Fontane's and Kafka's amorous correspondence: letters are sent late or not at all; letters cross and thereby create misunderstandings; older letters follow newer ones and thereby to this day confuse the chronology of the correspondence as it appears in critical editions; other letters simply never arrive. The retardation runs parallel with the acts of writing and of reading that are marked as well by belatedness. In other words: in Fontane's and Kafka's love letters one finds the perfect recipe for frustration.

With this, we come to the Fontanes' love letters. Emilie and Theodor Fontane's three-volume marital correspondence presents an admirably comprehensive manual of epistolary frustration and the ambiguous

---

23 Quintilian, *Institutes of Oratory; or, Education of an Orator*, trans. John Selby Watson (London: George Bell and Sons, 1907), VI.3.87.

24 Jacques Derrida, "Purveyor of Truth," *Yale French Studies* 52 (1975): 31–113, at 42.

aggression resulting from it.²⁵ Thus, the editors of the correspondence wonder "how this doubtlessly complicated marriage could function as a durable bond over almost fifty years without scandals."²⁶ But perhaps this question is already slightly off in that it neglects how our idea of love has been slightly off for a long time—since Romanticism, to be exact; for as Niklas Luhmann has demonstrated, since the Romantic period, our discourse of love has been premised on impossibility.²⁷ Maybe this explains to some extent why in the marital correspondence of the Fontanes we can never really separate epistolary violence from the eroticism of role-playing and creating tension. Lauren Berlant, in words that sound surprisingly close to Luhmann's, explains the dialectical dynamics of such seemingly masochistic forms of attachment:

> Modern lovers are defined by their desire to remain in proximity to clarity—not simplicity—of the form of love; the form of love is an intention—not a compulsion—to repeat being attached. ... This is why the sideways gaze, the held breath, the mumbled phrase, or the strange piece of paper can so disconcert the dynamics of an attachment. This is how intimates who repulse each other can remain coupled when it is no longer fun.²⁸

Over fifty-four years the couple exchanges letters because Fontane often worked far away from the family as a foreign correspondent. The marital correspondence displays all the crucial moves and counter-moves one needs to know in order to excel in "warfare with velvet gloves": the

---

25 Theodor Fontane and Emilie Kummer married on October 16, 1850. Their marital correspondence started one and a half years later, in April 1852. Today, the letters are part of the Fontane archive in Potsdam and have been edited by Gotthard and Therese Erler: Emilie and Theodor Fontane, *Der Ehebriefwechsel* (= Grosse Brandenburger Ausgabe) (Berlin: Aufbau-Verlag, 1998). In his introduction, Gotthard Erler focuses on the letters by Emilie Fontane because it is the first edition containing (some of) her letters. The marital letters have been carefully collected (with the exception of Fontane's adulterous Dresden period) and were at times reread and newly "selected"; during this elimination process many of Emilie's letters vanished, possibly by her own hand. Hannelore Schlaffer argues in "Die gesprächige Ehe," *Fontane-Blätter* 67 (1999): 75–91 that in Fontane's literary texts, marriage similarly is characterized by the "utopia" of an infinite conversation; yet, even the "reality" of his *fictional* marriages looks otherwise, so that Schlaffer calls Fontane "the author of unhappy marriages" (75).
26 Gotthard Erler, "Einleitung," Emilie and Theodor Fontane, *Der Ehebriefwechsel*, vol. 1: *Dichterfrauen sind immer so. 1844–1857* (= Grosse Brandenburger Ausgabe, ed. ibid. and Therese Erler) (Berlin: Aufbau-Verlag, 1998), vii–xxxiv, at xi.
27 In *Liebe als Passion*, Luhmann assumes that the code of the modern discourse of love still follows the Romantic emotional script to a large degree.
28 Lauren Berlant, *The Female Complaint: The Unfinished Business of Sentimentality in American Culture* (Durham, NC/London: Duke University Press, 2008), 15.

54   Ambiguous Aggression

rhetorical art of ambiguous aggression, of criticizing someone without criticizing someone. Let us take the following example: For Fontane, his wife's short letters are a constant source of disappointment. To make explicit his dream of an intimate communication seems to be out of the question; the unarticulated wish thus remains unfulfilled. This is why Fontane applies *Ambiguous Aggression Strategy No. 1*: translate love frustration into arrogance, try to spoil the unacknowledged object of desire!

> *My dear Emilie-of-my-heart,*
> *First, my cordial thanks for your friendly lines in the letter from the 4th of the month; that they were too short for me, and as I believe rightly so, goes without saying; I won't urge you, however, to change this because I know from experience that your letters lose their charm as soon as you get to the second page.*[29]

Ambiguous Aggressive Strategy No. 2: present accusations as neutral assessments, as both spouses do. *Strategy No. 3*: anticipate one another's opinion or behavior, thereby denying his or her freedom, futurity, and generally the possibility of change. *Strategy No. 4*: make casual reference to third parties—which can even be God, or the Lutheran equivalent "conscience"—as Emilie likes to whenever she criticizes her husband. The same maneuver equally comes in handy when parrying one's partner's passive-aggressive remarks, a gesture gracefully executed by Emilie in a letter she sends from her vacation:

> *My dear husband,*
> *How lucky I am that your letters, as amiable as they may be, deliver me little treatises on my mistakes and weaknesses, which I know in their entire, all too big appearance. This is because here, young and old alike consider me a true exemplum, even little Marta says: ach, Mum, but here everybody is just crazy about you.*[30]

---

29 Theodor Fontane to Emilie Fontane, London, May 13, 1852, Emilie and Theodor Fontane, *Der Ehebriefwechsel*, vol. 1, 40–45, at 40: "*Meine liebe Herzens-Emilie, Für Deine freundlichen Zeilen vom 4ten d.M. nimm zunächst meinen herzlichen Dank; daß sie mir zu kurz waren, und wie ich glaube mit Recht, versteht sich von selbst; doch dring' ich nicht in Dich das zu ändern, da ich aus Erfahrung weiß, daß der Reiz Deiner Briefe aufhört, so wie Du auf den zweiten Bogen kömmst.*"

30 Emilie Fontane in a letter to Theodor Fontane, Neuhof, July 21, 1867, *Der Ehebriefwechsel*, vol. 2: *Geliebte Ungeduld. 1857–1871*, 304–305, at 304: "*Mein lieber Mann, Es ist ein wahres Glück daß Deine Briefe, so liebenswürdig sie sind, mir kleine Abhandlungen über meine Fehler u. Schwächen bringen, die ich auch in ihrer vollen, nur zu großen Erscheinung erkenne; denn hier werde ich von Groß u. Klein für ein wahres Musterbild angesehen, selbst Martchen sagt: ach, Mama, hier mögen Dich Alle doch gar zu gern.*"

Ambiguous Aggression Strategy No. 5 is of grammatical relevance: the frequent use of the subjunctive mode. The most condensed example of this grammatical technique can be found in Fontane's novel *Irretrievable*, where the female protagonist complains (without complaining) to the pastor about her husband:

> And really, [my husband] would be the ideal of a man if he had ideals at all. Please excuse this wordplay, it forces itself upon me because this is how it is and no different, and I have to say it again .... Have to, I say, and if I don't want to avoid anything sharp and hurtful [*wenn ich nicht ... vermeiden möchte*], I would tell him .... But let's drop assumptions about what I would or wouldn't say ...[31]

The wife says nasty things, then takes them back, excusing her insults as language playing with itself, at times at the price of grammatical correctness. The formulation "if I don't want to avoid anything sharp," for instance, would actually have to be in the subjunctive *irrealis* if it were to be grammatically correct: "if I *wouldn't* want to avoid anything sharp." Fontane, nevertheless, chooses the negating auxiliary verb "don't": a false indicative hiding another subjunctive. This modal idiosyncrasy performs on the level of grammar what has its philosophical pendant in Hegel's critique of the "beautiful soul." This is because, for Hegel, the main deficit of the beautiful soul consists in its timidity: Goethe, Schiller, Jean Paul, and Schlegel's respective beautiful souls can only remain beautiful because they remain virtual, rather than becoming actual. The *grammatical* mode of this remaining virtual would be the subjunctive. This reading is sustained by the fact that in a later passage Christine's brother indeed refers to his sister disparagingly as a "beautiful soul, a posthumous Jean Paul character"[32] in what appears to be an allusion to Schlegel's critique of Jean Paul's female characters "His women have

---

31 Fontane, *Unwiederbringlich*, 14–15: "Und wirklich, (mein Mann) wäre das Ideal von einem Manne, wenn er überhaupt Ideal hätte. Verzeihen Sie diese Wortspielerei, sie drängt sich mir aber auf, weil es so und nicht anders liegt, und ich muß es noch einmal sagen .... Muß, sag' ich, und wenn ich nicht alles Spitze und Verletzliche vermeiden möchte, so würd' ich ihm sagen .... Doch lassen wir Vermuthungen über das, was ich sagen oder nicht sagen würde ...." Gottfried Honnefelder summarizes: "In keinem anderen Roman hat Fontane das Problem menschlicher Kommunikation und ihrer Grenzen so sehr im Medium des Briefwechsels sichtbar warden lassen wie in *Unwiederbringlich*." *Der Brief im Roman. Untersuchungen zur erzähltechnischen Verwendung des Briefes im deutschen Roman* (Bonn: Bouvier, 1975), 199; see also Claudia Liebrand, *Ich und die Anderen. Fontanes Figuren und ihre Selbstbilder* (Freiburg i.Br.: Rombach, 1990), 143–153.
32 Ibid., 38.

red eyes and are exempla, mannequins [*Gliederfrauen*] for psychological-moral reflections on femininity or enthusiasm [*Schwärmerei*]."[33]

All in all, the Fontanes' correspondence often reads like the grim competition between two martyrs. Ergo, *Ambiguous Aggression Meta-Strategy No. 6*: the one who loses wins. Who is the more powerful victim? Here, epistolary sensibility turns into mere sensitivity—one could also say: eighteenth-century *Empfindsamkeit* degenerates into *Empfindlichkeit*.[34] Who had more sleepless nights, who had colder days, the worse stomach flu, the more persistent cold? Who had to endure the more boring dinner party? Although Aaron Schuster assumes that "complaint serves to ritually exorcize the envious gaze of the Other,"[35] with the Fontanes the otherwise reliable apotropaic technique fails and even intensifies the rivalry—so that when Theodor complains, as he does so often, that other guests at a dinner party did not treat him with enough courtesy, Emilie complains in her letter about his continuous complaining.[36] To this complaint competition, Theodor adds another hurdle with *Meta-Strategy No. 7*: double bind communication. Gregory Bateson defines a double-bind as the causal connection of two irreconcilable demands. Non-compliance to these demands is punished with withdrawal of affection, even as it is impossible to leave the situation.[37] Let us take the following example: From London, Fontane admonishes his wife to write only happy letters. At this time, Emilie raises their children pretty much by herself; they have lost two children, and she does not have enough money to care for the rest. "Be cheerful, trusting,

---

33 "Seine Frauen haben rote Augen und sind Exempel, Gliederfrauen zu psychologischmoralischen Reflexionen über die Weiblichkeit oder über die Schwärmerei." *Kritische Friedrich-Schlegel-Ausgabe. Erste Abteilung: Kritische Neuausgabe*, vol. 2, ed. Ernst Behler, Jean-Jacques Anstett, and Hans Eichner (München: Schöningh, 1967), 246–247.
34 In *Diskurse der Empfindsamkeit. Zur Geschichte eines Gefühls in der Literatur des 18. Jahrhunderts* (Stuttgart: Metzler, 1988) Nikolaus Wegmann draws attention to the fact that the demand in sentimental epistolary communication to write spontaneously and freely presents a "normative principle" (76). The Fontanes are clearly acting out such a script—and yet *Empfindsamkeit*, according to Wegmann, strives for "tenderness" as a paradigm of interaction; in the Fontanes' letters, in distinction, strategies and theories of prudence (49), from which the epoch of sensibility tried to separate itself, persistently surface in comical ways.
35 Aaron Schuster, "Critique of Pure Complaint," in *The Trouble with Pleasure: Deleuze and Psychoanalysis* (Cambridge, MA: MIT Press, 2016), 1–26, at 3.
36 Roland Berbig writes about such an exchange, "Vom Nörgeln und Nöhlen. Eine beiläufige Betrachtung zu Fontane und Kempowski," *Fontane Blätter* 95 (2013): 120–134, at 121–122. The letters to which Berbig refers are dated from June, 1878 and to be found in: *Der Ehebriefwechsel*, vol. 3: *Die Zuneigung ist etwas Rätselvolles. 1873–1898*, 110–117.
37 Gregory Bateson, "Toward a Theory of Schizophrenia," in *Steps to an Ecology of Mind* (Chicago, IL/London: University of Chicago Press, 2000 [1972]), 201–228.

and abstain from sickly nagging," Fontane writes her, "then you shall remain young and, at least maybe, get silk dresses."[38] Untangling herself from this double bind, and simultaneously fighting back with her own double bind (complaining without complaining), keeps Emilie on her toes throughout the many years of correspondence.

The list of ambiguous aggressions would not be complete without *Meta-Strategy No. 8*: the substitution of amusement, pity, or sadness for aggression. When Theodor informs Emilie that he will not take her on any more travels because he is tired of Emilie telling him how to deal with "hosts, waiters, coachmen, porters, and castellans," he does not present this measure as punishment but as a "sad fact":

> You can imagine that I am not telling you this maliciously, my soul is free from any aggravation but perhaps you'll admit that I'm correct and find that I am describing quite accurately the sad fact of our continuous annoyance as soon as we enter the cab. ...
>
> Against my will I got into this contemplation; actually I wanted to write you just a short letter, and only nice and pleasant things; I also urge you not to want to perceive what I previously wrote as an accusation but only as the attempt of a psychological explanation.[39]

The irony, of course, consists in the fact that Theodor, who just accused Emilie of giving him too many instructions, now gives her instructions on how to read his words: i.e., *not* as accusations but only as explanations—and as a "quite accurate" explanation at that, of which the sixty-five-year-old wife is surely in bitter need. Theodor ties an additional double bind by formulating an accusation but at the same time forbidding his wife to read it as such. This allows Theodor to threaten his wife with vacation-revocation without having to take responsibility for this aggression. Rather than formulating an accusation that would have to be sustained by argument, Theodor rests on the unquestionable authority of scientific evidence, a "fact." But the etymology of "fact" (which comes from *facere*) calls attention to fabricatedness, fictitiousness, and metaphoricity, rather

---

38 Theodor Fontane in a letter to Emilie Fontane, London, July 3, 1856, *Der Ehebriefwechsel*, vol. 1, 325–326, at 326.
39 Theodor Fontane in a letter to Emilie Fontane, Berlin, July 9, 1862, *Der Ehebriefwechsel*, vol. 2, 236–238: "Du kannst Dir denken, daß ich Dir das nicht im Bösen sage, meine Seele ist frei von jeder Gereiztheit, aber vielleicht giebst Du mir Recht und findest, daß ich das traurige Faktum beständigen Aergers so wie wir gemeinschaftlich in die Droschke steigen, ziemlich richtig erkläre .... Wider Willen bin ich in diese Betrachtung hineingerathen; ich wollte eigentlich nur einen kurzen Brief schreiben und nur Freundliches und Angenehmes; ich bitte Dich auch dringend das Vorstehende nicht als Anklage sondern blos als Versuch einer psychologischen Erklärung auffassen zu wollen."

than self-evidence in the strict sense. As a sad trope, the "sad fact" in Fontane's letter presents an elliptical metonymy. The "sad fact" not only turns aggression into sadness but it anthropomorphically displaces this sadness onto the object. Alexander Kluge admonished readers of Fontane: "We do not honor Fontane if we count him as polite."[40]

Pleas for Interpretation

So much ambiguity does not simply go by unnoticed. Even though it might be most elegant to parry one ambiguity with another, until no one who is part of the conversation knows any longer what is being spoken of, there comes a point when someone asks the question "What should it mean?" (*Was soll das bedeuten?*)

> Dear wife,
> Today I got your lines—the nicest ones that I received in 5 weeks. You write: "everybody is spoiling you, only from here you would be treated meagerly." In the context, in which this phrase appears it can only relate to my correspondence with you, and there this comment again belongs to those enigmatic remarks in which you are … big. … What is it supposed to mean when you write to me short and solemnly in regard to a soiree of 3 people during which not even two bottles of Medoc Cautenac à 12 ½ silver pennies were drunk: "this is how I pictured our future." What shall I do with such a clause? From here you resume, very drily, with the remark "that we also finished your Maraschino." If maybe all of this isn't meant maliciously then I can only say: educated people express themselves in a way that their words cannot be misunderstood. I want to see the person who can read humor or harmlessness into two such sentences.[41]

---

40 "Wir ehren Fontane nicht, wenn wir ihn für höflich halten." Alexander Kluge, "Das Politische als Intensität alltäglicher Gefühle. Theodor Fontane," in *Fontane, Kleist, Deutschland, Büchner. Zur Grammatik der Zeit* (Berlin: Wagenbach, 2004), 7–19, at 7–8.

41 Theodor Fontane in a letter to Emilie, Berlin, August 15, 1876, *Der Ehebriefwechsel*, vol. 3: *Die Zuneigung ist etwas Rätselvolles. 1873–1898*, 69–71: "Liebe Frau, Heute früh erhielt ich Deine Zeilen—die freundlichsten, die ich in diesen 5 Wochen empfangen habe—und danke Dir dafür. Du schreibst: „alles verwöhnte Dich dort, nur von hier aus würdest Du knapp behandelt." Dem Zusammenhange nach, kann sich dieses nur auf mein Briefschreiben beziehn und da gehört denn diese Bemerkung wieder zu jenen rätselhaften Aeußerungen, an denen Du … groß bist. Was soll es heißen wenn Du mir, in Bezug auf eine aus 3 Personen bestehende Gesellschaft, in der noch nicht zwei Flaschen Medoc Cantenac à 12 ½ Sgr. getrunken wurden, kurz und feierlich schreibst: „so hatte ich mir unsre Zukunft gedacht." Was soll ich mit solchem Satze machen? Daran knüpfst Du dann, ganz trocken, die Aeußerung „dass wir also Deinen Maraschino ausgetrunken hätten." Wenn dies alles möglicherweise nicht böse gemeint gewesen ist, so kann ich blos sagen: gebildete Menschen drücken sich eben so aus, daß ihre Worte nicht mißverstanden werden können. Ich will den sehen, der aus zwei solchen Sätzen, wie die vorstehend citirten, Humor und Harmlosigkeit herauslesen kann."

The private letter incites an exegetic obsession; it creates a moment of acute epistemological uncertainty, of skepticism and testing. Theodor treats Emilie's letter like a secret text that is to be deciphered. Several times he quotes from the letter as if apotropaically repeating the phrases back to the origin of evil would bring out the truth. The "enigmatic remarks" of his wife put Fontane into a hermeneutic stupor: "What should this mean, what shall I do with such a clause?" ("Was soll es heißen? Was soll ich mit solchem Satze machen?"). Such requests for interpretation, of course, themselves require interpretation. If Fontane were his wife's analyst, one might say that he is making a scansion, a cut. Or, again with double bind theory, one could understand his requests for clarification as attempts to leave the emotionally messy communication situation and to have a meta-communication instead. However, what is problematic about the idea of "meta-communication" is that it suggests that it would be possible to give an explanation of an utterance that would be more literal than the utterance itself. Paul de Man warns of such questions about the "literal meaning" as well as of questions concerning the "rhetorical substance" of a statement. For all such questions are to be understood rhetorically, writes de Man:

> Any question about the rhetorical mode of a literary text is always a rhetorical question which does not even know whether it is really questioning. The resulting pathos is an anxiety (or bliss, depending on one's momentary mood or individual temperament) of ignorance, not an anxiety of reference ..., not as an emotive reaction to what language does, but as an emotive reaction to the impossibility of knowing what it might be up to.[42]

We ask for the meaning because of our own not-knowing, which might even make us anxious, or angry. Questions such as "What is it supposed to mean[?]," "What shall I do with such a clause?" are never to be taken at face value, de Man warns. At least for Fontane and Kafka, this hypothesis seems to be true. Even though Fontane demands "no irony," this (luckily) doesn't stop him from being ironic. Or, the irony of irony is that we cannot answer with certainty the question of Fontane's irony. Take his sentence "From here you resume, very drily, with the remark 'that we also finished *your* Maraschino!'" This sentence shows a lot of wit. For in the formulation "very drily" writing and drinking are rendered parallel; with the effect that "very dry ..." (*ganz trocken*) may not only refer to Emilie's sense of humor but also to the Maraschino—a dry fruit liquor, after the enjoyment of which (as well as of the Medoc Cantenac) Emilie will hardly have been "very

---

42 Paul de Man, "Semiology and Rhetoric," *Diacritics* (fall 1973): 27–33, at 33.

dry ...." Emilie's consumption of various alcoholic beverages stands in economic contrast with the figure of scarcity. Theodor assumes that Emilie feels only "curtly treated" ("knapp behandelt") by him because he has not written much. At the same time, he himself accuses Emilie's rhetoric of being scarce, in the sense of *brevitas*: "you write to me short and solemnly" ("*kurz und feierlich schreibst [du]*"). Both expenditure and scarcity (finishing the bottle, "*this* is how I pictured my life") come together in the idea of verbal ambiguity. For verbal ambiguity always alludes to *more*—but in as little space as possible. *Brevitas* (in the Latin sense of brevity and force) is characteristic for passive-aggressive statements: it is as if the sentence would want to flee the scene before it ends and the bomb explodes. Because of its beauty and its relation to brevity, let me cite here from one of Emilie's early letters to her husband, a mere six years into the marriage: "*This morning I received your kind letter from Paris. Your cordiality revives me a. I begin more and more to be content with the measure a. the type of your love.*"[43] Besides the more obvious hilarity of having to "content" oneself with the Other's love, and besides the oddity of Emilie not saying, as one might expect, that she is "more and more content" with her husband's love but rather that she *begins* more and more to content herself with it—note the subtle, still conceivable formal sideswipe: the abbreviation ("a." instead of "and") right after the word "measure." The brevity manages to convey that her husband's measure errs on the side of stinginess and that the latter puts the marriage at risk; for it is, after all, the very conjugal conjunction *and*, that "marries" two words to one another, which Emilie truncates.

Kafka's Letters to Felice

I will now turn away from Fontane and toward Kafka—a turn that may make some heads turn. The reason I say this is because surprisingly few attempts have yet been made to bring Fontane and Kafka into dialogue with one another. Now, this is understandable given that Fontane's realist portraits of social life from the second half of the nineteenth century are much more evenly tempered than the shrill grotesqueness of Kafka's twentieth-century world. But why then does Max Brod list Fontane among the "favorite authors" of the late Kafka?[44] And why then was there not in fact a single novel of Fontane's in Kafka's library, even

---

43 Emilie to Theodor Fontane, October 19, 1856, *Der Ehebriefwechsel*, vol. 1, 411–414, at 413; in German: "Heut Vormittag erhielt ich Deinen lieben Brief aus Paris. Deine Herzlichkeit erquickt mich u. ich fange immer mehr an, mit dem Maaß u. der Art Deiner Liebe zufrieden zu sein."
44 Max Brod, *Über Franz Kafka* (Frankfurt a.M.: Fischer, 1974), 46.

though he knew *Irretrievable*?[45] What we do find among Kafka's books are indeed four volumes of Fontane's letters.[46] "Kafka delighted in reading biographic and autobiographical works," writes Brod. "Fontane's letters were among his favorite readings, he knew them much more closely than the poetic works."[47] It is thus safe to say that Kafka knew Fontane's letters; he loved Fontane's letters. At one point, Fontane even becomes an *alter ego*, or a pseudonym, in Kafka's romantic correspondence. In four postcards[48] to his soon-to-be–ex-fiancée Felice Bauer, Kafka aligns himself with Fontane by quoting a long, bitter passage in which Fontane expresses to his old pen-pal Mathilde von Rohr deep discontent with his wife Emilie, who criticized him for having quit his job as standing secretary at the Academy of the Arts in Berlin after only one month:

> I had to decide whether—for the sake of external security—I wanted to live a dull, lightless and joyless life or, preferring the old insecurity, wanted to regain at least the *possibility* of happy hours. I chose the last option while my wife demanded the first from me. I would have to call this demand infinitely loveless if I didn't assume she calmed herself with the truism: one gets used to anything. That sentence is wrong.[49]

---

45 While Kafka's friend Minze Eisner was staying at the Baltic Sea, Kafka wrote her several letters, in which he mentioned Fontane and sent *Meine Kinderjahre*: "The small book by Fontane might have disappointed you in regard to the Baltic way of life, and maybe one has to know more of Fontane in order to really understand these memories, especially his letters. But most importantly, I am not really sure where this Baltic life took place—in the memoirs, or in one of his novels. Moreover, I don't quite recall the title of that novel—*Cecile* or *Irretrievable*, or another one, I don't know, I could check that in Prague." Matliary, end of March 1921. Kafka, *Briefe 1902–1924* (Frankfurt/M.: Fischer, 1958), 309–312, at 312.
46 Jürgen Born, *Kafkas Bibliothek. Ein beschreibendes Verzeichnis. Mit einem Index aller in Kafkas Schriften erwähnten Bücher, Zeitschriften und Zeitschriftenbeiträge* (Frankfurt/M.: Fischer, 1990).
47 "Kafka delighted in reading biographic and autobiographical works. Grillparzer's and Hebbel's diaries, Fontane's letters were part of his favorite reading; he knew them far better than the poetry by these authors." Brod, *Über Franz Kafka*, 99.
48 I am referring to the postcards on Fontane from August 17, 1916 and to three more from August 21, 1916, Kafka, *Briefe an Felice und andere Korrespondenz aus der Verlobungszeit*, 680 and 685–686.
49 Fontane to Mathilde von Rohr, Berlin, July 1, 1876, 164–166, at 164, see also the earlier letter on the same topic by Mathilde von Rohr from June 17, 1867, 162–164, *Theodor Fontane. Briefe*, vol. 3. *Briefe an Mathilde von Rohr*, ed. Kurt Schreinert und Charlotte Jolles (Berlin: Aufbau, 1963): "Ich hatte mich zu entscheiden, ob ich, um äußrer Sicherheit willen, ein stumpfes, licht- und freudeloses Leben führen oder, die alte Unsicherheit bevorzugend, mir wenigstens die *Möglichkeit* heitrer Stunden zurückerobern wollte. Ich wählte das letzte, während meine Frau das erstre von mir forderte. Ich würde diese Forderung unendlich lieblos nennen müssen, wenn ich nicht annähme, sie hätte sich in ihrem Gemüth mit dem berühmten Alltagssatze beruhigt: der Mensch gewöhnt sich an alles. Dieser Satz ist falsch."

One is reminded of the earlier passage from *Irretrievable*, in which Fontane's sanctimonious character Christine speaks badly of her husband to the priest, using the subjunctive all the while. In this instance, it is the author himself who complains about his wife to Mathilde von Rohr, who indeed lived in a convent. Here as well the subjunctive *irrealis* renders the critique of the spouse purely "hypothetical": Fontane "would" call his wife loveless if her behavior were not merely the result of a certain stoic *ethos*. Emilie's attitude, however, "is wrong"—in the indicative. So does this after all mean that Emilie is in fact loveless? Kafka writes a postcard to Felice about Fontane's "dreadful argument with his wife"[50] and quotes Fontane's letter almost in its entirety. Kafka ends the postcard with the sentence: "So today Fontane wrote you a postcard instead of me."[51] Although Felice is more professionally successful than either Kafka or Fontane she must have expressed understanding for Fontane's resignation; Kafka, however, cannot let pass Felice's sympathy for Fontane but instead has to "correct" it: "—Yes, Fontane! You must not do an injustice to his wife, in spite of how unjust she herself was, and how often."[52] The manner in which Kafka lectures Felice—pretending to have understanding for Emilie, only in the next moment to pronounce a much harsher verdict about her—mirrors the way in which Fontane superficially forgives his wife in the letter to Mathilde von Rohr, only then to scapegoat her. Kafka characterizes Fontane's (and in fact his own) style with the following succinct description: "All this is said casually, more lightly than it is meant, and it might even be meant more casually than it is in truth."[53]

For their part, Kafka and Fontane admonish their women that they shall write more, more quickly, and less ambiguously: "Dearest, don't

---

50 Kafka in a postcard to Felice Bauer, Prague, August 13, 1916, *Briefe an Felice und andere Korrespondenz aus der Verlobungszeit*, 680. Fontane's argument with his wife can be found in Fontane's *Briefe. Zweite Sammlung Erster Band*, 208–209.
51 Ibid., "So heute hat Dir also Fontane statt meiner geschrieben."
52 Kafka to Felice in postcards from August 21, 1916 in: *Briefe an Felice und andere Korrespondenz aus der Verlobungszeit*, 685–686, at 685 ("– Ja, Fontane! Du mußt der Frau nicht Unrecht tun, so sehr Unrecht sie selbst gehabt hat, und zwar oft"). At this point, Emilie's letters had not yet been published and so Kafka was only reading Fontane's complaints about her. In his introduction to the marital correspondence, Erler corrects the ungenerous view of Emilie—perpetuated by Fontane himself but also by Gerhardt Hauptmann's autobiography: Emilie as the nagging housewife lacking in understanding for her poet-husband. Hannelore Schlaffer resumes her review of the *Ehebriefwechsel*, at 143–144: "Where Emilie's appearance wins, Fontane's must lose …. Through the complete edition of the correspondence a new aspect of Fontane surfaces, who now appears a little bit less charming than the author of the poems, reports, and novels."
53 Ibid.: "Es ist das alles flüchtiger, leichter gesagt, als es gemeint ist, und es ist vielleicht sogar flüchtiger gemeint, als es in Wahrheit ist."

cause me worries, or at least uneasiness, through indeterminacies such as in the postcard from Saturday,"[54] Kafka asks of Felice. And in a desperate letter, in which Kafka reassures (or threatens) Felice that he feels "bound to her through infinite violence,"[55] he presses Felice:

> *If you can explain this to me in a positive sense, and not only by saying it's all in my imagination, then please, please, Felice, do it. Explain the letters of this kind and those that you didn't write. ... Among those written ... [is] the last one from Wednesday evening, which says nothing but "Erna scolds me all day long; she claims I spend the whole day writing in my room instead of 'in die Luft zu gehn.'" Dear Felice, what shall this mean, what shall be said with this?*[56]

What Kafka, taking on the role of the analyst, seems to be getting at is an ambiguity in Felice's letter, an ambiguity that one might call a "Freudian slip": for Felice brings in "Erna" as a third party, who might be introduced to free her from her writing obligations to Franz. One expects Felice to write that on her vacation she should go outside (*an die Luft gehen*), instead of sitting all day at her desk; but she actually writes, changing just one letter in the preposition—from *an* to *in*—that she would rather explode (*"in die Luft gehen"*) than write one more letter! What we have here is a "contamination,"[57] which is how Freud coins the inadvertant condensation of two expressions; every such case of parapraxis (among which he counts slips of the tongue as well as of the pen) is caused by "the repression of an intention to say something,"[58] following Freud, and tellingly most of the examples rendered by him in his study on the *Psychopathology of Everyday Life* (1901) are of the aggressive, obscene, or insulting kind.

---

54   Ibid., Kafka in a postcard to Felice from Prague, August 17, 1916, 682: "Liebste, mach mir nicht Sorgen oder wenigstens Unbehagen durch Unbestimmtheiten wie in der Karte vom Samstag."
55   Ibid., Kafka in a letter to Felice from August 9, 1913, 440–441, at 441: "mit unendlicher Gewalt verbunden fühle."
56   Ibid.: *"Kannst Du es mir erklären und im guten Sinn und nicht nur durch den Hinweis auf meine Einbildungen, dann bitte, bitte, Felice, tue es. Gib eine Erklärung für die paar geschriebenen Briefe dieser Art und für die Reihe der nichtgeschriebenen. Unter den geschriebenen ... (ist) dieser letzte vom Mittwoch abend, in dem nichts steht, als daß »Erna schilt den ganzen Tag mit mir, sie behauptet, ich verbringe den ganzen Tag im Zimmer mit Schreiben, anstatt in die Luft zu gehn.« Liebste Felice, was bedeutet das, was soll damit gesagt sein?"*
57   Sigmund Freud, *Zur Psychopathologie des Alltagslebens (Über Vergessen, Versprechen, Vergreifen, Aberglaube und Irrtum)* (Berlin: S. Karger, 1912), 42.
58   Sigmund Freud, "Die Fehlleistungen," in *Vorlesungen zur Einführung in die Psychoanalyse* (= Studienfassung, vol. 1, ed. Alexander Mitscherlich) (Frankfurt/M.: Fischer, 2000), 85.

Of all disciplines, media studies has shown most compassion with the exhaustion Felice must have felt. Hans-Georg Pott found out that during the time that Kafka lived in Prague and Felice in Berlin (from 1910 to 1914), the mail was delivered no fewer than eight times a day in Prague, whereas in Berlin, where Felice resided, it was "only" delivered twice a day. "He could pretty much bombard her with letters"[59] Pott concludes. Mobilizing an equally militaristic language, Bernhard Siegert alerts us (in a footnote) to the sadism that characterizes Kafka's excessive demand for correspondence:

> Kafka emphatically refused to ease this distress: once, when Bauer wanted to know when her letters were delivered so she would be able to calculate her letters as well (one learns from the enemy), Kafka answered with the demoralizing remark that her army was still at a preindustrial (quasi-mail-coach) level, "My poor dear one, you want to know when your letters arrive, so as to plan accordingly? But the mail is quite unpredictable; in Austria in particular it functions in a completely haphazard fashion, just like the telegraph game at summer parties."[60]

Again, we are at a point in which Kafka and Fontane's love letters are eerily akin to one another—namely in the strict organizational principles to which their partners must subject themselves for the sake of a swift and enjoyable response system. Gotthard Erler (together with his wife, the lector Therese Erler, the editor of Fontanes' marital correspondence) is quite explicit when describing Fontane's ruthless hunger for ever-more letters from his wife: "Writing letters and receiving letters for him is a daily element of life and therefore he tortures his partners, first of all Emilie, with a strictly organized system of correspondence; derivations from this system cause him despair, suspicion, and rage."[61] But Fontane and Kafka not only urge their lovers to write more—the women shall also write with less equivocation: "As you don't want to hear ... the undertone of what you say, I will repeat it to you loudly once more"[62] Kafka writes to Felice. But how can you be loud in a letter,

---

59 Hans-Georg Pott, *Die Wiederkehr der Stimme. Telekommunikation im Zeitalter der Post-Moderne* (Wien: Sonderzahl, 1995), 77.
60 Bernhard Siegert, *Relays: Literature as an Epoch of the Postal System 1751–1913*, trans. Kevin Repp (Stanford, CA: Stanford University Press, 1999 [1993]), 300. The letter to which Siegert refers is from December 5–6, 1912 and can be found in: *Briefe an Felice und andere Korrespondenz aus der Verlobungszeit*, 89.
61 Erler, "Einleitung," xxxii–xxxiii, at xxxii.
62 Kafka in a letter to Felice from August 11, 1913, *Briefe an Felice und andere Korrespondenz aus der Verlobungszeit*: "Du willst den Unterton in dem, was Du sagst..., nicht hören, also wiederhole ich es für Dich laut noch einmal."

i.e., in a silent medium? How can you repeat an undertone loudly without it ceasing to be an undertone? Felice writes less and less, and complains about Kafka's "cruelty." In one of the last letters to be exchanged between them, Kafka writes:

> Dearest,
> but this I still have to tell you, you've read my Sunday letter only fleetingly, it's not possible otherwise, there was enough nasty stuff in the letter (I will explain it to you some time), and I'm happy about the fleeting reading and ask you to not read it again at the end—but there is no word, mustn't be a word about cutting the noose between us. Dearest, I am not so crazy to give the verdict on myself or to paint it up against the wall, on myself who I belong more to you than my picture around your neck. How could you read something like that into my letter, with what kind of eyes did you read it?[63]

Kafka's little epistolary hell gives us further glimpses as to how double bind communication works, how allusions immediately withdraw from interpretation. In Kafka's letter, demands and interdictions, scolding and praise are inextricably tied to one another: "You haven't read my letter!"/"Don't read my letter!"; "I was mean to you!"/"How come you say things aren't great between us?" The assurance that things are just fine between him and his fiancée is embedded in a semantic minefield of death threats: "there is no word, mustn't be a word about cutting the noose between us." With the same "noose" (*Strick*) he metonymically ties "my picture on your neck." Although these words shall presumably make the fiancée feel at ease, in combination with phrases such as "up against the wall" ("an die Wand"), or "the verdict" they instigate quite the contrary effect. "Peace doesn't need letters"[64] Kafka writes in one of his last letters to Felice.

The previously cited letter ends with the uncanny question: "with what kind of eyes did you read it?" A question that on the one hand

---

63 Ibid., Kafka in a letter to Felice, February 17 to 18, 1913, 303–305, at 304: "*Liebste, aber das muß ich Dir noch sagen, Du hast meinen Sonntagsbrief nur flüchtig gelesen, anders ist das nicht möglich, es war Widerliches in dem Brief genug (ich werde Dir das noch bei Gelegenheit erklären), und ich bin über das flüchtige Lesen froh und bitte Dich, ihn nicht am Ende noch einmal zu lesen—aber von einem zwischen uns bestehenden und vielleicht zerreißenden Strick kann dort, darf dort kein Wörtchen gestanden sein. Liebste, ich bin doch nicht so irrsinnig, selbst das Urteil über mich zu sprechen oder an die Wand zu malen, über mich, der ich Dir mehr gehöre, als mein Bild an Deinem Hals. Wie konntest Du etwas Derartiges in meinem Briefe lesen, mit welchen Augen hast Du das gelesen?*"
64 Kafka in a letter to Felice from August 15, 1913, *Briefe an Felice und andere Korrespondenz aus der Verlobungszeit*, 445–446, at 446.

displaces all responsibility to the "eyes" of the reader and on the other hand narrows the focus through the implicit order that the one who truly loves can read nothing but love between the lines. As if this wouldn't confuse the reader enough, the question furthermore suggests that one needs some kind of mirroring to know one's eyes are really one's own. Kafka in fact offers to Felice an epistolary reflection—but a reflection that shows her own body, her own eyes, to be mere prostheses, her perceptions to be inaccurate. After all, following Barbara Johnson, every interpretation of a letter becomes more complicated through the fact that the relation between sender and addressee is symmetrical. This symmetry becomes a problem as soon as we are interpreting a letter because the constant back and forth of the positions starts to resemble the psychoanalytical scene of transference: "The message I am reading may be either my own (narcissistic) message backwards or the way in which that message is always already traversed by its own otherness to itself or by the narcissistic message of the other."[65] Hence, we *never* know whether we are reading with our own eyes, or with those of the Other (if this difference still exists at all).

Kafka's Letters to Milena

This complexity only increases when Kafka starts corresponding with his Czech translator and soon-to-be lover, the journalist Milena Jesenská. In contrast to the correspondence with Felice, here rules a "balance of terror." One indicator for this is that Kafka compares Milena's "psychological observations" and the "delicacy" of her style to none other than Fontane in his travel reports and letters.[66] Now, it is no longer only Kafka who (as in the postcard to Felice) lets Fontane speak in his place. Milena (supposedly) also writes like Fontane, with the effect that Fontane writes to Fontane. Thus rendering the readings all the more confusing: whereas Kafka had driven Felice into emotional vertigo, reading Milena's letters has a radically derealizing effect upon him:

---

65 Barbara Johnson, "The Frame of Reference: Poe, Lacan, Derrida," *Yale French Studies* 55, no. 56 (1977): 457–505, at 503.
66 Max Brod reports that Milena wrote articles on Viennese life, on society talk, on books, on female fashion, on the daily news, as well as on psychological reflections: "Kafka couldn't find enough words of praise to emphasize the subtlety, liveliness, and stylistic resolve of these articles; he liked to compare these articles to the letters as well as the travel reports by Fontane, one of his favorite authors." ("Kafka konnte gar nicht genug Lobesworte finden, um die Feinheit, die Lebendigkeit, die stilistische Gelöstheit dieser Artikel zu erheben, die er gerne mit den Briefen und Reiseberichten Fontanes verglich, eines seiner Lieblingsautoren.") Brod, *Über Franz Kafka*, 194.

But then I read the letter carefully, i.e. Sunday's letter I read carefully, the reading of Monday's letter I will save until your next letter, it contains things that I cannot bear to read exactly .... There's only one thing left for me to ask from you, to answer me right away, one word is enough but it must be one that blunts the sharp edges from Monday's letter—and makes them readable. ...

I just read again Sunday's letter, it turns out to be more terrible than I thought after my first reading.[67]

How shall one make something more "readable" after having already read it? How readable is "readable"? Readability appears as the lowest degree of interpretation: the almost physical precondition that the written text is at all "bear(able)" to read. In order to guarantee this, the author Kafka tries to control latency: Milena is first asked (*"There's only one thing left for me to ask from you"*), then ordered (*"one word is enough but it must be one"*) to *"blunt the sharp edges."*

Perhaps you have noticed that Kafka's report on his process of interpretation contains the same comical *Kippfigur* as Fontane's country outing and the reading of the letters in *Unwiederbringlich*: in Kafka, first Sunday's letter appears harmless (at least more harmless than Monday's letter), but then, with some delay, the interpretation explodes: *"it turns out to be more terrible than I thought after my first reading."* In the letters to Milena, Kafka develops his own "two senses of interpretation": the first, fleeting, or rushed, reading, the second, careful, exact reading. Like in the famous letter in *The Castle*, the first reading tends to bring good, the second bad news.

Even the economic aspect, of which Fontane reminded his wife in the Maraschino-letter in which she might have written in an ambiguous manner, returns in Kafka: on the one hand we have again formulations of scarcity (*"save," "There's only one thing left for me," "one word is enough"*), and on the other hand this "one word" by Milena has to be the total word—the absolute condensation—that makes everything else clear, univocal. Soon Kafka will not ask Milena anymore for only one

---

67 Kafka to Milena Jesenská from Meran on June 3, 1920, Kafka, *Briefe an Milena*, ed. Jürgen Born and Michael Müller (Frankfurt/M.: Fischer, 2011), 42–44: "Dann allerdings las ich den Brief genau, d. h. den Sonntagsbrief las ich genau, das Lesen des Montagsbriefes hebe ich mir bis zu Ihrem nächsten Brief auf, es kommen Dinge drin vor, die ich genauer zu lesen nicht ertrage ... Es bleibt mir jetzt nur übrig Sie zu bitten, mir noch gleich hierher zu antworten, es genügt ein Wort, aber es muß ein solches sein, das allen Vorwürfen in dem Montagsbrief die Spitzen abbricht, und sie lesbar macht ....—Ich habe noch einmal den Sonntagsbrief gelesen, er ist doch schrecklicher als ich nach dem ersten Lesen dachte."

word that makes every other word superfluous but to take back whole sentences:

> *I have only one favor to ask from you: In today's letter from you there are two very hard sentences. ... Could you, Milena, take them back somehow, explicitly take them back—the first one only in parts, if you want to, but the second one in its entirety? ... There is even a third sentence in your letter that might be still more directed against me than the ones I quoted. The sentence about the sweet-stuff that is bad for one's stomach.*[68]

Just as in the letter before, it doesn't stay with *"only one favor"* but the one favor is followed by a second one (*"There is even a third sentence"*); the favor becomes a suggestion (*"if you want to"*), then turns into a command (*"but the second one in its entirety"*). The encroaching directions to the female writer, the censorship and requests for amendments, are slightly comical because of the role-switch they are attempting to bring about: the addressee (Kafka) is eager to substitute for the sender and, as a recipient, thereby becomes the sender of the letter. We can only guess what Milena might have written back because her letters have been lost.[69] But that a comparison to *"sweet-stuff that is bad for one's stomach"* (*"magen-verderbenden Zuckerzeug"*) would drive the hunger-artist Kafka up the wall seems obvious. Now, Milena shall take back this statement, she, so to speak, shall eat the "sweet-stuff" herself. But how shall that work? After all, a written sentence can only be revised through further additions, corrections, excuses, assertions: "I didn't mean it that way." The difficulty of such a revocation expresses itself in Kafka's desperate repetition: *"take them back somehow, explicitly take them back."* And still, there persists a certain tension; for although Kafka gives Milena orders in the end, he also assumes that she is the sovereign over these words: that she can take them back *ad libitum*, show mercy, turn back the wheel of time.

Two Genders, Two Economies of Interpretation

Let us return to de Man once more and to his critique of the obsolete question of the "literal or figurative" character of *"literary texts."* Thus, now—belatedly—the question: is a letter by the author a literary

---

[68] Kafka in a letter to Milena, Prague, August 4–5, 1920, *Briefe an Milena*, 185–186: "Nur eine Bitte habe ich: In Deinem heutigen Brief stehn zwei sehr harte Sätze .... Könntest Du Milena sie irgendwie zurücknehmen, ausdrücklich zurücknehmen, den ersten, wenn Du willst, nur zu einem Teil, den zweiten aber ganz?... Ja, noch ein dritter Satz steht in Deinem Brief, der vielleicht noch mehr gegen mich gerichtet ist, als die angeführten. Der Satz von dem magen-verderbenden Zuckerzeug."

[69] The only remaining letters from Milena Jesenská are published in: "Ich hätte zu antworten tage- und nächtelang." *Die Briefe von Milena*, ed. Alena Wagnerová (Frankfurt/M.: Fischer, 2005).

product? Most likely, we would affirm this question. But then how about the letter of the wife, or the author's lover? Can we call her letters "literary"? And does she enjoy the same liberties of literature? Or, do the lover's letters become treacherous when they as well indulge in poetic ambiguity, become equivocal, "unreadable"? *"[E]ducated people express themselves in a way that their words cannot be misunderstood"*—a statement like this by Fontane contains a judgment that makes one wonder who it is who makes the rules of the games, or the criteria. The answer is: the male author.[70] Whoever thinks that we are dealing with nineteenth- or early-twentieth-century problems here is mistaken. Just recently Chris Kraus expressed her dismay about similarly gendered double standards in a conversation about Kathy Acker: "I think it's a terrible thing that we still expect a consistency of women that we don't expect of men. Women would be criticized for inconsistency whereas in a male writer or thinker it's an admirable part of a nuanced picture of a person."[71] One of these construed expectations is directed at the economy of interpretation—an economy that has two sexes in Fontane as well as in Kafka: on the one hand a female, material, circular economy of the *oikos*, in which one drinks Maraschino and eats sweet stuff, and on the other hand the strictly spiritual economy of man.[72] It seems as if Fontane and Kafka find the mixing of these two economies almost unsavory. We sense a kind of masculine resistance that solidifies in the attempt to install a hermeneutics—be it by reference to the authority of science (Fontane) or to the kabbalistic idea of an absolute word or letter (Kafka).

One might be reminded at this point of the greatest of all (passive-) aggressive epistolary novels, *Les Liaisons dangereuses*. For—as both Barbara Vinken and Ulrike Vedder have elucidated—in Laclos' novel,

---

70 To quote Zadie Smith from "F. Kafka, Everyman," *New York Review of Books* 55, no. 12 (July 17, 2008): "Kafka's mind ... went wondrously fast—still, when it came to women, it went no faster than the times allowed."

71 Chris Kraus in conversation with Chloe Stead about Kathy Acker; http://www.anothermag.com/design-living/10096/chris-kraus-on-post-punk-literary-icon-kathy-acker (last retrieved August 22, 2017).

72 Here not only Kafka's famous affinity to Flaubert becomes apparent—Fontane too shows an affinity for the French writer. After all, Flaubert also tried, despite feelings of disgust, to teach his lover Colet a presumably more ascetic, more male style of writing: "Good style, valorized as male, is described as hard, hairy, and muscular .... Poor style, on the other hand, is denigrated as female; it is soft and fatty." Janet Beizer, *Ventriloquized Bodies. Narratives of Hysteria in Nineteenth-Century France* (Ithaca, NY/London: Cornell University Press, 1994), 78. On the prejudice that female writing is inferior to male style because of the former's excessive materiality, see Barbara Hahn in "'Weiber verstehen alles à la lettre'. Briefkultur im beginnenden 19. Jahrhundert," in *Deutsche Literatur von Frauen*, vol. 2, ed. Gisela Brinker-Gabler (München: C.H. Beck, 1988), 13–26.

too, Valmont questions the Marquise de Merteuil "Qu'avez-vous donc voulu dire?" after reading and rereading her letters ("J'ai beau vous lire et vous relire") because her irony collides with his literality.[73] Yet, all this is still the product of the fantasy of one, male author. The pleas and mandates for a hermeneutics by Fontane and Kafka, i.e., two literary authors, in contrast appear themselves anti-literary in character. The battle between the female lover, or wife, and the male author is fought around the question of whether the literary belongs to clear signification or to ambiguity. Is the literary on the side of control, or the giving up of control? Of course, distinctions like these are regressive, especially when talking about an author like Kafka, a master of ambiguity. And yet, this opposition is instituted where the author function collides with the function of the jealous lover; that is, where affect merges with critique. At this point, the female companion turns into an object of literature. One can call this bad critique because it is *too* affective, jealous—but at the same time Fontane and Kafka show that critique is always already libidinal. The libido of the author is always literary.

---

[73] Pierre-Ambroise-François Choderlos de Laclos, *Les Liaisons dangereuses* (= *Œuvres complètes*, ed. Laurent Versini) (Paris: Gallimard, 1979 [1782]), 3–386, at LXXVI, 149; Barbara Vinken, *Unentrinnbare Neugierde. Die Weltverfallenheit des Romans* (Freiburg: Rombach, 1991), 188–189; Ulrike Vedder, *Geschickte Liebe. Zur Mediengeschichte des Liebesdiskurses im Briefroman "Les Liaisons dangereuses" und in der Gegenwartsliteratur* (Köln: Böhlau, 2002), 131–134.

DOMESTIC VIOLENCE

Four Home in Hiding: Scenes of Domestic Violence

"That hurts me and the mother more than it hurts you."[1] Haneke

To those who have suffered domestic violence it may feel like an insult to see it subsumed under the title *"ambiguous* aggression," alongside two milder forms of social violence—flirtation and passive aggression—which also become objects of reflection during the nineteenth and early-twentieth centuries. *What is ambiguous about my suffering?* someone might ask with justifiable irritation. Therefore let me first clarify, somewhat defensively, that it is in no way my intention to diminish or trivialize the violence of domestic violence. So, for the rest of this chapter, allow me to go on the offensive. Calling domestic violence "ambiguous" is a provocation, and a necessary one, if one wants to be alert to the perfidious character of this violence, which begins with its name: how are we to read the name "domestic violence"? Does the name insinuate that "domestic violence" deals with a domesticated or tamed kind of violence? Even if we were to translate the word "domestic" more literally, as an adjective of the Latin noun *domus* for "home," we still would subscribe to the idea that domestic violence would be fenced off from other forms of structural violence, such as state violence, racism,

---

1 "Das tut mir und der Frau Mutter mehr weh als euch," says the father to his son after whipping him, in Michael Haneke's *The White Ribbon* (*Das weiße Band*, 2009), a movie about a German small town in the long nineteenth century. An earlier version of this chapter was published under the title "Ambige Aggression—Häusliche Gewalt im Realismus," *Weimarer Beiträge* 61, no. 2 (fall 2015): 181–201.

misogyny, heteronormativity, etc.² As a consequence, there is currently a push among North American feminists to speak of "public terror" instead of domestic violence. This makes a lot of sense given that, to quote the writer and activist Soraya Chemaly, "more than half of the 100-plus mass shootings in the United States between January 2009 and June 2014 involved the killing of an intimate partner or family member. Nine of the ten deadliest mass killings in the US in the past fifty years were perpetrated by men with histories of domestic violence."³ The push for recognizing domestic violence to be a form of terror was commented upon by the social scientist Shatema Threadcraft with an appropriately bitter irony: "This move is strategically brilliant, as terror is a problem toward which we are completely comfortable devoting conservable resources."⁴

The name "domestic violence" already has a certain diminishing, downplaying, or even "gas-lighting" quality that may in fact aggravate the difficulty of creating awareness around the issue. This difficulty of naming is no mere side-effect but rather is constitutive for domestic violence's particular mode of *hurting* (transitive and intransitive). Where does it hurt? First, the intransitive meaning of *hurting*: as someone experiencing family violence, you will hurt not only physically but will be subjected to a feeling of derealization: estranged or excluded, not only from your own family but from the very idea of "family"; as a consequence, you will have to mourn those ideals often tied in the first instance to that of family (love, tenderness, protection,

---

2   On the contrary, both Hegel, in §§260–262 of *Elements of the Philosophy of Right*, ed. Allen W. Wood, trans. H. B. Nisbet (Cambridge: Cambridge University Press, 1991 [1820]), 282–286 and Luhmann regard the family as an executive function of the state, with Luhmann concluding: "The family exaggerates society." "Sozialsystem Familie," in *Soziologische Aufklärung*, vol. 5 (Wiesbaden: Verlag für Sozialwissenschaften, 2005), 196–217: 205.
3   Soraya Chemaly, "America's Mass Shooting Problem Is a Domestic Violence Problem," *The Village Voice*, November 8, 2017, https://www.villagevoice.com/2017/11/08/americas-mass-shooting-problem-is-a-domestic-violence-problem; by the same author: "In Orlando, as Usual, Domestic Violence Was Ignored Red Flag," *Rolling Stone*, June 13, 2016, https://www.rollingstone.com/politics/news/in-orlando-as-usual-domestic-violence-was-ignored-red-flag-20160613; see also Pamelah Shifman and Salamishah Tillet, "To Stop Violence, Start at Home," The Opinion Pages, *New York Times*, February 3, 2015, www.nytimes.com/2015/02/03/opinion/to-stop-violence-start-at-home.html; Melissa Jeltsen, "We're Missing The Big Picture On Mass Shootings," *Huffington Post*, August 25, 2015, www.huffingtonpost.com/entry/mass-shootings-domestic-violence-women_us_55d3806ce4b07addcb44542a (all last retrieved March 6, 2018).
4   Shatema Threadcraft, "North American Necropolitics and Gender: On #BlackLivesMatter and Black Femicide," *South Atlantic Quarterly* 116, no. 3 (July 2017): 553–579.

care, nourishment, safety, loyalty, education, pedagogy, etc.). We cannot overestimate the binding and blinding effect of this ideological framework—at which point, the distinction between intransitive and transitive *hurting*, between *how someone hurts* and *how someone is hurt*, breaks down, because it becomes increasingly clear that the ideology by which we live enables the reproduction of this particular hurt. Note that we have not yet even arrived at the more spectacular, physical violence that is dealt first-hand. We will see that what is missing from scenes of domestic violence in general is such a distinct, univocal violence, committed by one actor alone. Instead, domestic violence is portrayed as ambiguous because it is entangled in complicit structures, ideologies, and institutions, and complicated by the presence of witnesses and bystanders.

If domestic violence plays tricks with our perception, shifts accountability and opens doors for denial then this means that domestic violence entails a representational or aesthetic problem. It is a reminder that categories like "representation" or "aesthetics" are not reserved for "frivolous" or beautiful things but that they actually decide about what appears to us, what becomes visible, readable, audible, perceptible. Of course, there are infinite reasons why a person may witness a situation of domestic violence without giving testimony to it—one of the main culprits is our well-meant respect for other people's private sphere; this almost religious belief instilled in us to respect the autonomy of "the family" is based upon an all-too-literal adherence to the distinction between private and public. In regard to the historical scope of this book, it is noteworthy that this very distinction became quasi-institutionalized by the rise of the bourgeoisie in the nineteenth century. Hence, Larry Wolff in his study on child abuse in Freud's Vienna can simultaneously report that in the late-nineteenth century societies against cruelty to children were founded, court trials held, newspaper articles published on especially gruesome cases—but that it would nevertheless take until the 1960s for public awareness to really shift; Wolff blames the distinction of public–private in helping us "repress" domestic violence:[5]

> Historians know very little about the history of childhood, of relations between parents and children. They know still less about the cruel and painful side of that history, the history of the abuse that children have suffered. Past centuries have left us little evidence to construct that history, for the brutalization of children was always a strictly private family matter, unrecognized as a public social evil.[6]

---

5   Larry Wolff, *Postcard from the End of the World: Child Abuse in Freud's Vienna* (New York: New York University Press, 1995 [1988]), 6.
6   Ibid., 4.

Still today, we have strong reservations against seemingly infringing on someone else's privacy (even that of a child or a battered person) by reporting a case of domestic violence. If bourgeois citizens were understandably concerned with how to protect themselves from an absolutist state and, as a reaction, separated private life from public life, then we nowadays grapple with the question as to how we can protect the private sphere from itself, i.e., from its (apparent) auto-aggression—even though this sphere is never simply private.

What could a scholar of literature possibly achieve in this regard? No more and no less than what we usually do: to work on enhancing legibility. In my readings, I will in a first step draw attention to the linguistic techniques by which violence is rendered ambiguous and, in a second step, speculate as to what symptomatic reaction formations (e.g., denial, not-knowing, uncertainty) follow from such ambiguously violent situations. Bear with me: literary examples are already hard to take, but examples from "real life" are far more difficult to cope with. Nevertheless, I would like to call into memory the 2018 case of the Turpin family; in the conversations about this case, the question was repeatedly raised as to how nobody could have noticed the abuse of no fewer than thirteen children. There had been plenty of indicators: when the family moved away from Texas, their former neighbors remained silent in spite of finding the vacated home full of feces and beds with ropes tied to them;[7] the Turpins' neighbors in California described the thirteen children and young adults as looking starved, scared to talk, invisible, filthy, and added that they were "walking in circles late at night"[8] in the living room. Still, nobody intervened. Yet the same community showed great alertness when it came to the condition of the Turpins' garden, eagerly reporting that the "yard was unkempt with overgrown weeds prompting a code violation."[9] What made the denial of the children's suffering possible appears to have been, among other

---

7   Molly Hennessy-Fiske and Paloma Esquivel, "Dead dogs, filth and ropes tied to beds: Inside the Turpins' home in Texas before they moved to Perris," *LA Times*, January 21, 2018, http://www.latimes.com/local/lanow/la-na-perris-texas-20180120-story.html (last retrieved March 6, 2018).
8   Kristine Phillips and Marwa Eltagouri, "Parents of captive Turpin siblings barred from contacting their 13 children," *The Washington Post*, January 25, 2018, https://www.washingtonpost.com/news/post-nation/wp/2018/01/24/captive-turpin-siblings-often-marched-in-circles-in-their-house-at-night-former-neighbor-says/?utm_term=.802eb2dc9bb7 (last retrieved March 1, 2018).
9   Samantha Schmidt and Lindsey Bever, "How a malnourished teen escaped a house full of chains and freed her 12 siblings," *The Washington Post*, January 16, 2018, https://www.washingtonpost.com/news/morning-mix/wp/2018/01/15/police-rescue-13-siblings-from-california-house-parents-charged-with-torture/?utm_term=.2e99fe2a91a0 (last retrieved January 18, 2018).

things, a peculiar economy of visibility and invisibility, by which the abuse of children was displaced onto a garden.

Now, the case of the Turpin family is exceptional in that it made it into the news as "The California House of Horrors." The former blindness has been overcompensated by ubiquitous broadcasting: the sheer number of children—thirteen, a baleful number—excessive cruelty, Christian fanaticism, a father with a creepy haircut, a mother's grin; all this set against the backdrop of the Californian sun apparently makes for a good story. Aristotle already knew that nothing works better on our emotions than fear and pity instilled by some hefty family cruelty:

> We must now decide what incidents seem dreadful or rather pitiable. ... Now if an enemy does it to an enemy, there is nothing pitiable either in the deed or the intention, except so far as the actual calamity goes. Nor would there be if they were neither friends nor enemies. But when these calamities happen among friends, when for instance brother kills brother, or son father, or mother son, or son mother—either kills or intends to kill, or does something of the kind, that is what we must look for.[10]

Reading Aristotle, one would think that there is nothing better than a good story of domestic violence and that therefore people would indeed "look for" situations of family abuse and be alert to them. And yet, we know that this is not the case, quite the contrary. This is because Aristotle—like today's media—only has exceptional cases in mind: in Greek tragedy, for instance, the family violence of people of exceptional status, kings, and demigods. What we are left with is the worrisome insight that the representation of domestic violence is caught in a doublebind: whereas we only notice domestic violence when it is exceptional, it by definition belongs to the ordinary (hence, it is questionable whether Aristotle's examples would qualify as "domestic violence"). The ordinary, however, elides us if we do not pay close attention to it, precisely because it *is* ordinary.

*

This is where realism and realist literature come in. Realism grapples with the problem of how to make the ordinary appear as such and thus gravitates to domestic violence as an example of just such an invisible, ordinary phenomenon. Again, to speak of domestic violence in German-language literature may seem hyperbolic given how few overt instances of it there are in the canon. This is especially true if we search before 1945, i.e., before the break with the *Vaterland* enables also literary

---

10 Aristotle, *Poetics, Aristotle in 23 Volumes*, vol. 23, trans. W. H. Fyfe (London: William Heinemann Ltd., 1932), 1453b.

breaks with fathers, mothers, even children (I am thinking here of Peter Weiss' *Farewell to the Parents* [*Abschied von den Eltern*, 1961], Ingeborg Bachmann's *Malina* [1971], or Elfriede Jelinek's *The Piano Teacher* [*Die Klavierspielerin*, 1983]). For the longest time, though, physical conflicts within the family were not perceived as violence. Rather authors like Hans Sachs, J. M. R. Lenz, or August von Kotzebue presented domestic violence as genuinely comical in its bodily articulation and unsophistication; in Kotzebue's *The Sufferings of the Family of Ortenberg* (*Die Leiden der Ortenbergischen Familie*, 1804) it becomes a running joke that if the nagging housewife Barbara does not shut up she will either be whipped with the hunting whip or spat upon.[11] And then there is of course Kleist whose *œuvre* as a whole is devoted to the destructiveness of the family as an institution.[12] But we have to wait until realism for a literary movement—and not just a single author—to open the still relatively new institution of literature to the everyday and thus to the family, and with this also to approach the family, its violence and its affects, in a critical manner and as an aesthetic challenge.[13] For one thing because, as Jameson explained, storytelling and affect are intimately intertwined in realism; this is especially true when family violence is narrated, so that it becomes very difficult, in fact nearly impossible, to tell the two apart. Yet this is precisely what some might expect from a critical literary analysis. The second reason that it is so difficult to read these moments—aside from the emotional toll it takes—is that they hide in the text. In "The Child in the Broom Closet," inspired by Ursula Le Guin's short story "The Ones Who Walk Away from Omelas," Elizabeth A. Povinelli begins with an instance of domestic violence to shed light on the invisibility of what she calls the "quasi-events"[14] of ordinary life. Povinelli adumbrates Le Guin's image of an abused child in a broom closet, an everyday horror silently accepted by the community,

---

11   August von Kotzebue, *Die Leiden der Ortenbergischen Familie*, vol. 2 (Frankfurt/Leipzig: Kummer, 1804 [1785]), 68–70.
12   "Kleist gibt zu denken ..., welche unbewältigte und als solche verkannte Gewalt in die häuslichen Verhältnisse, domestic issues, eingeht." Anselm Haverkamp, *Latenzzeit. Wissen im Nachkrieg* (Berlin: Kadmos, 2004), 137. In *Die zerbrochenen Bilder. Gestörte Ordnungen im Werk Heinrich von Kleists* (Würzburg: Königshausen & Neumann, 1989). Joachim Pfeiffer makes an inventory of the incidents of domestic violence in Kleist (38).
13   According to Fredric Jameson, realism emerges between the "genealogy of storytelling and the tale" and "its future dissolution in the literary representation of affect. A new concept of realism is then made available when we grasp both these terminal points firmly at one and the same time." *The Antinomies of Realism* (London/New York: Verso, 2015 [2013]), 10.
14   Elizabeth A. Povinelli, "The Child in the Broom Closet," in *Economies of Abandonment: Social Belonging and Endurance in Late Liberalism* (Durham, NC/London: Duke University Press, 2011), 13.

in order to illustrate the hermeneutical and ethical challenge of staying with this everyday suffering: "As a result any ethical impulse dependent on a certain kind of event and eventfulness—a crisis—flounders in the closet. How does one construct an ethics in relation to this kind of dispersed suffering?"[15]

The Battles around Domestic Violence (Droste-Hülshoff)

Realism is ethical in this precise sense; it stays with the ordinary. At the very beginning of German realism stands Annette von Droste-Hülshoff's *The Jew's Beech* (*Die Judenbuche*, 1842), which features two haunting scenes of domestic violence. In the novella, two women flee the same abusive husband within a two-year timespan; each time, we as readers see a wife taking flight from her home in disarray, in a death-drive-like compulsion to repetition. I will abstain from adding another reading here but would like to make some remarks on the discussion around family violence in *The Jew's Beech*, because the debate strikes me as at once exceptional and exemplary: exceptional in that it leads at all to a critical controversy about domestic violence;[16] exemplary in that this discussion highlights both the typical pitfalls and the hidden potential of literary reflections on the subject.

Starting with the negative, most of the secondary literature is oblivious toward the novella's aesthetic character; its critical attention is almost entirely spent on a classic either/or discussion about victims vs. perpetrator. What provokes this blindness toward the literary in the case of Droste-Hülshoff's novella is an utterance the second wife "is said to have declared."[17] On the wedding eve, the latter supposedly proclaims that if her husband should ever mistreat her like he did his first wife, she should be blamed for it;[18] upon which, the narrator laconically comments that the woman "had over-estimated her powers" (*The Jew's Beech*, 91). A surprising number of critics take these statements at face value; that is, as proof of "female hubris." Other, more feminist, readings oppose this interpretation.[19] But no matter which of these two

---

15 Ibid., 4.
16 Cora Lee Nollendorfs, "'... kein Zeugniß ablegen': Woman's Voice in Droste-Hülshoffs *Judenbuche*," *The German Quarterly* 67, no. 3 (summer 1994): 325–337.
17 Annette von Droste-Hülshoff, *The Jew's Beech*, trans. Lionel and Doris Thomas (= *German Novellas of Realism*, vol. 1), 88–132, at 91.
18 Ibid: "'A woman who is ill-treated by her husband is stupid or worthless; if I live to regret it, say it's my own fault," in *Die Judenbuche* (= *Historisch-kritische Ausgabe*, vol. 5,1, ed. Winfried Woesler) (Tübingen: Max Niemeyer, 1978), 7: "Eine Frau, die von ihrem Manne übel behandelt wird, ist dumm oder taugt nicht; wenn's mir schlecht geht, so sagt, es liege an mir."
19 See Gertrud Bauer Pickar, "The Battering and Meta-Battering of Droste's Margreth: Covert Misogyny in *Die Judenbuche*'s Critical Reception," *Women in German Yearbook* 9 (1994): 71–90.

positions one takes, one gets stuck in a moralizing back and forth about whether the wives' suffering was self-inflicted or not.

The question of who is the victim and who is the perpetrator not only misses out on the aesthetic dimension of the literary text, it also distracts us from what is truly perplexing—that is, the question itself. The curious fact that responsibility becomes questionable in Droste-Hülshoff's text tells us more about the effects of domestic violence than any taking of sides ever could. What is really noteworthy in *Die Judenbuche* is the ambiguity of domestic violence, as Martha Helfer has demonstrated in a most attentive reading.[20] If we take the two cardinal scenes of family violence in *Die Judenbuche*, then it is noteworthy that we as readers are excluded from the scene of abuse; instead of witnessing how the husband batters his wives, we see only the fleeing women, one bleeding and on her way to her parents, the other in deep distress and displaying enigmatic behavior.[21]

After Droste-Hülshoff's text, it is not long before the reader finally gains access to the scene of violence in the literary canon. And yet, we will see in the following examples that witnessing the aggression does not make it appear less ambiguous—but that it requires more artful depiction, not on the level of the plot as in Droste-Hülshoff's case so

---

20 Martha B. Helfer's "Wer wagt es, eitlen Blutes Drang zu messen?': Reading Blood in Annette von Droste-Hülshoff's *Die Judenbuche*," *The German Quarterly* 71, no. 3 (summer 1998): 228–253. In her careful analysis of the violence in *Die Judenbuche*, Helfer abstains from speculating about the source of violence, and instead meticulously lays out how structures like secrets and enigmas withdraw violence from representation. Helfer traces several secrets that are laid out in the text and puts forward for consideration that the reason why the second wife enters the abusive relationship could also be that she intended to distract from her incestuous relationship with her brother, which finally would have led her to kill her husband.

21 Shortly after the first wedding, the narrator records: "On the following Sunday, however, the young wife was seen running through the village to her people, screaming, covered in blood, abandoning all her new household utensils." *The Jew's Beech*, 90–91. In German: "[A]m nächsten Sonntage sah man die junge Frau schreiend und blutrünstig durchs Dorf zu den Ihrigen rennen, alle ihre guten Kleider und neues Hausgerät im Stich lassend." Droste-Hülshoff, *Die Judenbuche, Historisch-kritische Ausgabe*, 5. In the second incident, too, the narrator only depicts the traces of the domestic dispute from outside the house: "[S]oon he was to be seen often enough staggering across the road into the house, making a deafening noise inside so that Margret hurriedly closed doors and windows. On one such evening—now no longer a Sunday—she was seen rushing out of the house without cap or neckerchief, her hair hanging wildly about her head" 91; in German: "[B]ald sah man ihn oft genug quer über die Gasse ins Haus taumeln, hörte drinnen sein wüstes Lärmen und sah Margreth eilends Tür und Fenster schließen. An einem solchen Tage—keinem Sonntage mehr—sah man sie Abends aus dem Hause stürzen, ohne Haube und Halstuch, das Haar wild um den Kopf hängend." *Die Judenbuche*, 5–6.

much as in rhetorical as well as narratological registers. The examples that I will analyze to prove my point are short scenes taken from Adalbert Stifter's story "Granite" ("Granit") from the story collection *Colorful Stones* (*Bunte Steine*, 1853) and from Gottfried Keller's *Romeo and Juliet of the Village* (*Romeo und Julia auf dem Dorfe*, 1871); those who read at the borders of the canon might recall Theodor Storm's *Ein Doppelgänger* (1887); almost everybody will expect Gerhart Hauptmann's naturalist study *Flagman Thiel* (*Bahnwärter Thiel*) to be part of the discussion. The latter appeared only one year after Storm's novella (1888) and one year before Arno Holz and Johannes Schlaf's gruesome take on fatal neglect and abuse of an infant in *Papa Hamlet* (1889), which gives way to a number of expressionist texts picking up on the subject, such as Walter Hasenclever's *The Son* (*Der Sohn*, 1916). And because I conceive of Robert Walser as in some regards a late-realist author, I will conclude my reflections with a reading of *The Assistant* (*Der Gehülfe*, 1908), which, in my eyes, presents one of the most thought-provoking texts to read in the context of domestic violence.

This limited—though by no means complete—number of examples shows that domestic violence is almost a non-topic, which of course is not to say that it does not exist. Rather, the rarity of its depictions can be taken as a sign either of the fact that domestic violence is so common that it is not worth mentioning, or that it is too much of a taboo to address. These hypotheses coexist with one another insofar as violence in the family is usually handed out with a self-erasure kit. I investigate literary scenes that reflect upon this erasure, while at the same time remaining identifiable as portraits of domestic violence in that they demonstrate how the space of the family can make violence appear ambiguous. The family, in these texts, shows and denies violence at the same time and thereby increases the violence.

From the way in which I have framed this introduction, it will have become clear that I am not pursuing a traditional trauma reading. That is, even though we will be dealing with representations of traumatic experiences, I chose not to immerse myself in one literary text alone and to do an extended close reading—although one could certainly do that. But my own interest is more of a formalist kind so that, in this chapter, we will move rather quickly through four scenes of domestic violence by Stifter, Keller, Hauptmann, and Walser. What I seek to gain from this focused overview is to assemble something like a short catalogue of the common features of domestic violence in literary realism (and in Walser's case early modernism). Is there something like a poetics of domestic violence, a shared arsenal of specific narrative perspectives, tropes, style, syntax, and other structures?

Hyperbaton: Master Trope of Domestic Violence (Stifter)

What could possibly be "ambiguous" about domestic violence? In Stifter's *Granite* we find a first example to help us ponder this question: depending on how trustworthy one deems the viewpoint of the child, one can either read the following quote as the depiction of a mother who brutally beats her son's feet with rods, or—if one is more skeptical towards the child's description of "the castigation" (*"die Züchtigung," Bunte Steine,* 27)—as an exaggerated representation of a mother cleaning the dirty feet of her son. The scene thus productively complicates an overtly simple conception of realism as purely mimetic; it rather proves Eric Downing's claim that "'realism' entails a recognition of the inherent loss or reality," and that moreover this "self-conscious, somewhat self-deconstructive dimension … is intrinsic to realism, and almost inseparable from what we value as *literary* realism."[22] In the respective scene, the narrator remembers himself as a little boy, coming home to his mother with feet darkened with pitch:

> When she saw me coming and striding forward in this way, she jumped up. She remained hovering for a moment, either because she so admired me or because she was looking around for an instrument with which to receive me. Finally she cried: "What does this unholy son in the flesh [*eingefleischter*] have on him today?"
>
> And to keep me from going farther forward she hurried toward me, lifted me and carried me, ignoring my fright and her apron, out into the vestibule. There she set me down, and from under the loft steps, where we had to put all the switches and branches we brought home because they were not allowed anywhere else and where I myself had recently collected a large number of these things in recent days, she took whatever she could grab, and whipped my feet with it so long and so violently until the whole litter of switches, my pants, her apron, the stones on the floor, and everything around were full of pitch. Then she let me go and went back into the parlor.[23]

---

[22] Eric Downing, *Double Exposures: Repetition and Realism in Nineteenth-Century German Fiction* (Stanford, CA: Stanford University Press, 2000), 6 and 13. Though Downing's study focuses on moments of repetition that, more literally, capture this dual, conflicting nature of realism, his general claim still proves true.

[23] Adalbert Stifter, *Granite*, trans. Jeffrey L. Sammons, *German Novellas of Realism*, vol. 1 (New York: Continuum, 1989), 7–34, at 9–10. "Da sie mich so kommen und vorwärts schreiten sah, sprang sie auf. Sie blieb einen Augenblick in der Schwebe, entweder weil sie mich so bewunderte, oder weil sie sich nach einem Werkzeuge umsah, mich zu empfangen. Endlich aber rief sie: 'Was hat denn dieser heillose, eingefleischte Sohn heute für Dinge an sich?' Und damit ich nicht noch weiter vorwärts ginge, eilte sie mir entgegen, hob mich empor und trug

The narrative perspective of this passage perfectly reflects the (dys)-functions of family violence: Stifter chooses to use a first-person narrator, but one whose voice has an authorial quality in that his descriptions have the function of trying to understand his mother's actions. As an effect of this, the son appears just as impotent on a diegetic level as he appears omnipotent in a narratological regard; this is to say that the son has an infinite, even improbable, empathy with his mother even when she turns violent in his eyes. This omni-empathy or over-proximity of the narrator is tied to a claustrophobic excess of binding that can be explained by way of unorthodox psychoanalysis: we owe to Sándor Ferenczi the crucial psychological insight that a child is likely to identify with its parental aggressor, including in cases of "unbearable punishments": "Through the identification, or let us say, introjection of the aggressor, the latter disappears as part of the external reality, and becomes intra- instead of extra-psychic."[24] Which is to say, domestic violence presupposes a particular mode of relation—an over-connectedness with the Other that ultimately yields a certain disconnect. According to Gregory Bateson and Alice Miller, any relation presupposes a prior distance constituted by two distinct positions of self and Other.[25] A destructive excess of binding, as Stifter imagines it here, not only manifests itself in relation to the Other (e.g., the mother) but it produces a crisis in the subject, a self-disconnection. With Freud,

---

mich, meines Schreckes und ihrer Schürze nicht achtend, in das Vorhaus hinaus. Dort ließ sie mich nieder, nahm unter der Bodenstiege, wohin wir, weil es an einem andern Orte nicht erlaubt war, alle nach Hause gebrachten Ruten und Zweige legen mußten, und wo ich selber in den letzten Tagen eine große Menge dieser Dinge angesammelt hatte, heraus, was sie nur immer erwischen konnte, und schlug damit so lange und so heftig gegen meine Füße, bis das ganze Laubwerk der Ruten, meine Höschen, ihre Schürze, die Steine des Fußbodens und die Umgebung voll Pech waren. Dann ließ sie mich los, und ging wieder in die Stube hinein." Adalbert Stifter, "Granit," *Bunte Steine*, 21–60, at 26–27.

24 Sándor Ferenczi, "Confusion of Tongues Between the Adults and the Child (1933)," trans. Michael Balint, *International Journal of Psychoanalysis* 30 (1949): 225–230, at 227–228.

25 Gregory Bateson argues in "Toward a Theory of Schizophrenia," that schizophrenia emerges from certain family situations, in which the mother (I would say "the parent") is arbitrarily "controlling the closeness and distance between herself and her child" (213). This confusing situation causes over-proximity of the dependent child toward the mother as well as for the child to abandon his or her own feelings and perceptions. Alice Miller a little later made a similar point in *The Drama of the Gifted Child. The Search for the True Self*, trans. Ruth Ward (New York: Basic Books, 1997 [1979]); Miller gives to consideration that a child who has to blind out negative experiences and to instead empathize with the neglecting parent suffers an "inability to experience consciously certain feelings of his own" (9).

one would speak of a lack of primary (i.e., normal or necessary) narcissism,[26] for which the peculiar hesitance of the first-person narrator to say "I"—instead of "me"—would be symptomatic. In the end, narratology functions almost too symptomatically as an approach if one intends to analyze the forms of ambiguity that accompany domestic violence. This is because narratology perfectly mirrors, and thus in a way also repeats, the dysfunction of the family—in this case, the boy's lack of self-connectedness. Although narratology enables us to understand better the specific form of blindness evoked by domestic violence, it does not allow us to have a glimpse beyond this blindness.

In order to avoid this doubling, I would now like to transpose the problem from the register of narrative perspective into a rhetorical register. The advantage of rhetorical analysis in this regard ironically lies in its very limitation: rhetoric does not know of consciousness and thus does not take the bait of empathy. If we approach Stifter's passage anew via rhetorical analysis then we also get to see from anew how, for a moment, the child thinks that his mother "remained hovering for a moment, either because she so admired me or because she was looking around for an instrument with which to receive [or conceive, BNN] me [*mich zu empfangen*]." In the eyes of the child, his mother is first *in der Schwebe*, in suspension—not unlike a Marian apparition embodying the idea of Immaculate Conception, one might pun (*unbefleckte Empfängnis*). Then she grasps the child—and the child comes to grasp that in the place of the expected praise or a hug he is instead receiving a beating.

The boy's initial optimistic misinterpretation of the scene would be funny if the turn of events were not so grim; Stifter's narrator shares this tragic naiveté with the young protagonists of Gottfried Keller's most famous novella *Romeo and Juliet of the Village* in the story collection *Seldwyla Folks* (*Die Leute von Seldwyla*), which appeared roughly twenty years after Stifter's story. In Keller, the state of not-knowing encompasses both the daughter who is beaten and the father who beats her:

> ... and he struck her in the face several times, without really knowing why, so that both children ran home in great sadness and weeping, and neither did they really know why they were sad nor why they had been so merry before; because the roughness of the

---

26 "Narzißmus in diesem Sinne wäre keine Perversion, sondern die libidinöse Ergänzung zum Egoismus des Selbsterhaltungstriebes, von dem jedem Lebewesen mit Recht ein Stück zugeschrieben wird." Freud, *Zur Einführung des Narzißmus* (= *Gesammelte Werke*, ed. Anna Freud a.o., vol. 10) (London: Imago Publishing, 1946), 138.

fathers, in itself rather new, not yet had been understood by the unsuspecting creatures and could not move them in any deeper way.²⁷

The children's ignorance or "innocence" in the face of (their later) love as well as of the violence that they suffer (the *Grimmsches Wörterbuch* translates *arglos* with the Latin *innocens*) works like a blinder or a Freudian "Reizschutz" that wards off most of the traumatic experiences strung together paratactically in this long sentence. Rainer Nägele perceptively notes that Keller's sentences in general have the habit of "skipping ... along the surface, which makes it so difficult to describe their peculiar effects. Only sometimes, when one of these sentences enters the scene a bit more severely, even stamping its way in, it resounds as if hollow and uncanny."²⁸ This affective hollowness, in the passage from *Romeo and Juliet of the Village*, goes together with the becoming-unreadable of emotive memory. The temporal adverb "yet" ("not yet had been understood") suggests that there exists a latency period for an emotional concept like that of "aggression" to solidify in the psyche and to break through the child's protection shield. In his reading of *The Three Righteous Combmakers*, Nägele more generally warns in regard to the people of Seldwyla that

> ... innocence becomes the most terrible thing thinkable[,] ... the perverse par excellence. ... [I]t is the experience of a world of sin that has been stamped with Christianity, a world in which

---

27 "... und er gab ihr, ohne zu wissen warum, einige Ohrfeigen, also daß beide Kinder in großer Traurigkeit und weinend nach Hause gingen, und sie wußten jetzt eigentlich so wenig, warum sie so traurig waren, als warum sie vorhin so vergnügt gewesen; denn die Rauheit der Väter, an sich ziemlich neu, war von den arglosen Geschöpfen noch nicht begriffen und konnte sie nicht tiefer bewegen." Gottfried Keller, *Romeo und Julia auf dem Dorfe* (1871), *Die Leute von Seldwyla*, vol. 1 (= *Sämtliche Werke. Historisch-Kritische Ausgabe*, vol. 4, ed. Walter Morgenthaler) (Zürich: Stroemfeld, 2000), 87. In his translation, Wolf von Schierbrand overcompensates and fills in the moments of not-knowing in Keller's text: "... he struck her harshly in the face without giving any reason. So that both little ones went home weeping and sad; yet they were both still so much children that they scarcely knew at this time why they were so sad or knew before why they felt so happy. As for the rudeness of their fathers they did not understand the underlying motive of it, and it did not touch their hearts." *Seldwyla Folks: Three Singular Tales* (New York: Brentano's Publishers, 1919), 210–211.
28 Rainer Nägele, "Keller's Cellar Vaults: Intrusions of the Real in Gottfried Keller's Realism," in *Rethinking Emotion: Interiority and Exteriority in Premodern, Modern and Contemporary Thought*, ed. Rüdiger Campe and Julia Weber (Berlin: de Gruyter, 2014), 187–201, at 192.

innocence can only appear as the phantasmagoria of a radical forgetting of oneself and of the world.[29]

In other words, it takes time for aggression to mature, to be acknowledged, and for the child to be able to make aggression an object of knowledge. But who or what is it that is actually being forgotten in the example from Keller? And what is protected through this forgetting? Is it really the children? After all, the narrator reports that they suffer "great sadness" when returning home. But it is true that we read that the children cannot grasp the reason for their sadness—and this very absence of a reason can indeed be life saving if the source of suffering is the family, on which a child's survival depends.

We witness a similar, possibly protective censoring mechanism in Stifter's *Granite*: here, the mother's aggression initially not only goes by unrecognized by the boy but he even translates her aggression into an act of grace. From the very outset of the story, the latter is introduced as a story of *Pech*, meaning not only "pitch" but also "mishap." If one takes this second connotation seriously then the aggression, to which the son is subjected, is first depersonalized and abstracted from the mother and then awarded a lapidary, metaphysical quality. Given that the instrument for beating the boy is a set of rods, one might also feel reminded of the biblical proverb 13:24 "a father who spares the rod hates his son, but one who loves his son brings him up strictly." This proverb, which interprets sensitivity as hate and violence as love is exemplary for the Judeo-Christian transvaluation of values, which more generally filters acts of violence through familial paradigms of love and education. Even Walter Benjamin still belongs to this tradition with his enigmatic remark in *Critique of Violence* that pedagogical violence presents one of the few manifestations of divine violence performed by human beings.[30]

---

29 Ibid. The fact that I offer a Freudian reading of the scene from Keller indicates that I do not share Nägele's view that Keller's characters are a-psychological.

30 "The educative power, which in its perfected form stands outside the law, is one of its manifestations. These are defined, therefore, not by miracles directly performed by God, but by the expiating moment in them that strikes without bloodshed and, finally, by the absence of all law-making." Walter Benjamin, "Critique of Violence," in *Reflections: Essays, Aphorisms, Autobiographical Writings*, ed. Peter Demetz, trans. Edmund Jephcott (New York: Schocken Books, 1986), 277–300, at 297; "Zur Kritik der Gewalt," *Aufsätze, Essays, Vorträge: Gesammelte Schriften*, vol. II.1, ed. Rolf Tiedemann (Frankfurt/M.: Suhrkamp, 1999): 179–203, at 200. For Benjamin, pedagogical violence is a violence of pure means, which can be taken as a critique of the Platonic concept of pedagogy, in which violence is always a means to an end. As the ends, however, do not justify the means, Benjamin tasks us to think about this positively: if we assume that the alibi for violence is that it is pedagogical when really it is just violence (i.e., without an end), then Benjamin transvalues this thought by claiming that it is divine violence. Reading Benja-

If we want now to approach this scene through rhetorical analysis, we are likely to notice the quite enormous hyperbaton: a trope that appears with striking regularity in scenes of domestic violence. The reason for this can be found in Longinus' description of the emotional atmosphere evoked by hyperbata, because for Longinus hyperbaton reflects and elicits extreme emotions:

> It [hyperbaton] is a very real mark of urgent emotion. People who in real life feel anger, fear, or indignation ... (it is impossible to say how many emotions there are; they are without number), often put one thing forward and then rush off to another, irrationally inserting some remark, and then hark back again to their first point. They seem to be blown this way and that by their excitement, as if by a veering wind.[31]

The image of "blowing ... as if by a veering wind" makes more readable a persistent motif that otherwise remains somewhat in the air: flying. What is the connection between domestic violence and flying? As a matter of fact, elevated movements come up in all but one of the textual examples discussed in this chapter: Stifter's mother is "hovering" ("in der Schwebe," 22); Storm's mother in *Der Doppelgänger* "flew into a corner of the room"[32] when her husband attacks her, and even in Robert Walser's *The Assistant* the narrator makes an "Anflug"[33] (literally "a descent"), i.e., an approach, or a futile attempt, to keep the husband from abusing his wife. Approaching flying only thematically, however, does not adequately attend to the ways in which these hyperbata actually function; rather, the emotional register is deeply intertwined with the syntactical and epistemological. Consequently, when reading a hyperbaton, the syntax too requires us to "fly" over textual areas without knowing where we will end up; the obvious reason for these "fly-over zones" is that the units of the sentence are divided. Hyperbaton is

---

min's argument in a historical context, Eva Geulen takes his words as an objection to attempts in the nineteenth century to bring educational matters under the control of the police: "Legislating Education: Kant, Hegel and Benjamin on 'Pedagogical Violence'," *Cardozo Law Review* 26 (2004/05): 943–956, at 947.

31 Longinus, "On Sublimity,"*Classical Literary Criticism*, ed. D. A. Russell and Michael Winterbottom (Oxford/New York: Oxford University Press, 1989 [1972]), 166–167.

32 "... flog in eine Ecke des Zimmers," Theodor Storm, *Ein Doppelgänger* (= *Sämtliche Werke: Novellen 1881–1888*, vol. 3, ed. Karl Ernst Laage) (Frankfurt/M.: Deutscher Klassiker Verlag, 1987), 517–579, at 547.

33 Robert Walser, *Der Gehülfe* (= *Sämtliche Werke*, vol. 10) (Frankfurt/M.: Suhrkamp, 1985 [1908]), 87.

in this regard a very German trope, I would boldly infer, given the German language's capability to form extremely long sentences through integration of subordinated clauses; one could even wonder what the preponderance of hyperbata tells us about "German emotions." For if according to Longinus emotions form syntax and vice-versa then one might want to add a chapter of German emotions to Longinus and ask: what emotions are possible in German?

One understanding of hyperbaton is that it performs a division of meaning, and hence creates a state of not-knowing. Hyperbata have the effect that understanding becomes a matter of time. Longinus writes on Demosthenes that the transpositions performed by his hyperbata ...

> produce not only a great sense of urgency but the appearance of extemporization, as [the author] drags his hearers with him into the hazards of his long hyperbata. He often holds in suspense meaning which he set out to convey and [and now starts Longinus's own hyperbaton], introducing one extraneous item after another in an alien and unusual place before getting to the main point, throws the hearer into a panic lest the sentence collapse altogether, and forces him in his excitement to share the speaker's peril, before, at long last and beyond all expectation, appositively paying off at the end the long due conclusion; the very audacity and hazardousness of the hyperbata add to the astounding effect. There are so many examples that I forbear to give any.[34]

While the effect of Longinus' ironic non-example of a hyperbaton feels hardly traumatic, in the passage from *Granite* the "extemporization" yielded by hyperbaton could be linked to a traumatic belatedness. In Stifter, the condition of the child's not-knowing what his mother is up to extends over no less than six lines, six lines that separate the announcement of what might happen from the sudden turn to (what the child deems to be) the catastrophe.

But there is still more that binds hyperbata to the bursting of family bonds. When reading hyperbata, Quintilian states succinctly, "the sense cannot be ascertained but by uniting the two separate parts."[35] It is not least this dialectical tension between interruption and resumption, which makes hyperbaton the master trope of domestic violence, because domestic violence, too, binds through dissolution. Like in a moment of domesticated violence, in hyperbaton the experience of division is only transitory; the reason for this is that the moment of

---

34 Longinus, "On Sublimity," 167–168.
35 Quintilian, *Institutes of Oratory*, book VIII, chap. 6, 66.

indecision, of hovering, of separation and disorder, is belatedly undone when the main clause comes together again, as in a family reunion. The question is which of these two acts is more violent: the separating of what presumably ought to be together, or the uniting of what was violently broken up? Longinus in his deliberations on hyperbaton still presupposes the existence of a "natural order of thought," and even more generally the existence of "things which are by nature completely unified and indivisible."[36] Likewise, Quintilian establishes that hyperbaton is a transposition—literally a *"transgressio"*—of the "natural order" of words; though only a little later Quintilian demurs "that there is no real bond of union" anyway. This moment is key: for Quintilian thus at the same time accepts and suspends the effectivity of this order. If we now apply Quintilian's tropological wisdom to the problem of domestic violence—a state of dis-order, formalized as hyperbaton—then hyperbaton would be the symptom of a seemingly unnatural falling apart of the family, even as this trope at the same time reminds us of the fact that there is in the first place no natural unity or bond between words or between people.

Tropes are spatial constructions, and in *Granite* this spatial dimension of the hyperbaton exceeds the limits of syntax in a dance-like jump, or flight: the mother darts to her child, she lifts it and carries it over to a place "out of the field," in a kind of *décadrage*. The people in the scene are driven by aerial movements—*schreiten, springen, schweben, eilen, heben, tragen*—movements oscillating between ground and air, walking and flying.[37] If earlier we took notice of the violent side of hyperbaton, then it is now time to take record of the disturbing beauty of the scene, its sublime terror. In fact, the dance-like verbs in Stifter function as literary terms as well: *tragen* (to carry over) is linked to metaphor; *schreiten* (to stride) to the *Schreittanz*/sonnet (i.e., the classic depiction of two separated lovers); *springen* (to jump) divides and connects two lyrical lines qua enjambment (*Zeilensprung*); and *Hebung* (to lift) is a stressed syllable in lyrical language. All this amounts to the fact that Stifter employs a highly poetic language on the level of lexicon in order to evoke something like a choreography. This is riveting for two reasons: first, if the movements of the mother draw their energy from a poetic vocabulary, then literature would partake in the aestheticization and

---

36 Longinus, "On Sublimity," 167.
37 One might be reminded here of Cathy Caruth's reading of Kleist's *Über das Marionettentheater* in "The Falling Body and the Impact of Reference (de Man, Kant, Kleist)," in *Unclaimed Experience: Trauma, Narrative, and History* (Baltimore, MD/London: Johns Hopkins University Press, 1996), 73–90, at 75–76. Caruth explains the gracefulness of Kleist's marionettes with their being "antigrav," as Kleist has it, i.e., not subjected to Newton's law of gravity but instead flying and hovering.

anestheticization of violence. After all, the eloquence and elegance of literature are in tension to what happens in the scene: "a child is being beaten." Other than in Stifter's literary tableau, it was precisely the literal, *anti-literary* character of this merely descriptive formula "a child is being beaten" that left Freud perplexed when he listened to patients who had fantasies of children being beaten without any context or linguistic ornament—a fantasy that Freud then came to incorporate into the smooth operating system of the theory of seduction.[38]

The vocabulary of high literature in Stifter is remarkable insofar as we are talking about realist literature, and one usually does not associate realism with literariness or style but with lack of style; this, at least, was Georg Lukács' fear, on which he elaborated in his seminal essay "Narrate or describe?" Lukács warned that realism was always on the verge of regressing into a mere enumeration of details that threatens to corrode the narrative function.[39] Thus, realism is supposed to strive for transparency (and even when magical moments occur in realist texts they tend to be framed as rumors, manipulation, or superstition). Things are different in the quote from *Granit*: the texture of the text is so pronounced that—contrary to Lukács' worries—the aesthetic appears to be displaced into the diegetic; language itself becomes more present rather than what it represents. A way of coming to terms with this literariness of realism—and thus of making rhetoric realistic—is by saying that the scene depicts a psychological disturbance in the child. But still there remains a creeping feeling that realism in these lines is abandoning its chief task—description—just as the mother abandons her child. The issue of abandonment is, of course, pertinent when a parent abuses a child, or allows a child to be abused. But Stifter's scene goes deeper in that it stages literature's own abandonment, its own looking or turning away from description. In this way, Stifter performatively repeats and intensifies the ambiguity of violence as well as the violence of ambiguity.

---

38 Freud, "'Ein Kind wird geschlagen' (Beitrag zur Kenntnis der Entstehung sexueller Perversionen)," in *Studienausgabe*, vol. 7 (Frankfurt/M.: Fischer, 2000 [1915]), 229–254.

39 Lukács, "Erzählen oder beschreiben? (1936)," 199. Lukács argues here that realism cannot fulfill its historical mission if it restricts itself to a naturalist enumeration of details. In "On Realism in Art," Jakobson had named precisely the detail—i.e., the logic of contiguity or metonymy—as realism's formal key feature (24). For Lukács, though, realism cannot dispense of the categories of experience, narration, and fiction, because without them the possibility of identification is forestalled. Barthes made still more explicit than Lukács this dialectical struggle between the anarchic abundance of details and narration, between necessity and contingency ("The Reality Effect," in *The Rustle of Language*, trans. Richard Howard [Berkeley/Los Angeles, CA: University of California Press, 1989], 144–146).

Semantic Field: Systematic Beating (Hauptmann)

The next analysis contains yet another technique of literary unaccountability: Gerhart Hauptmann's *Flagman Thiel* is *the* exemplary German text on the topic of domestic violence. It is a story of denial, surpassed only by the author's own forces of denial in the face of National Socialism.[40] *Flagman Thiel* is the psychological study of a loving father who nevertheless closes his eyes to the abuse that his son Tobias suffers at the hands of Thiel's second wife. The reason for this denial is as dated as it is tacky: the gateman, we learn, is sexually dependent on his wife and thus cannot bring himself to "man up" to her. Instead, he represses his son's abuse. We are thus talking about the novella as an "unheard-of event," insofar as *Flagman Thiel* is all about the not-hearing, not-talking, and first and foremost about the not-seeing of domestic violence. The boy's name, "Tobias," highlights this blindness: reminiscent of the son's name in *The Book of Tobit* where the son, with divine help, cures his father's blindness and vindicates the "demon of lust." Nothing of this sort happens in Hauptmann's version of the story; here there is neither divine nor parental intervention. The father remains "blind" to his child's suffering. The gateman is usually at work when his son is abused, and thus out of sight, though he cannot help but to detect the boy's bruises. One day, however, Thiel has to return home early because he forgot his lunch; upon approaching the family house the father hears the soundtrack of domestic violence and, unlike the visual sense, the auditory at first forces itself upon him:

> "What, you merciless, heartless scroundrel! ... Just you wait—just you wait. I'll teach you to mind. You'll never forget." For a few moments there was silence. Then a sound could be heard like the beating out of clothes. And the next instant another hailstorm of abuse was let loose. ...
> "Shut your mouth!" when a slight whimper had been audible. "If you don't shut your mouth, I'll give you a portion from which to feed off for eight days."
> The whimpering did not subside. The flagman felt his heart pounding in heavy, irregular beat. (Hauptmann, *Flagman Thiel*, 312)[41]

---

40 Peter Sprengel, *Gerhart Hauptmann. Bürgerlichkeit und großer Traum. Eine Biographie* (München: Beck, 2012), especially chap. 10.

41 Gerhart Hauptmann, *Flagman Thiel*, trans. Adele S. Seltzer, *German Novellas of Realism*, vol. 2, ed. Jeffrey L. Sammons (New York: Continuum, 1989), 304–330, at 312; the passages where I felt that I had to alter Seltzer's translation are the address ("Was, du unbarmherziger, herzloser Schuft!"), which she translates very freely as "You horrid little beast, you!" and the last sentence, which she renders as: "I'll give you something that'll keep you going a whole week." I will return to the

And yet, Hauptmann's omniscient narrator, who almost exclusively takes the viewpoint of the father, manages to neutralize these violent sounds, too, by translating *qua* another *as if* ... formula into noises of domestic work: the beating out of clothes ("wie wenn Kleidungsstücke ausge*klopft* würden"). In his prose-piece "Knocking" ("Klopfen"), Robert Walser, who knew Hauptmann personally, similarly has his narrator suspect that the sound of household "Klopfen" serves as a cover-up for family brutalities: "There is knocks again. Apparently it's a carpet on which someone is working. I envy all those who practice flogging harmlessly."[42] Or also: "Possibly his wife is beating him a little like a piece of furniture [*bemöbelklöpfelte*] and hooding him a little [*behäubelte*]. One is better off not saying too much about this."[43]

If in Stifters' *Granit* the narrative voice of the son was over-empathic with his mother, then this scene from Hauptmann performs the reversal: the father is not "with his son," not even in his imagination. Rather, he seems eager to erase the child's body from the scene so that nothing is left of him but his clothes. And like in Stifter, the mother's aggression is camouflaged through housework. When her husband appears in the doorway and wants to confront his wife, she cunningly uses Thiel's hesitation in order to turn the tables by vociferously accusing him of sneaking up on her. The way this moment is formulated is quite peculiar: whereas the translation reads "she recovered herself sufficiently to address her husband with violence" (Hauptmann, *Flagman Thiel*, 313) a more literal translation would read: "[she] finally manned up enough [*ermannte sich*] to turn on [*anzulassen*] her husband forcefully [*ihren Mann heftig anzulassen*]."[44] Not only does the violent mother become

---

strangeness of the dialogues toward the end of the chapter. The original reads: "'Was, du unbarmherziger, herzloser Schuft! ...—na, wart nur, wart, ich will dich lehren aufpassen!—du sollst dran denken.' Einige Augenblicke blieb es still; dann hörte man ein Geräusch, wie wenn Kleidungsstücke ausgeklopft würden; unmittelbar darauf entlud sich ein neues Hagelwetter von Schimpfworten. ... 'Halt's Maul!', schrie es als ein leises Wimmern hörbar wurde, 'oder du sollst eine Portion kriegen, an der du acht Tage zu fressen hast.' Das Wimmern verstummte nicht. Der Wärter fühlte, wie sein Herz in schweren, unregelmäßigen Schlägen ging." *Bahnwärter Thiel* (= *Sämtliche Werke. Centenar-Ausgabe*, vol. 6, ed. Hans-Egon Hass) (Berlin: Propyläen, 1963), 35–68, at 46.

42 Robert Walser, "Klopfen," in *Wenn Schwache sich für Starke halten* (Zurich/Frankfurt/M.: Suhrkamp, 2011), 199–200, at 199: "Da klopft's schon wieder. Anscheinend ist's ein Teppich, der bearbeitet wird. Ich beneide alle die, die sich im Prügeln harmlos üben."

43 Walser, "Die Allee," *Wenn Schwache sich für Starke halten*, 98–101, at 101: "Womöglich bemöbelklöpfelte und behäubelte ihn seine Frau ein bißchen. Man tut gut, nicht zu viel hierüber zu sagen."

44 "(Sie) ermannte sich endlich so weit, ihren Mann heftig anzulassen," Hauptmann, *Bahnwärter Thiel*, 47.

masculine but the verb that describes her action is *anlassen*—a verb to be used to indicate violent speech as well as the starting of a seemingly self-propelling engine. We will come back to this point.

Yet, if the beatings are removed from the text's diegetic eye, they are still present in a different way because the word *schlagen* is dispersed throughout the text. First, in a prolepsis toward the beginning of the novella, the narrator mentions that with the birth of her own child, the stepmother's love for Tobias "turned into unmistakable dislike" (Hauptmann, *Flagman Thiel*, 308), in German "*schlug* ... in unverkennbare Abneigung um*" (*Bahnwärter Thiel*, 41), with *schlagen* meaning "beating." Second, this prolepsis is literalized a little later in the passage cited, when the noises of the beating inside the house also "beat" the father's ear ("A volley of violent, jangling tones assailed [*schlug an*] his ears," 312).[45] Third, we learn at the end of the scene that the father's heart is beating heavily ("The flagman felt his heart pounding in heavy, irregular beats [*Schlägen*]," 312). Fourth, even the signal echoes the unseen event when it "rang with three shrill beats [*Schlägen*]"[46] (314). Hauptmann employs what Empson calls "the method of reiterative imagery,"[47] i.e., the construction of a field of signifiers that creates a latent *Leitmotiv*. The question is what function the reiterative imagery of *beating* has in *Flagman Thiel*. Do the variations of the verb *to beat* work as transitory devices of empathy, echoing the boy's anguish? Or, is the beating rather to be read as a form of guilt-tripping: the "bad conscience" tormenting the "bad father"? Given Hauptmann's life-long obsession with the figure of Christ, the bell tolling three times is probably a not-so-subtle allusion to Peter's repeated denial of Jesus before the rooster crows three times. But we must interrupt the sentimental joys provided by the biblical allegory right here in order to take notice that we are shifting away from the object of the beating, the boy.

These kind of diversionary maneuvers seem to be symptomatic in texts on domestic violence. What is happening here could be interpreted as another case of hyperbaton, called *hypallage*: a particular type of inversion by which the adjective shifts from the expected noun to another. A classic example of *hypallage* is in Virgil's *Aeneid*, where Rome is first evoked as "altae moenia Romae"[48] so that "altus" ("high") oddly

---

45 "Ein Schwall ... misstönender Laute *schlug* an sein Ohr," *Bahnwärter Thiel*, 46.
46 My translation. Seltzer translates more freely "the signal rang shrilly, three times," *Flagman Thiel*, 314; *Bahnwärter Thiel*, 48.
47 William Empson, *The Structure of Complex Words* (Cambridge, MA: Harvard University Press, 1989 [1951]), 67–68.
48 Virgil, *Aeneid 1–6. English and Latin*, trans. H. R. Fairclough (Cambridge, MA: Harvard University Press, 1999), book 1, l. 7.

modifies "Roma" instead of the "walls": "the walls of high Rome."[49] The idea appears to be that the thought of Rome's magnificence upsets the poet's grammatical sense. In Hauptmann, it is not an adjective that shifts but the word *beating*, which is displaced from the boy to his surroundings. As such, it would perform a kind of abstraction; for if the enabling father is portrayed as being subjected as well to beating, then this might just be another way of saying that it always hurts "the family" the most when one of its members has to be subjected to violence—comparable to the scene in Michael Haneke's *The White Ribbon* (2009) where the father first whips the son and then explains to the son that it hurts the parents the most to whip him. Instances like these are typical features of double bind communication where every negative injunction is immediately negated, as in Gregory Bateson's example "Do not see me as the punishing agent."[50] Another, more abstract, way of saying the same is to say: in Hauptmann, the net-like structure around the word *beating* reflects a particular form of aggression, which results from the very ambiguity of domestic aggression. The source of this ambiguity lies in the idea of the family as a system: a system of total inclusion, as Luhmann has it,[51] a system of uninhibited communication in the most extreme way, a system that seems to have the capacity of neutralizing violence. This is because the family, *qua* structure, is always both "subject" and "object" of its own violence. Though we might deem the break the gesture of violence par excellence, in the case of the family this break takes place in an enclosed place, a break within a circle, to speak in formal terms. Thus, Ohad Parnes, Ulrike Vedder, and Stefan Willer in their book on *The Concept of Generation* purport that "The literature of the nineteenth century focuses on the family not as a unified system or discourse, but rather as a framework full of tension and conflict, which

---

49 Heinrich Lausberg, *Handbook of Literary Rhetoric*, ed. David E. Orton and R. Dean Anderson (Leiden/Boston/Köln: Brill, 1998 [1960]) categorizes "altae moenia Romae" for *alta moenia Romae* as a *hypallage adiectivi*, in which "the adjective that fits the superordinate noun is placed in the genitive," §606, 306.
50 Gregory Bateson states in "Toward a Theory of Schizophrenia" that the classic double bind consists of a primary negative injunction that is added by a second injunction, which is in conflict with the first: "Verbalization of the secondary injunction may, therefore, include a wide variety of forms; for example, 'Do not see this as punishment'; 'Do not see me as the punishing agent'" (207).
51 Niklas Luhmann, "Jenseits von Barbarei," in *Modernität und Barbarei. Soziologische Zeitdiagnose am Ende des 20. Jahrhunderts*, ed. Max Miller and Hans-Georg Soeffner (Frankfurt/M.: Suhrkamp, 1996), 219–230. According to Luhmann, it has historically been the family's task to make inclusion a continuous, plausible process (221). In "Sozialsystem Familie," Luhmann states that the family exaggerates society by still performing the inclusion of the entire person ("Inklusion der Vollperson") (199).

has something of a picture-puzzle character";[52] and indeed what makes representations of domestic violence in the nineteenth century so perplexing is precisely *both* the unity or system character of the family *and* the sense that the family is in disarray.

Maybe we could go so far as to read Hauptmann's excessive use of the word *schlagen* (beating) not only as an inversion and misattribution of a word to another noun akin to *hypallage* but also as literalizing the percussive aspect of this trope. In that sense the repeated beating is linked to rhythm—that is precisely force, rather than semantics, or possibly the alternation between the semantic and the anti-semantic. It really is a kind of meta-figure, insofar as the beating (*Schlag*) would seem to be a figure of reiteration—reiteration also in the sense that we could hear the percussive beating in *Flagman Thiel* as echoing another uncanny beating from Goethe's *The Recreations of the German Emigrants* (*Unterhaltungen deutscher Ausgewanderten*, 1795). In the novella "The Knocking"[53] an orphan girl grows up in an aristocratic family. As a young woman, she rejects all her suitors in order to stay with the family. But now a ghostly beating sound sets in wherever the young woman walks in the house. The narrator describes the sound first as "the knocking" ("das Klopfen"), then as "the pounding" ("das Pochen," which Goethe, in his works, uses both for blood circulation but also for the movement of a hammer), and finally as "the beats" ("die Schläge").[54]

> Outraged by this circumstance and by the disarray, the nobleman determined upon adopting strong measures. He took down his large hunting-whip from the wall, and swore that he would flog the girl to death if he heard the knocking one more time. From this time forth she could go through the house without the slightest molestation, and the knocking was never heard again. (Goethe, *The Recreations of the German Emigrants*, 289)[55]

---

52 Ohad Parnes, Ulrike Vedder, and Stefan Willer, *Das Konzept der Generation. Eine Wissenschafts- und Kulturgeschichte* (Frankfurt/M.: Suhrkamp, 2008), 151.
53 Johann Wolfgang von Goethe, "The Knocking," in *The Recreations of the German Emigrants*, trans. Thomas Carlyle (London: John C. Nimmo, 1903), 288–289; in German: "Das Pochen," in *Unterhaltungen deutscher Ausgewanderten, Werke. Vollständige Ausgabe*, vol. 6 (Stuttgart: Cotta, 1958), 634–639.
54 Ibid., 635.
55 I am mostly adhering to Carlyle's translation. "Entrüstet über diese Begebenheit und Verwirrung, griff der Hausherr zu einem strengen Mittel, nahm seine größte Hetzpeitsche von der Wand und schwur, daß er das Mädchen bis auf den Tod prügeln wolle, wenn sich noch einzigmal das Pochen hören ließe. Von da an ging sie ohne Anfechtung im ganzen Hause herum, und man vernahm von dem Pochen nichts weiter." Goethe, *Unterhaltungen deutscher Ausgewanderten*, 636.

The chronology between the two texts is reversed: whereas in Goethe the percussive sound is answered with a threat of domestic violence, in Hauptmann the violence suffered at the hands of the stepmother occurs first and is then echoed by other sorts of beating.[56] Furthermore, one might object that in Goethe's "The Knocking" the threat of violence is not realized; rather, as a threat (in Benjamin's sense) the threat of whipping the young woman to death is part of law-preserving violence, in this case preserving the law of the father. As described in Benjamin's elaborations on the threat in *The Critique of Violence*[57] this threat presents itself as fateful and hence becomes so powerful that it silences the text, brings the novella to a forcedly harmonious, one wants to say "Kleistean" ending, in which the death threat of the father is righted as a form of protection of his adopted daughter.

Although the scenes that we examined are largely depictions of movement, there is also a small amount of dialogue, which either announces an attack, or (in Walser) comments upon it. Can we even still call those lines "dialogic" given that no one replies—the other is silenced—and the spoken word thus goes over into physical actions? And is this what Luhmann had in mind when he described the system of the family as being characterized by a demand for "uninhibited communication"?[58] As a general rule, physical contact seems to occur in moments when verbal communication is perceived as not sufficing any longer. Goethe is especially sensitive to these jumps or short-circuits in the communication patterns, with Tasso being the most (in-)famous example of someone who violates the rules of etiquette: he first challenges Antonio to a duel, then inappropriately embraces the princess, thereby substituting physical for verbal communication.

In our examples of domestic violence, however, it is not only the physical "communication" that violates rules of conduct; rather the spoken language, too, breaks rhetorical rules of what is appropriate, but this time in terms of style. In Stifter, the raging mother (a farmer's woman) shouts with apocalyptic pathos, "What does this unholy, son in the flesh have on him today?" ("Was hat denn dieser heillose,

---

56 Similarly, in *Papa Hamlet* by Arno Holz und Johannes Schlaf (Stuttgart: Reclam, 1963 [1892]) the murder of the infant by his father is announced in a cracking sound of the basket, in which the baby lies ("... der ganze Korb war in ein Knacken geraten," 61); afterwards, the killing is echoed through a repeated knocking ("K—lopft da nicht wer? ... K—lopft da nicht wer?" 62) as well as through further cracking sounds ("seine knackenden Finger," "Eine Diele knackte," 62).
57 Benjamin, "Zur Kritik der Gewalt," 188.
58 In "Sozialsystem Familie," Luhmann defines "Familie als Sozialsystem mit enthemmter Kommunikation ...; man kann zum Beispiel nicht fragen: Warum fragst Du das? Die Enthemmung selbst ist durch Hemmungen geschützt" (195).

eingefleischte Sohn heute für Dinge an sich?") In Storm's *Ein Doppelgänger* the unleashed husband (a worker and former prisoner) equally lays the theological jargon on thick before slapping his wife: "'Do you want to deride me, woman? ... So God help you!' John cried out and raised his fist."[59] In *Flagman Thiel*, the stepmother—a former milk-maid (also called "the creature" ["*das* Mensch"] or "an animal," *Flagman Thiel*, 306)[60]—seems to speak from an opera stage when addressing her stepson with the words "you heartless, merciless scroundrel! ... I'll give you a portion from which to feed off for eight days" (*Flagman Thiel*, 312). These are not merely insults but *aesthetic* insults: bad writing, trash—or, in less trashy, Latin, terms: *inconcinnitas*, i.e., an inelegant, unsuitable, or awkward style, often associated with hyperbaton. My intention here is not, however, to take on the role of a critic who passes judgment on the literary quality of these scenes. Instead I have Benjamin's words from the *Origin of the German Mourning Play* in mind: if we want to grasp a certain *form*, then those artworks are most helpful, which otherwise might appear incomplete or even insufficient; the reason for this is that in "bad art," the form becomes visible; it shines through like a skeleton.[61] It is in this specific sense that we can learn from these pieces of dialogue: in a first step, the "unsuitableness" of these addresses obviously pertains to the social milieu but more generally to a debased language that crosses over with high literary style. Second, the result is a mixture of *genus sublime* and *genus humile*. Third, given that rhetoric is all about the right speech for the right occasion, we must ask ourselves: what is it about the occasion that causes confusion of words and styles, of the sublime and the ridiculous? For a scene of persuasion, we do not even know who the addressee is in the speech acts of domestic violence: is it God, the one who is being beaten, or even the reader?

What is certain is that we have violence, and violence is always to some degree metaphysical in character, which is especially true for domestic violence if one is to believe Benjamin. This metaphysical aspect of violence is famously embodied, for example, by the raging God of Genesis; but if the God of Genesis who promises Noah, after having killed almost all of mankind, "to not do it again" already seems a little off, then Storm's abusive husband, who makes the same promise

---

59 "'Willst du mich höhnen, Weib? ... So helf dir Gott!' schrie John und hob die Faust." Storm, *Der Doppelgänger*, 546–547.
60 Hauptmann, *Bahnwärter Thiel*, 38, 39.
61 "Die Form selbst, deren Leben nicht identisch mit dem von ihr bestimmter Werke ist, ja, deren Ausprägung bisweilen umgekehrt proportional zu der Vollendung einer Dichtung stehen kann, wird gerade an dem schmächtigen Leib der dürftigen Dichtung, als ihr Skelett gewissermaßen, augenfällig." Walter Benjamin, *Ursprung des deutschen Trauerspiels* (= *Gesammelte Schriften*, vol. I.1), 203–409, at 238.

until he finally kills his wife, just seems pathetic. To be fair, these speech acts occur in different contexts: whereas God's speech act is addressed to the world, the husband's cries resound in the home: a feminine, if not castrated space. As a consequence, the degree of violence seems to be at odds with the location, so that Adorno cautions in his aphorism "Philemon and Baucis" how quickly the domestic tyrant degenerates into a "henpecked husband [*Pantoffelheld*]."[62] One could add, similarly, that the violence of the mother in Stifter and Hauptmann cannot even be perceived as such but is instead framed as housework: cleaning feet in Stifter, beating clothes in Hauptmann.

Energy: Poetics of Unaccountability (Keller, Walser)

I have not said much about what are maybe the two most dominant discourses of rendering domestic violence ambiguous: first, the discourse of theology that justifies suffering as martyrdom, and second, Freud's theory of seduction that has at least the potential of conceiving victims as seducers. Both discourses appear to be fairly recognizable. In comparison, it is much harder to develop a vocabulary for a third type of ambiguity that I tried to approach in the last section: energy. Although energy gives momentum to Stifter's scene of domestic violence, although it drives the frantic movements, it is hard to comprehend energy because of its high degree of abstraction. If we represent domestic violence as an energetics then we are talking about abstract patterns, movements of beauty and terror, of formation and deformation. Abstraction too is a form of forgetting, indeed a domestication. In Hauptmann's *Flagman Thiel*, the rail network that encompasses the engine-like stepmother constitutes just such an abstract, energetic pattern; Storm's and Stifter's fascination with electricity and lightning can be plugged in here;[63] and at this point it seems hardly coincidental that the novel to which I want to turn now, Robert Walser's *The Assistant* (*Der Gehülfe*), ends with the electricity station turning off the power in the abusive household.[64] Although it is well known that authors such as Robert Musil or Alfred Döblin derive their poetic language by wiring it up with discourses of energy, the alliance between domestic violence and energy in realist (and in Walser's case modernist) texts is particularly notable. One might refer to Anson Rabinbach's study *The Human Motor*, in which Rabinbach refers to nineteenth-century science and

---

62 Theodor W. Adorno, "Philemon und Baucis," in *Minima Moralia. Reflexionen aus dem beschädigten Leben* (Frankfurt/M.: Suhrkamp, 2001 [1951]), aphorism 111, 325–326, at 325.
63 See Michael Gamper, "Stifters Elektrizität," in *Figuren der Übertragung*, ed. Michael Gamper and Karl Wagner (Zürich: Chronos, 2009), 209–234.
64 See Robert Walser's short piece "Energisch," *Wenn Schwache sich für Starke halten*, 200–201, at 201: "Man besinne sich, eh' man energisch wird."

philosophy, Helmholtz and Marx, but also to Marey's dynamic physiology in *La Machine animale* (1873), which Rabinbach summarizes with the phrase: "the body is a theater of motion"[65]—quite an apt description of what is happening in the violent family scenes that we have read so far.[66] In the context of energy, even the flight-motives in Stifter's *Granit* become newly legible—after all, Rabinbach mentions that many inventors of the nineteenth century were fascinated with the problem of flight.[67]

But let us finally turn to Walser: in *The Assistant*, a young man, Joseph Marti, is hired as the assistant of an innovator/con-artist. As Joseph lives with the innovator's family, he witnesses on a daily basis the abuse of children as well as abuse by and of the mother. One day, the husband hits his wife after she makes a critical comment at the dinner table:

> He, however, turned on her so savagely that it made her collapse, head first upon the table; she immediately rose up to her full height and walked away with a delicate stride. (Walser, *The Assistant*)[68]

Compared to Stifter's scene of domestic violence, in which the son tries to make sense of what is happening to him, the reflections on domestic violence in *Der Gehülfe* are much more devoted to the perplexing relation between causality and intransparency. In only one sentence, and one of moderate length at that, the narrator describes the instance of domestic violence, and yet this sentence is hard to grasp. We again have a hyperbaton that puts understanding on hold ("head first upon the table") because it separates the action ("He ... turned on her") from its

---

65 Anson Rabinbach, *The Human Motor: Energy, Fatigue, and the Origins of Modernity* (Berkeley/Los Angeles, CA: University of California Press, 1992 [1990]), 97.
66 See also Elizabeth R. Neswald's chapter on biophysics: "Ein als Kraftmaschine begriffener Körper war kein Organismus mehr und mußte nicht auf ganzheitliche Prinzipien der Physik und Wechselwirkungen hin erforscht werden." Elizabeth Neswald, "Körpermaschinen," in *Thermodynamik als kultureller Kampfplatz. Zur Faszinationsgeschichte der Entropie 1850–1915* (Freiburg i.Br.: Rombach, 2006), 310–318, at 314.
67 Ibid., 97–98.
68 Bernofsky's translation does not capture the strange passivity of this sentence: "He, however, turned on her so savagely that she collapsed face down upon the table, but she immediately then rose up to her full height and withdrew somewhat primly." Robert Walser, *The Assistant*, trans. Susan Bernofsky (New York: New Directions, 2007); "Er aber fuhr sie so grausam hart an, daß es sie, den Kopf voran, auf die Tischplatte niederstreckte, worauf sie sich hoch aufrichtete und mit sanft gesetzten Schritten davonging." Walser, *Der Gehülfe*, 87.

effect ("that it made her collapse"). But what really causes confusion is the verb *anfahren* on account of its ambiguity: *anfahren* in its intransitive, more literal sense means "starting an engine." Indeed, the verb seems to literally start an engine: the husband-innovator turns on a machine that smashes the wife's head down on the table; the woman immediately rises up again, and moves like a vector towards the door, as if nothing had happened to her—sheer energy. Within this uninterrupted chain-reaction, the energy runs through three different pronouns and agents (*er, es, sie*), binding these pronouns together in one fluid, biophysical movement.

But we have to be more exact: Walser actually uses *anfahren* in a transitive manner: *er fuhr sie ... an*, which can mean: "he drove into her," or "he collided with her," like one Newtonian body is pulled *qua* attraction towards another. Yet, *er fuhr sie ... an* also means: "he shouted at her," which indicates a violent use of language. We thus have the same strange polysemy of "violent speech" and "starting an engine" as in the verb *anlassen*, which Hauptmann used when describing the action of the violent mother: "[she] finally manned up enough to turn on [*anzulassen*] her husband forcefully" (Hauptmann, *Bahnwärter Thiel*, 16). Like Hauptmann, Walser keeps all of these connotations of *anfahren* (or *anlassen*) in vibration and lets them charge the semantic field. By now, we have identified three parallels between Stifter, Hauptmann, and Walser: 1) the hyperbaton, 2) the chain reaction, 3) language as force. I would like to stay with this third aspect a little longer. Just like Stifter associates the violent mother with poetic language, Walser has the violent father use performative speech. Furthermore, many of the examples in the *Grimmsches Wörterbuch* for *anfahren* in the sense of "to shout at" are taken from the theological context. Hence, *jemanden anfahren* seems to be such a powerful way of speaking that it borders on a (divine) performative. Likewise, Stifter's mother addresses her son as the Anti-Christ. This performative dimension gets to the real oddity of the phrase "He, however, turned on her so savagely that it made her collapse, head first upon the table." The husband shouts at his wife "cruelly hard," and in this formulation the figurative verb has literal consequences: the word unfolds a self-propelling energy with enough power to first hit the woman's head on the table and then to lead her out of sight.

As in that of the other two authors, Walser's writing on domestic violence brings up the question of literature's complicity—even more so maybe because the novel is called, after all, *The Assistant*. In Stifter, Hauptmann, and Walser energy functions as an aesthetic formula that creates beauty as well as terror and hence presents one more blind spot in the history of repression. This means, however, that the way these (late) realist authors stage domestic violence is less about the traumatic experience of being beaten than it is about the trauma of unaccountability: energy rolling through the room like a thunder bolt, people losing control, flying and crashing, getting knocked down, and standing up again.

If Luhmann calls the family "a closed system as a closed-off system"[69] then this formulation also resonates with the second law of thermodynamics, which was authored around the same time as our literary examples: in a closed system, the energy level stays the same. Soon after, in the second half of the nineteenth century, the concept of entropy is formulated, which is directly related to the second sentence of thermodynamics: in a closed system, the entropy (or the amount of chaos) increases or stays the same but it does not diminish. One feels compelled to read the idea of entropy—the death of warmth—as a scientific allegory of domestic violence.[70] But as in the case of violence in the family, for the concept of entropy, too, a major objection would be to say that there is nothing like a "closed system." And thus, even if we want to represent it we have to retreat to fiction; in this case literature.

The two scenes of family violence in *Romeo and Juliet of the Village*, written by Walser's own literary father-figure Gottfried Keller, illustrate the idea of the family as a closed system in a most instructive way. Right before the first time that the father struck his daughter in the face he is said to have "whistled to her"[71] through his fingers and then slapped her across the face. Not much ambiguity here. But if we take the language into consideration, as we should, then Keller's phrasing appears quite odd: he omits the preposition "to" (*pfeifen nach*, i.e., to whistle *to*). Due to the absence of the preposition, the illusion is created that there was no distance to bridge in the first place but that father and daughter were one: "he [the father] whistled (to) the girl shrilly and imperiously through the finger" ("pfiff er (zu) derselben schrill und gebieterisch durch den Finger," *Romeo und Julia auf dem Dorfe*, 87). In the second scene of abuse, something quite similar happens. When Vrenchen's father detects her in the field kissing Sali, the son of his arch-nemesis, the father beats his daughter and pulls her by the hair while the young Sali tries to come to her rescue:

> Sali dodged and sprang back a few paces, terrified of the wild man, but immediately jumped back to the old man when he saw that the latter instead of himself now took hold of the trembling girl, dealing her a violent blow that the red garland flew down,

---

69 "(E)in geschlossenes System als eingeschlossenes System," Luhmann, "Sozialsystem Familie," 190.
70 I say "compelled" because (not only) Elizabeth R. Neswald cautions that "(d)er Topos 'Entropie als Metapher' ist selbst zu einem Gemeinplatz geworden." *Thermodynamik als kultureller Kampfplatz*, 16.
71 "Romeo and Juliet of the Village," trans. von Schierbrand, 210.

and wrapped her hair around his hand in order to drag her along and mistreat her further.[72] (Keller, *Romeo and Juliet of the Village*)

Like in the first example, what makes this brutal scene equally aesthetically fascinating in the original German is that through its mere grammatical form the sentence mirrors the system-character of the family. In the two depictions of the father's abuse of his daughter that we have come across, Keller chooses formulations that keep the relations between pronouns ambiguous—with the outcome that we as readers might be under the impression that father and daughter were but one grotesque body. More likely, however, we translate the strangeness of the formulation into a more "familiar" language like this: "he grabbed the trembling girl, slapped her in the face so that the red garland flew down, and wrapped her hair around his hand in order to sweep her along with him and to continue to abuse her." The English rendition fails to convey the ambiguity of the Swiss-German original. To begin with, in the quote from Keller the effect of the strange neuter form of "girl" (*das* Mädchen) is twofold: one may take the repeated use of the neuter pronoun instead of "the girl" to imply that the father relates to his daughter but as a thing (literally: "in order to sweep *it* along with him and to continue to abuse *it*"). But things do not end quite here because the final part of the sentence makes reference to the girl through pronouns in the dative and accusative, so that an overtly literal translation would go: "dealing *him* a violent blow" ("*ihm* eine Ohrfeige gab") "and wrapped *his* hair around his hand" ("*seine* Haare um die Hand wickelte"). As Keller decided to use the neuter formulation "the girl" and, at that, does so in two cases that are shared by both neuter and masculine genders, he achieves a fascinating gender overdetermination. The effect of this overexposure is that one could mistake the girl for a masculine entity, i.e., for her father, which means that the father would be slapping *himself* and would be torn by *his* own hair. In that way, one could argue that the masculine and neuter pronouns hide the abuse of the feminine. To return now to the system-character in scenes of family violence: just as the grammatical cases become interchangeable and genders start to merge, so too the family in these strange sentences by Keller comes to appear as one closed system. In this sense, the passages of abuse from *Romeo and Juliet of the Village* would be a cynical

---

72 "Sali wich aus und floh einige Schritte zurück, entsetzt über den wilden Mann, sprang aber sogleich wieder zu, als er sah, dass der Alte statt seiner nun das zitternde Mädchen faßte, ihm eine Ohrfeige gab, daß der rote Kranz herunterflog, und seine Haare um die Hand wickelte, um es mit sich fortzureißen und weiter zu mißhandeln." Keller, *Romeo und Julia auf dem Dorfe*, 118.

commentary on the pathetic commonplace notion that it is always the *whole* family that suffers when it is "forced" to abuse one of its members.

At this point, it is time to draw attention to a methodological dilemma: because if we agree that the discourse of systems and energy systems often frames the representation of domestic violence, then the effect of this is that any distinction between agents—classically, the opposition of "victims" and "perpetrators"—becomes impossible. If Rabinbach describes the "vision of a society powered by universal energy,"[73] then on a moral level, the effect of mixing the discourses of energy and violence is ambiguity. But how do we respond to this decentralization of violence? Questions of responsibility and accountability are rendered obsolete. But this critique itself could be criticized as moralizing insofar as moralism would presuppose that we are referring to subjects that have total freedom, and that could therefore be subject to accusation. That is, if we talk about how violence and violent language obscure subject positions then we implicitly assume that there is a prior agent, an agent that would thus be hidden by language. Paradoxically, psychoanalysis would be the solution, because Freud's concepts of the unconscious and of psychic reality resist the idea of a willful subject. Moreover, we could ask: do we even know if violence has an origin?

Where do we come out in this argument? When analyzing scenes of domestic violence, should we argue in favor of a willful, responsible subject that can then be accused of wrongdoings? Or, shall we submit to a logic that conceives of violence as ubiquitous? The problem of reading domestic violence is that it is unsatisfactory to have an argument in which violence is just an anonymous structure—but, equally, we wouldn't do justice to these texts if we were to present violence simply as an individual, psychological choice. In the same way, it would be too easy to treat language as either totally non-referential or as entirely referential in the sense that the reader would just have to read for some origin of violence that is hiding somewhere between the lines.

Walser seems to be well aware of this problem of writing on domestic violence that arises from the lack of a formula, the reaching for a formula, and the messing up of the formula:

> "You just hurt your wife," Joseph made so bold as to remark, suddenly feeling a sense of gentlemanly chivalrousness. "Hurt

---

73 Rabinbach, *The Human Motor*, 1.

her—what rubbish! It's a tiny world being injured there," Tobler replied. (Walser, *The Assistant*, 87)[74]

Instead of big emotions, in Walser we face apathy in the face of the antiquatedness of bravery (*Ritterlichkeit*), apathy as expressed by the perspective's constant zooming out from the scene of violence—in Stifter, Storm, and Hauptmann by way of theological references and in Walser through cosmological allusions to microcosm and macrocosm. One might rightly object that Walser had an emphatic understanding of the idea of "small worlds," but in *Der Gehülfe* neither the husband nor the abused and abusive wife embody this empathetic approach to life. Rather, when the mother in Walser's novel finally "rose up to her full height and walked away with a delicate stride," then she appears more as a continuation of the old tradition that Heine puts straight in *Deutschland. Ein Wintermärchen*:

They still strut around so stiffly,
as upright as a candle and finely combed,
as if they'd gulped down the stick
with which they'd once been beaten.[75]

---

74 Strangely, Bernofsky translates "What you just *said* hurt your wife!" right after the passage in which the husband smashed his wife's head on the table, as if the violence had only been metaphorical: ",Sie haben ihrer Frau wehgetan', wagte Joseph in einem Anflug von weltmännischer Ritterlichkeit zu sagen. ,Ach was wehgetan! Da ist eine kleine Welt verletzt', erwiderte Tobler" (Walser, *Der Gehülfe*, 87). This is just one more example of a disturbing tendency of translations—documented in the footnotes of this chapter—to resist or even repress moments of domestic violence by taking them figuratively or rendering them comical (see the final quote from Heine), or by literalizing the complex question of agency (as happens in the translations of Keller and Walser).
75 "Sie stelzen noch immer so steif herum,/so kerzengerade geschniegelt,/als hätten sie verschluckt den Stock,/womit man sie einst geprügelt." Heinrich Heine, *Deutschland. Ein Wintermärchen* (Stuttgart: Reclam, 1974 [1844]), Caput III. Again, the translations make light of the violence that is so clearly indicated by the word *verprügelt* (beaten; flogged) and sacrifice it for the rhyme as "wheedling" (Bowring) or switches the whole register to horseplay when referring to "the corporal stick/Old Fritz knew how to handle" (Reed).

SYMPHONIC AGGRESSION

Five "What Murderously Peaceful People There Are": On Aggression in Robert Walser

The question of how to live sprouts and withers all over the writings of the Swiss modernist author Robert Walser; some people even consult his texts as a "philosophy of life."[1] Given the high degree of reflection that Walser's texts reach when they turn to the subject of life and practices of the self, as readers interested in how affect represents itself we cannot expect to encounter any "raw emotions" here—if indeed there ever existed such a thing. Instead, those who studied affects in Walser speak of sublimated forms: Elias Canetti wrote about Walser's hidden anxiety,[2] Susan Sontag on depression,[3] Jörg Kreienbrock on politeness,[4] Jan Plug on shame,[5] Marianne Schuller on ritualization of love,[6] Jens

---

1 I am taking a certain distance here from more immediate identifications of Walser with the philosophy of life, like Martin Suter, *Die Lebensquelle. Lebensphilosophie und persönlicher Mythos im Spätwerk Robert Walsers* (Lang: Bern a.o., 1984) or Hubert Thüring, "Lebensphilosophie im Zeichen des Glücks," in *Robert Walser Handbuch. Leben—Werk—Wirkung*, ed. Lucas Marco Gisi (Stuttgart: Metzler, 2015), 344–350.
2 Elias Canetti, "Aufzeichnungen zu Robert Walser (1973)," in *Über Robert Walser*, vol. 1, ed. Katharina Kerr (Frankfurt/M.: Suhrkamp, 1978), 12–13.
3 Susan Sontag, "Walser's Voice," in *Selected Stories*, trans. Christopher Middleton (Manchester: Carcanet New Press, 1982), vii–ix, at viii.
4 Jörg Kreienbrock, "Höflichkeit im Zeichen der Nuance," in *Kleiner. Feiner. Leichter* (Zurich: Diaphanes, 2010), 83–122.
5 Jan Plug, "Shame. On Language. *Snow White*, Benjamin," in *They Have All Been Healed: Reading Robert Walser* (Evanston, IL: Northwestern University Press, 2016), 17–56.
6 Marianne Schuller, "Briefe an Frieda Mermet," *Robert Walser Handbuch*, 224–230.

Hobus on love's sublimation[7] (to name but a few). Hardly ever is there any word of aggression. The single exception is that of sado-masochism, which attempts to convert aggression into a coded game ("More on this later," as one of Walser's last characters, the robber, would say).[8]

When dealing with Walser as an author concerned with "how to live," the omission of aggression is all the more surprising given that since antiquity the question of life has included strategies to help the self regulate its affects, particularly aggressive impulses.[9] What to do with our anger, social beings that we are? How best to face others' aggressions? These questions must have accompanied Walser throughout his life; why else would his literary texts spread out in front of us like a field for experimentation to test different approaches to aggression? And yet if this is the case, one might wonder, then why is it that nobody talks about Walser's literary aggressions? First, the author's tragic biography produces a certain blindness on this matter: solipsism, social decline, mental illness, attempts at suicide, twenty-three years in a closed asylum, death in the snow. Certainly enough misery to prompt pity in interpretations of the author's life and letters like Coetzee's elegy on Walser: "His own uneventful yet in its way harrowing life was his only true subject."[10] Second, if this study undertakes to trace "ugly feelings" such as passive aggression, envy, resentment, or schadenfreude then this approach starkly contradicts the image of Walser and his characters as radically passive or even pacifist, an image painted early on by Hermann Hesse: "If poets like Walser were the 'leading minds' then there would be no war. If he had a hundred thousand readers the world would be a better place."[11] Years later, Susan Sontag still advertised this pacifist image of Walser: "The moral core of Walser's art is the refusal

---

7 Jens Hobus, "'Was soll ich mit Gefühlen anfangen, als sie wie Fische im Sand der Sprache zappeln und sterben zu lassen?' Emotionen als ästhetisches Phänomen im Werk Robert Walsers," in *Sentimentalität und Grausamkeit. Ambivalente Gefühle in der skandinavischen und deutschen Literatur der Moderne*, ed. Sophie Wennerscheid (Berlin: LIT, 2011), 229–241, at 240.
8 Wolfram Groddeck offers an overview on "Masochism" in Walser in *Robert Walser Handbuch*, 332–336.
9 See Seneca's "On Anger (De Ira)," in *Moral* Essays, vol. 1, trans. John W. Basore (Cambridge, MA: Oxford University Press, 1928) or Galen of Pergamum's *On the Passions and Errors of the Soul*, trans. Paul W. Harkins (Columbus, OH: Ohio State University Press, 1963), 38: "A man cannot free himself from the habit of anger as soon as he resolves to do so, but he can keep in check the unseemly manifestations of his passion."
10 J. M. Coetzee, "The Genius of Robert Walser," *The New Yorker*, November 2, 2000.
11 Hermann Hesse, "Poetenleben (1917)," in *Über Robert Walser*, vol. 1, ed. Katharina Kerr (Frankfurt/M.: Suhrkamp, 1978), 57–58, at 58.

of power; of domination."[12] Although Sontag's hyperbolic praise of Walser's "radical passivity" recently has met some resistance by Ben Lerner,[13] the emotionally one-dimensional, if not castrating, portrayals of Walser persist; yet those readers who embrace the author so seemingly tenderly forget about the violence inherent to any idealization—especially when this idealization occurs in the name of ideals such as "passivity" or "innocence."

With the notion of "innocence" I come to one of the most influential, and at the same time most elliptical, writings on Walser in recent years: the three little entries on Walser in Giorgio Agamben's *The Coming Community*. Although Agamben discerns the "ambiguity" of "Walser's creatures"[14] he falls short of this insight when praising "the natural innocence of his creatures."[15] This is because there is actually nothing ambiguous about innocence: innocence presents a state before the split, which, however, is structurally necessary for ambiguity to come into being. Likewise, if Agamben raves that "nothing is more foreign to Walser than the pretense of being other than what one is," then the question arises how one could possibly separate the pretense from what one is—a question that goes right to the heart of Walser's reflections on how to hide, provoke, or even try to own one's aggressions. Hence, my polemical decision to read Walser's literary texts through the lens of concepts such as "pretense," "dissimulation," and "ressentiment," i.e., through the very terms the validity of which many readers of Walser have contested.[16] Contrary to what Agamben and his (unacknowledged) precursor Walter Benjamin have argued, I intend to show how Walser is exploring pretense and ressentiment as something that cannot be transcended. Third, and perhaps most importantly, there is an epistemological problem that pertains to this book as a whole because it arises more generally from reading ambiguous aggression. One could think about this relation by analogy to Nietzsche's argument

---

12 Sontag, "Walser's Voice," viii.
13 Ben Lerner challenges Sontag's judgment in "Robert Walser's Disappearing Acts," *The New Yorker*, September 3, 2013.
14 Giorgio Agamben, *The Coming Community*, trans. Michael Hardt (Minneapolis/London: University of Minnesota Press, 2003 [1990]), 31.
15 Ibid., 32.
16 Agamben's reading of Walser through "the history of salvation" (*The Coming Community*, 31), the idea of a *"renovatio* of the universe" and the "irreparable" (39) would not be thinkable without Benjamin asserting about Walser's characters that *"they have all been healed"* in "Robert Walser," *Aufsätze, Essays, Vorträge*, ed. Rolf Tiedemann (= *Gesammelte Schriften*, vol. 2.1) (Frankfurt/M.: Suhrkamp, 1977), 324–328, at 327. Benjamin goes on to wonder "why the seemingly most playful of all poets was the favorite author of the relentless [*unerbittliche*] Franz Kafka." Maybe one first has to pay attention to Walser's own "relentlessness" to make sense of this affinity.

in *The Birth of Tragedy*: if Greek serenity exists only to fend off a more primal or primary Dionysian energy, so too might one say that Walser's politeness is but the outer surface of his literary aggression—though as with Nietzsche, one should note that the genetic narrative ("this before that") may be better rethought as a structural account ("no this without that").

There arise further complications: as a literary author, Walser complements the existential dimension with a formal one, to the effect that his literary texts serve as an existential principle as well as an aesthetic program. There is no sentence by Walser in which this double-tone is not audible; his voice unifies in disharmony the existential naïveté of the one who seeks sincere answers to life with a formal irony that quickly spirals out of our control.[17] Which is to say, if we thought art was exclusively about detached contemplation, i.e., about pure form, then Walser turns out instead to be a Nietzschean; if, however, the poet tells us "You must change your life" then the ironist replies that it is impossible to do so—Walser is in this regard closer to Kafka than to Rilke. Indeed, although one usually associates the aesthetics of life with immediacy, Walser's literary scenes of ambiguous aggression deny us an immediate access to any kind of affective truth; but what they grant us instead is insight into how to *read* for life-strategies, how to read the exempla. Such knowledge is practical but it nonetheless implies mediation—the paradox of a wisdom that is practical yet which cannot simply be applied. Walser thereby avoids a simple "either or" of formalism or life and instead follows Nietzsche's track—maybe this is what Max Brod had in mind when he said "After Nietzsche, there had to come Walser."[18] Walser's ambiguous aggression is situated right between literary formalism and practices of life. For this reason, in the readings

---

17 Hendrik Stiemer cautions against taking Walser's "ironic naiveté" at face value, thereby neglecting its staged quality: *Über scheinbar naïve und dilettantische Dichtung. Text- und Kontextstudien zu Robert Walser* (Würzburg: Königshausen & Neumann, 2013), 63–65; see also Peter von Matt, "Wie weise ist Walsers Weisheit?," in *Robert Walsers "Ferne Nähe." Neue Beiträge zur Forschung*, ed. Wolfram Groddeck (München: Wilhelm Fink, 2007), 35–47, at 46–47: "Im belehrenden Gestus, der Walsers Werk durchzieht, operiert der Autor fortwährend mit den Trümmern der Mentorrede. Bald zitiert er sie, bald kehrt er sie um. Er kann sie ironisieren, dann tut er wieder so, als nehme er sie ernst. ... Aber die Momente der Erschütterung beim Lesen in Walsers Büchern? Die Momente, die wir alle kennen, wenn unser Fühlen und Erkennen gleichzeitig erfasst und aufgewühlt sind? Er gibt sie, weiß Gott, aber sie lehren uns nicht das richtige Leben oder das 'artige' Verhalten, um Walsers vertracktes Lieblingswort zu zitieren."
18 Quoted after Christopher Middleton, "Introduction," in *Jakob von Gunten*, trans. Christopher Middleton (New York: Penguin, 1999), 5–17, at 9.

of Walser that follow, I draw from psychoanalysis as well as rhetoric, because both methods offer paradigms to connect formalism to questions of how to live that otherwise might appear to be in conflict with one another.

Let us now examine a selection of scenes from Walser's œuvre that model different ways of dealing with aggression. I will proceed through the scenes according to their time of creation so that we get a sense of development in his literary approach to aggression: starting with an early letter from Walser to his sister Lisa from 1898 and ending with passages from the aforementioned, posthumously published, experimental novel *The Robber* (*Der Räuber*, 1925–26), written in micro-script. Notwithstanding the date of production of a text, they all share the common feature that a narrative voice gives instructions as to how to cope with aggressive affects—and each time the answer changes. By the end of this closing chapter we will have traversed a wide range of ambiguous aggressions: starting off with an ambiguous plea for cursing, we will then discuss teasing, sublimation, dissimulation, resentment, and will close our tour of ambiguous aggression with ambivalence.

Cursing (Letter to Lisa Walser)

This chapter started with an early warning: if one reduces Walser to the tragic moments in his biography and reads his works too sentimentally, then one likely misses out on the indeed wonderfully broad kaleidoscope of affects that Walser's œuvre spans. A letter comes in handy, which Walser in 1898 wrote to his sister Lisa: Lisa, the oldest of the eight siblings, a school-teacher, on whom the burden fell not only to take care of the "mother's melancholia"[19] until her death in 1894 but who also hosted her brother for longer stretches of time. Speaking of pity, it is a pity that Lisa's letters did not survive, but judging from Robert's response we can safely deduce that he was eager to bring about at *Wechsel der Töne*, i.e., an alternation of tone, to speak in Hölderlin's idiom:

> Dear Lisa!
> … How are you? Your 1) letter sounds a bit me-lan-cho-lic. Really, what's gotten into you? If I were a stupid fellow, I would say: ha, I don't understand that, but if I were totally stupid, then I would join into your moonlight-pale [*mondscheinblassen*] laments. But because I am (let's hope) neither stupid nor totally

---

19 W. G. Sebald, "Le Promeneur Solitaire: A Remembrance of Robert Walser," in *A Place in the Country: On Gottfried Keller, Johan Peter Hebel, Robert Walser and Others*, trans. Jo Catling (New York: Penguin, 2015), 117–153, at 120.

stupid, I simply shout: My goodness! [*Donnerwetter*] Lisa, yes, my Lord! My goodness! [*Herrgottsdonnerwetter*] and nothing else.— Cursing is swell in such cases, I can tell you.[20]

The letter sets out with the usual address line, "Dear Lisa!" amplified by a drum-like exclamation mark, as if Robert were trying to shake the melancholic from her heavy thoughts by shouting her name: "Lisa!" Likewise, the subsequent question "How are you?" seems to be less a sincere inquiry about her well-being than his request to repeal what Lisa must have previously stated about her not-so-well-being. In spite of the sister's melancholic letter fittingly having been lost, those who are familiar with Walser's texts should not have too hard a time ventriloquizing Lisa's me-lan-cho-ly; after all, Lisa's laments form a constant, if not notorious element of Walser's literary, emotional repertoire. Wherever one suspects a character of channeling Walser's oldest sister—be it, most famously, Hedwig in *The Tanners* (*Die Geschwister Tanner*, 1907) or Lisa Benjamenta in *Jakob von Gunten* (1909)—these female characters combine an unapproachable gravitas with barbed-hooked reproaches. According to Walser's later guardian and supporter Carl Seelig, it is especially *The Tanners* "where the character of the teacher [and sister Hedwig] is the intimate image of this matron-like altruist who is willing to sacrifice herself."[21] Indeed, in Robert's anti-melancholic letter to Lisa, one hears a certain echo of a passage in *The Tanners* where Hedwig, upon Simon's departure, demands from her brother *not* to write to her because she would rather enjoy the melancholic[22] "lack" or "loss" of his presence than his usual "neglect" of her. "The female complaint *is* a discourse of disappointment," writes Lauren Berlant in what reads like a commentary on Lisa Tanner's letter to her brother, "But where love

---

20 Walser to his sister Lisa, Zurich, May 5, 1898, *Briefe*, ed. Jörg Schäfer and Robert Mächler (*Das Gesamtwerk*, vol. 12/2, ed. Jochen Greven) (Geneva: Kossodo, 1975), 9–10, at 9; in German: "Liebe Lisa! … Wie geht es dir? Dein 1. Brief klingt ein bischen [sic] me-lan-cho-lisch. Ja, was steckt nur in dir? Wenn ich nun ein dummer Kerl wäre, so würde ich sagen: ha, das versteh ich nicht, aber wenn ich ganz dumm wäre, so würde ich in deine mondscheinblassen Klagen einstimmen. Aber da ich (hoffen wir es) weder dumm noch ganz dumm bin, so schreie ich einfach: Donnerwetter, Lisa, ja Herrgottsdonnerwetter, und weiter nichts.— Fluchen ist in solchen Fällen famos, sage ich dir."
21 Carl Seelig, "25. Mai 1944," *Wanderungen mit Robert Walser*, 77–81, at 77: "… wo die Gestalt der Lehrerin Hedwig das innige Abbild dieser opferwilligen, hausmütterlichen Altruistin ist."
22 Freud defines melancholy as a reaction towards the experience of a loss, in which the I remains unconscious of the loved object—the loss of a loss. "Trauer und Melancholie (1917 [1915])," in *Studienausgabe*, ed. Alexander Mitscherlich a.o., vol. 3 (Frankfurt/M.: Fischer, 2000), 193–212, at 193–194.

is concerned, disappointment is a partner of fulfillment, not an opposite."[23] Now let us listen to Lisa:

> Now, when you will be away from me, which as a matter of fact must happen soon, do not write to me. I don't want it. You shall not think that you would have to be obliged to send me notice about your further whereabouts. Neglect me, like you used to do. How should writing help us? I will continue to live here and will relish in thinking occasionally that you were here for three months. The region will lift me up and will show me your picture. I will visit all the places that we both found beautiful, and I will find them even more beautiful; because a mistake, a loss, only makes the things more beautiful. Both I and the region will lack something, but this lack and even this mistake will press even more intimate sentiments upon my life.[24]

It appears as if Hedwig is not only the most annoyingly passive-aggressive character in Walser's novels but also an annoying melancholic at that, an observation that brings a ruthless emotional hermeneut to wonder whether not melancholy may sometimes serve as a cover-up for passive aggression. This at least would be one way to make sense of Robert's reaction to his sister's letter: forcing Lisa to get out of her emotional comfort zone, blowing her cover, demanding from her to trash all sadness and to try instead a taste of anger. (Of course, the other option is that the brother is simply being a jerk.)

What is clear is that Robert provokes Lisa by cursing at her, by insulting her: he rejects the commonplace idealization of melancholy as gentled by reflection and instead ridicules melancholy as a state of advanced stupidity. This polemic in itself is not as stupid as it might seem; after all, Albrecht Dürer's famous emblem *Melencolia I* challenged the topos of "Saturnian genius" by depicting a female, winged allegory

---

23 Lauren Berlant, *The Female Complaint: The Unfinished Business of Sentimentality in American Culture* (Durham/London: Duke University Press, 2008), 13.
24 "Wenn du nun, was ja bald geschehen muß, von mir fort bist, so schreibe mir nicht. Ich will es nicht. Du sollst nicht meinen, du müßtest verpflichtet sein, mir von deinem ferneren Treiben eine Nachricht zukommen zu lassen. Vernachlässige mich, wie du es früher auch getan hast. Was sollte uns beiden das Schreiben nützen? Ich werde hier weiter leben und es als einen Genuß empfinden, öfters daran zu denken, daß du drei Monate lang da warst. Die Gegend wird mich emportragen und mir dein Bild zeigen. Ich werde alle die Orte aufsuchen, die wir zusammen schön gefunden haben, und ich werde sie noch schöner finden; denn ein Fehler, ein Verlust macht die Dinge noch schöner. Mir und der ganzen Gegend wird etwas fehlen, aber diese Lücke und selbst dieser Fehler werden meinem Leben noch innigere Empfindungen aufdrücken." *Die Geschwister Tanner*, 178.

of melancholy surrounded by instruments of knowledge. According to Erwin Panofsky's interpretation of Dürer's thought-image this "Melancholia is neither a miser nor a mental case, but a thinking being in perplexity. She does not hold to an object which does not exist, but to a problem which cannot be solved."[25] Fittingly, Dürer's dumb-founded, winged, female *Melencolia* reappears in Walser's last novel, *The Robber* (*Der Räuber*), in the description of a "copper-engraving-like"[26] widow called "silly":[27] *ein Dummchen*, just like Robert implicitly calls Lisa "*dumm*" in his letter. The widowed ninny from *The Robber* is depicted as winged and nocturnal (*[n]achtvogelhaftscheu[]*), even vampire-like, again just like the "moonlight-pale" Lisa after the loss of her husband-like brother:

> She [the widow] fell silent, and in this moment had something of the aura of one of Dürer's female figures, a sort of night-bird shyness, a flying-over-the-seas-in-the-dark, a soft inner whimpering. ... Ninnies can sink their teeth into a tenacious silence that can never be surpassed, they are unmatched in their predilection for tactful behavior. It might almost seem they are being tactful out of spite, or in defiance, and with unwavering decorum they consume morsel after morsel of their own sorrow at the disappointments that have befallen them. No one excels in this like so-called ninnies. Could it be they love their own pain?[28]

For the sake of a more synthetic comparison of the three quotes on melancholy it is crucial to note the constant displacement of affects: in his letter, Robert tries to sell Lisa aggression as an alternative to melancholy; in the passage from *The Tanners*, we meet in Hedwig a melancholic and a master of double binding at that ("Don't write to me!" and "You always neglect me!"); in *The Robber*, we learn that ninnies love their pain and refine it with "defiance" and "scorn." One reason why readers of

---

25 Erwin Panofsky, *The Life and Art of Albrecht Dürer* (Princeton, NJ: Princeton University Press, 1955 [1943]), 163.
26 "[E]twas Kupferstichhaftes," Walser, *Der Räuber*, 39.
27 Robert Walser, *The Robber*, trans. Susan Bernofsky (Lincoln, NE: University of Nebraska Press, 2000), 24.
28 Ibid., 26; "Sie schwieg und bekam dabei etwas, das auf einer Frauenfigur von Dürer schwebt, so etwas Nachtvogelhaftscheues, in der Finsternis die Meere Überfliegendes, etwas in sich hinab Wimmerndes. ... Dummchen können sich in eine Schweigsamkeit verbeißen, wie man's nicht besser tun kann, sind Meisterinnen in der Lust an taktvoller Aufführung. Sie führen sich gleichsam wie zum Trotz, wie zum Hohn taktvoll auf und essen an ihrem Weh über die ihnen zugeflogenen Enttäuschungen Stückchen für Stückchen mit gleichmäßigem Anstand. Gerade die sogenannten Dummchen sind dessen fähig. Lieben sie etwa ihren Schmerz?" *Der Räuber*, 40.

Walser's are well-advised to double-check whether his texts motivate the melancholy to which we might at times feel given is because Walser himself, as it turns out, is highly suspicious about the lures of melancholia. The way in which he displaces affects presupposes that affects do not follow a substitutive "either … or" logic but rather one of "both … and." To put it in more spatial terms, Walser's texts construct layers of affects—however, these layers are not hierarchized in the sense that one layer of affect would be closer to "the truth" than the other; rather, affects cover each other up or hover between foreground and background. In the correspondence of Robert and Lisa Walser, sadness takes over the stage while aggression is banished into the background—an arrangement typical for the nineteenth and early-twentieth centuries, insofar as sadness was regarded (and still is) as socially more acceptable for women than anger.[29]

But we have not yet said a word about Robert's curse: "My goodness! (*Donnerwetter*) Lisa, yes, my Lord! My goodness! (*Herrgottsdonnerwetter*) and nothing else." ("Donnerwetter, Lisa, ja Herrgottsdonnerwetter, und weiter nichts.") Robert taunts his sister to bring her aggression on stage, first with the ambiguous phrase "Donnerwetter," which according to the *Grimmsches Wörterbuch* alternatively may function as an acknowledgement (like the contemporary "wow!") or as a curse, if one reads the outcry as the ellipsis of the ancient "you shall be struck by a thunderstorm." The subsequent shift to "Herrgottsdonnerwetter" is a decision for this aggressive variant, which adds God, i.e., real "blasphemous power,"[30] to the equation. We hear the German turn-of-speech "to release a thunderstorm" (*ein Donnerwetter loslassen*) roaring between the lines: all hell shall be let loose through the sheer force of one's excitable speech! And yet Walser would not be Walser if he did not take this rage back in a flash that makes light of the previous blasphemy—the ironic litotes "and nothing more" appears to cradle the curse to sleep.

One cannot but wonder from where this aggressive energy arises in the first place. I would argue that for Walser it is the *form* of the curse, less than its divine content, that awakens aggression. As a speech act,

---

29 "A dominant way for women to express anger is, as present-day psychologists observe, to shed tears. Tears here stand for desperation, grief, and sadness, i.e. for emotions described as passive, self-referential and asthenic. They thus perfectly fit the nineteenth-century notion of women as weak, powerless human beings." Ute Frevert, *Emotions in History—Lost and Found*, 96; Frevert explains how women and rage were for the longest time regarded as incompatible; thus, Friedrich Schlegel argued in *Theorie der Weiblichkeit*, ed. Winfried Menninghaus (Frankfurt/M.: Insel, 1983), 127 that the average women is incapable of rage.

30 Arnd Wedemeyer, "Herrschaftszeiten! Theopolitical Profanities in the Face of Secularization," *New German Critique* 105, 35, no. 3 (autumn 2008): 121–141, at 126.

the curse is "interminable and excessive,"[31] as Björn Quiring pointedly states; there is even something parodic about the curse's overstretching of language insofar as the curse calls upon an archaic performativity of language in which we no longer believe. As if to compensate for this impotence, the curse piles words on and on. And with this we finally put our fingers on the heart of the aggression. German, with its logorrheic capacity for gluttony, can pile words into lengthy compound-formations, their very length becoming the proof of their ineffectivity; yet however impotent these compounds may be, they bring about another phatic or emphatic effect. I would like to draw attention to the fact that Walser uses compounds usually either in an ironically sentimental or outright cynical way. In Walser, compounds therefore function as the town-signs of fake idylls that overexpose and condense places and narratives. If you trust, or even better, if you agree with me that a) for Walser, compounds frequently have an aggressive edge and that b) compounds appear frequently in the writings on and to his sister Lisa (e.g., "mondscheinblass," "Donnerwetter," "Herrgottsdonnerwetter," "Kupferstichhaftes," "Nachtvogelhaftscheues") then one must wonder: what is it that binds these three figures together—family, the compound word, and aggression? I would dare to say that it is actually the very force of binding and Walser's purported refusal of forming relationships (*Bindungsangst*), which Peter von Matt labeled *qua* another composite as *"Beziehungsverweigerung."*[32] Carl Seelig, who upon Lisa's death became Walser's guardian, reports with horror how Walser in lapidary fashion pathologized and ultimately rejected his dying sister's wish for her brother to visit her in the hospital; here too, it is a compound word, i.e. a *bound* word, which paradoxically cuts the chord between brother and sister: Walser dismisses Lisa's plea as an

---

31 Björn Quiring, *Shakespeare's Curse: the Aphorias of Ritual Exclusion in Early Modern Royal Drama*, trans. Michael Wrinkler and Björn Quiring (New York: Routledge, 2014), 3.

32 Peter von Matt compares Walser's letters to Frieda Mermet to Kafka's letters to Felice: "When one approaches these letters one must not allow oneself to be deceived by the sympathy towards the author. Otherwise, one easily overlooks the dimensions of coldness and rejection that also form a decisive part of these letters. One has to know something of the hard and dangerous Walser in order to grasp the strange compendium. ... Walser's letters to Frieda Mermet are a play with distance following a highly developed method. ... When he makes an extensive compliment to Mrs. Mermet that inevitably must deepen the relationship, he subsequently diverts inadvertently to the description of very young, lovely girls, with an excitement that is openly offensive. This doesn't rely on sadism but on the principle of sabotaging a relationship." "Wer hat Robert Walsers Briefe geschrieben?", in *"Immer dicht vor dem Sturze ..." Zum Werk Robert Walsers*, ed. Paolo Chiarini/Hans Dieter Zimmermann (Frankfurt/M.: Athenäum, 1987), 98–105, at 100–102.

oversensitivity-phenomenon ("*Überfeinerungserscheinung*"[33]) for which his family's childlessness (*Kinderlosigkeit*) is to be blamed. And yet, the very attempt at unbinding cannot but tighten another bind: for what better way to say farewell to his sister, i.e., a "matron-like altruist who is willing to sacrifice herself"[34] than to give her the gift of staying in her guilt-debt and thus honoring the life-long psychic wars of siblings?[35] By denying his sister's dying plea Walser agrees to receive once more her reproaches, even to enlarge them with those coming from his new father-figure Carl Seelig.[36] And maybe, just maybe, something in the brother was hoping for a remainder of resistance: a remainder that screams and kicks, that cannot so easily be incorporated into the guilt-machinery, and which would become the spark of aggression, which would light up the death bed and galvanize the beloved melancholic sister with a jolt of anger.

---

33 Carl Seelig, "2. January 1944," *Wanderungen mit Robert Walser*, 68–77, at 72.
34 Ibid., 77. Walser ironically addresses the relation between motherhood, sacrifice, and worrying in "Verlorener und wiedergefundener Glaube," *Wenn Schwache sich für Starke halten*, 322–327: "Ah, and such a worried mother plays also a role, or for all I care a little background-role (*Hintergrundsröllchen*), with which she is totally content. It is based in the structure of society that mothers betimes habituate modesty." The British essayist and child-psychologist Adam Phillips gives a hilarious example from a conversation he had with a patient, a boy of ten: "Intending to say 'What are the worries?' I in fact said to him, 'What are worries?' Quite naturally puzzled by the question, he thought for a moment, then replied triumphantly, 'Farts that don't word,' and blushed. I said, 'Yes, some farts are worth keeping.' He grinned and said, 'Treasure.' For this boy worrying was a way of holding on to something, a form of storage. It transpired from our conversations that worries were like gifts he kept for his mother, and he was fearful of running out of them. What better gift to give to one's mother— especially if she was unsure of herself—than a worry she could resolve and so feel fully empowered as a good mother?" "Worrying and Its Discontents," in *On Kissing, Tickling, and Being Bored: Psychoanalytic Essays on the Unexamined Life* (Cambridge, MA: Harvard University Press, 1993), 47–58, at 47.
35 In *The Robber* the narrator comments on the addictive joy of making reproaches as well as of the privilege of receiving them: "Making reproaches can become an addiction that one can ridicule, and someone corrected is spiritually always better off than the one who corrects, who actually is rarely anything but suffering. … Having to allow oneself to be criticized, there's something about that which is amusing" (Walser, *Der Räuber*, 132).
36 Here we find a parallel between Walser's rapport to his sister and that of his esteemed precursor Heinrich von Kleist to his sister; in both cases the motherly, caring sister draws the brother's anger on her by depriving them of the privilege of self-sacrifice. On Kleist's sacrificial rivalry with this half-sister Ulrike see Barbara Natalie Nagel, *Der Skandal des Literalen. Barocke Literalisierungen bei Gryphius, Kleist, Büchner* (München: Wilhelm Fink, 2012), 155–158.

Teasing (Jakob von Gunten)

The practice to which Walser subjects his older sister Lisa is that of "teasing" or "tantalizing," in German *Reizen*. Not by coincidence teasing is probably also what first comes to mind when one thinks of ambiguous aggression in Walser's texts; it is something like the *lingua franca* of Walser's protagonists who laugh off the attacks of those bossing or slapping them around but who also take immense pleasure and relief from the fantasy that it was their own tantalizing that brought about this violence in the first place. Indeed, teasing could serve as an umbrella concept for all three of the social forms of ambiguous aggression, which we have investigated up to this point: for instance, if one reads Walser's literature through the notion of "passive aggression" then this concept circumscribes the power dynamics, i.e., the master–slave dialectics, which call for a tease. If the notion of "passive aggression" was invented, in the military,[37] due to a desire for punishment on the side of the law then this tells us something about the effect that teasing has on the law: teasing emanates from the fantasy of seducing the law to show its face and to render visible the violence on which the law is grounded.[38] One could thus say that teasing is the small, rebellious attempt to reappropriate aggression.

Although the passive-aggressive side of teasing is especially characteristic of the younger protagonists in Walser's earlier writings, there is clearly a flirtatious side to *Reizen* as well, one that never loses its *Reiz* or thrill—be it in Walser's novels, prose pieces, or late micro-scripts. Walser is a constant tease, so to speak, and teasing therefore becomes a point of intersection for all three social forms of ambiguous aggression (flirtation, passive aggression, and domestic violence), which so far we have been trying to separate from one another, with more or less success. How do we have to imagine such an overexposure of various forms of ambiguous aggression? Walser's most famous novel, *Jakob von Gunten* (1909), delivers the most outrageous answer to this question—not only by feeling out the affective economy of *Reizen* but also its confusingly passive aggressive, flirtatious, and even abusive undertones: "I tempt [*reize*] the law to rage,"[39] boasts the beaten Jakob, "How much fun [*Lust*] it is for me to tempt [*reizen*] those who exercise power into fits of rage."[40] As in English, the word *Lust* in German implies sexual pleasure or passion. The quote thus makes apparent the structural affinity that

---

37 See more on the military background of the notion of "passive aggression" in the chapter on passive aggression, 44–46.
38 Walter Benjamin, "Zur Kritik der Gewalt," *Aufsätze, Essays, Vorträge: Gesammelte Schriften* II.1, 42–66.
39 Walser, *Jakob von Gunten*, 28; in German: "Ich reize das Gesetz zum Zorn."
40 Ibid., 44; in German: "wieviel Lust es mir bereitet, Gewaltausübende zu Zornesausbrüchen zu reizen."

exists between flirtation and masochism (insofar as this latter, according to Deleuze, works to humiliate the law),[41] which explains why *Jakob von Gunten* is still able to elicit some outrage on account of the sadomasochistic dynamics between the headmaster of the *Institute Benjamenta* and the precocious Jakob. In general teasing is just as much linked to passive aggression as it is to flirtation:[42] for like flirtation, teasing aims at evoking sexual aggression. Walser's "Koketterie"[43] can express itself in the desired slap from a powerful woman, in her jealous husband's intimate anger, or in a schoolgirl's indignant rebuff; what is crucial, however, is that just like flirtation, teasing is never consummated but remains a potentiality.

If Walser is nonetheless able to strike a spark from this low-cooking type of sexual aggression then this is because he does not distinguish between different contexts; this is to say that while a public flirtation is pleasurable, maybe even exciting, moving the same dynamics into the domestic or educational realm and staging it between children and adults can be unsettling. The first lines from Walser's prose piece "Die kleine Berlinerin" give us a poignant example: "Today papa boxed my ears, of course he did it very paternally, tenderly";[44] thus brags "the little girl from Berlin" with a certain pride. The sentence contains in a nutshell the relationship between father and daughter, a rapport of teasing, incestuous undertones, and the double-binds linked to sadomasochism. The prototype of Jakob lingers over all these haplessly cunning creatures and their fantasies: the powerless who brag that they know how to "seduce" their parents or educators into abusing them, who prefer to imagine themselves as attracting violence, rather than helplessly being given over to it; they all dream of the superiority of the one who knows how to tame his or her aggressions and can, at the same time, tease out the aggression of others.

The ambiguity of teasing becomes really problematic at the point when the parent exploits the child's alleged teasing as justification for abuse, as is the case in Walser's second novel *Der Gehülfe* (1908). Few scenes in literature are as heartbreaking as the depictions of physical abuse that the neglected girl Silvi has to endure from her parents as

---

41 Gilles Deleuze, "Humor, Irony & the Law," in *Masochism: Coldness and Cruelty & Venus in Furs*, trans. Jean McNeil (New York: Zone Books, 1991 [1967]), 81–90.
42 We investigated the link between teasing (as *Sticheln*) and flirtation in the chapter on the terrors of flirtation in the context of Corinna's flirtation in Fontane's *Frau Jenny Treibel*, 37.
43 Hermann Hesse, "Robert Walser (1909)," *Über Robert Walser* 1, ed. Katharina Kerr (Frankfurt/M.: Suhrkamp, 1978), 52–57, at 53.
44 "Heute hat mir Papa eine Ohrfeige gegeben, natürliche eine echt väterliche, eine zärtliche." Robert Walser, "Die kleine Berlinerin," in *Aufsätze* (Frankfurt/M./Zürich: Suhrkamp, 2012), 88–97, at 88.

well as her nanny; after Marti, the assistant, finally confronts the wife of his boss about the maltreatment, the mother lectures her daughter at the night-bed:

> To Silvi she said goodnight with a grimace [*mit verzogenem Gesicht* = with a malformed face], adding that she should pull herself together and stop giving her mother cause to be harsh with her; then she, too, would be treated lovingly. It was a terrible shame the way she forced people to be stern with her and punish her over and over.[45]

Just as in the earlier chapter on domestic violence in this book on *Ambiguous Aggression*, here too accountability is displaced: the mother justifies her violence by suggesting that she was provoked by her unruly child. In order to make palpable the mother's double-binding maneuver, Walser refers to both mother and daughter with the pronoun "she"—the same technique that we examined in scenes of family abuse in Keller's *A Village Romeo and Juliet* where it had the effect that the positions of abuser and abused become interchangeable. Walser gives the revolving blame machine another spin by using the grammatical confusion in order to *correct* the mother's attempt to shift the responsibility: i.e., the order that "she should control her temper better" could (and should) be directed at the violent mother. One could go so far as to say that Walser succeeds in smuggling in a small, passive-aggressive counter-history to Freud's seduction theory. This tiny rebellion is joined by the phrase "with a malformed face" ("mit verzogenenm Gesicht"): even though the turn of speech *das Gesicht verziehen* ("to grimace"; "to contort" or "to screw up one's face") is common in German, it is rarely used as a participle; instead, the participle *verzogen* usually appears in the context of the paternal rebuke *verzogenes Gör* (spoiled brat). The displacement of this phrase has the effect that the mother's implicit accusation ("You spoilt brat tantalized me into abusing you") is turned back upon the accuser: it is the mother whose face bespeaks her own being a brat.[46]

---

45 Robert Walser, *The Assistant*, trans. Susan Bernofsky (New York: New Directions, 2007), 244; "Zu Silvi sagte sie, indem sie ihr mit verzogenem Gesicht gute Nacht sagte, sie solle sich besser zusammennehmen und ihr keine Ursache mehr geben, streng mit ihr zu sein, sdann sei man auch gut zu ihr. Es sei ein Jammer, wie man sie behandeln und immer wieder strafen müsse." *Der Gehülfe*, 244.
46 "Walser scheut sich nicht, auch in die allerausgetretensten Begriffspantoffeln zu steigen, um in ihnen nach seinen eigenen Melodien zu tanzen. All die 'Leerheiten, Widerlichkeiten, Seelen- und Herzlosigkeiten auf seiten dieser schwatzhaften Moderne' ... nimmt Walser in seine Texte auf, er umtänzelt sie leichtfüßig, ohne moralisch zuzuschlagen, er glossiert sie von außen, um sie von innen her auseinanderbrechen." Peter Utz, "Robert Walser," in *Deutsche Dichter des 20. Jahrhunderts*, ed. ibid. and Hartmut Steinecke (Berlin: Erich Schmidt, 1994), at 205–206.

Nietzsche's famous dictum that nihilism is "this uncanniest of guests"[47] aptly describes Walser's art of teasing: as a practice of ambiguous aggression, teasing is an everyday phenomenon that has the potential to imbue traditional formations of power with a sense of alienation, however momentary. Teasing advances in Walser to the position of a quotidian, poetic strategy of provoking people to the point where they take off their mask (*prosopopeïa*) and reveal their anger, a profane form of *aletheia*, the art of teasing out uncomfortable emotional truths.

Sublimation ("The Hatchitti")

As you will have noticed by now Walser's protagonists don't get angry. "Generally, it is ridiculous how quickly certain people can get angry," one of his minor narrative voices marvels, and immediately disperses this brief excursus with a light-minded "Oh well!"[48] Or, in a "Letter from one Man to another Man": "Better try to love where someone else, a man less prudent and strong, would hate."[49] Among the limited number of Walser's novels, *The Assistant* (*Der Gehülfe*) presents the only exception from this rule: being employed by a violent choleric, Joseph Marti has to witness and endure so many injustices that he vents his anger at certain points; Marti has to pay dearly for these brief moments of outrage that, worst of all, simply peter out. All other of Walser's main characters reliably retreat to irony as a default mode.

The fact, however, that a phenomenon is ubiquitous—like ambiguous aggression in Robert Walser—does not make it necessarily easier to examine because whenever we are faced with the overwhelming presence of a phenomenon it becomes more difficult to isolate this trait from other text structures. Hence I would like to continue my deliberations with the analysis of the little-regarded prose piece, "The Hatchitti" ("Die Hutchitti"[50]): a text rather untypical for its author, insofar as ambiguous aggression becomes a foreground-phenomenon here. "The Hatchitti" was written after Walser had returned from Germany to his hometown Biel, where he lived from 1913 to 1920 with little means.

---

47 Friedrich Nietzsche, *The Will to Power*, ed. and trans. Walter Kaufmann and R. J. Hollingdale (New York: Random House, 1967), 7; "Der Nihilismus steht vor der Tür: woher kommt uns dieser unheimlichste aller Gäste?" in *Der Wille zur Macht* (= *Kritische Studienausgabe*, vol. 12, ed. Giorgio Colli und Mazzino Montinari) (München: dtv, 1999), 125.
48 "Es ist überhaupt lächerlich, wie schnell manche Leute zornig werden können. Ei nun!" Robert Walser, "Besetzt," in *Träumen. Prosa aus der Bieler Zeit 1913–1920* (= *Sämtliche Werke*, vol. 16) (Zurich/Frankfurt/M.: Suhrkamp, 1985), 275–277, at 277.
49 "Versuchen Sie lieber, zu lieben, wo ein anderer, weniger Besonnener und Starker, hassen würde." Walser, "Brief eines Mannes an einen Mann," *Aufsätze*, 12–13, at 12.
50 Walser, "Die Hutchitti," *Träumen*, 248–249.

The text is shaped by negative representations and permanent relativizations, which makes sense given that its object is repressed anger, i.e., that which remains unsaid or maybe even unfelt; in fact, "The Hatchitti" is probably the most obscure of Walser's titles: *Hutchitti*—a word as inscrutable as Kafka's *Odradek*, with which it shares not only its linguistic origin in dialect or jargon but also the fact that both Chitti and Odradek arise from the world of children's play and become uncanny when they start haunting the adult world. "Does madam know what a chitti is?" Walser teases his long-time platonic love interest Frieda Mermet—his sister Lisa's best friend—in a cheeky or even rather impudent letter about teasing young waitresses.[51]

Walser's first-person narrator remembers "a reprehensible, mischievous, and willful game" that he and his friends used to play: the boys would rob one of them of his hat and throw it into the bushes. The victim would then refuse to pick up his hat and, pretending he did not care, start walking home "chittigly, or in good [high] German resentfully" (*grollend*) while only "raging pretty softly" ("hübsch sachte zürnend"). At some point, however, the boy would run back in order to pick up his "poor hat" "gently and humbly." This first part of the text is dominated by adjectives and adverbs—nothing unusual for Walser, whom the poet Christian Morgenstern, editor of Walser's first novel *The Tanners* (*Die Geschwister Tanner*, 1907), admonished: "You love to pile on predicate words making the mistake of saying, without necessity, two, three times the same thing."[52] However, the amount of adjectives and adverbs in "The Hatchitti" is remarkable even for Walser and moreover the rhetorical device of *accumulatio* stands in contrast to the brief definitions provided by the narrator of Chitti as "rage on account of a hat" ("die Hutchitti [Wut wegen eines Hutes]") as well as "wrath on account of hurt pride" ("Zorn wegen verletzten Stolzes"). In German, the use of the genitive prompted by the genitive preposition *wegen* (because of; on account of) always brings about a certain elevation of language and

---

[51] Walser in a letter to Frieda Mermet, Aug. (?) 1924, *Briefe*, 218: "Does madam know what is a Chitti? In any case something arranged, aimed. One sits there and all of a sudden one sees, right in front of oneself, the possibility of being chitty. The waitress e.g. does not want to pick up the umbrella from the floor for you. One knows exactly that she won't do it but for that very reason one appeals to her to do so. Now the Chitti arises, and it gets bigger from minute to minute. Dainty cavaliers come to defend the chitty girl of the chitty *Robert Walser* by way of their posture and countenance. What is so wonderful about the Chitti is the exact foreknowledge: now we have one ... The beautiful thing with Chittinen— which by the way are not city-Bernian but have quasi international cache—is that in silence one laughs about them terribly. ... Ordinary life can be so much fun if one only displays some playful pleasure (*Spiellust*)."

[52] Christian Morgenstern to Robert Walser, Obermais near Meran, mid-September 1906, *Briefe*, 41–45, at 43.

in the definitions of Chitti the neutral, quasi-scientific tone of causation resembles that of a judge or a referee. It is thus all the more perplexing when the same rational narrator takes an almost sadistic pleasure in the x-raying of irrational affects in the victim of the prank. Obsessive emotional circumscription is just another discipline of the art of teasing, through which Walser's characters relate to the world.

Once the boy returns with his hat, the other boys make fun of him "for his very incautious, pathetic anger or Chitti." And who would not laugh about a *Hut-Wut* (hat-anger)—a rhyme that sounds like one from a children's book, which makes the anger ridiculous? One can trace this pairing of aggression and laughter in the etymology of the Swiss dialect-word "Chitti," which translates as "resentfulness" or "grumbling" but which is also related to the words "chipper" and "chitter" meaning "laughter." The Swiss-German *Idiotikon* explicitly registers that "to be chitti" is a *result* of having been ridiculed or teased in the sense of being "sore." And yet, as readers we do not get to witness the boy's anger because the aggressive outburst itself is absent; thus we have to believe the narrator that, as a rule, the boy's *Chitti* increases his sense of humiliation so much that it "almost break[s] the boy apart."

At this point the line breaks off as well, forcing the text to start another paragraph, with the narrator's voice acquiring an even older, authorial tone: "O, such a Chitti is horrendous. Secret, gritty grudge, deep silent raging are something very, very bad." Now we are the children who have to be lectured about some "very, very bad" behavior: how not to hold on to grudges because they escalate quickly and may eventually lead to wars. Note that the text was first published in a newspaper during the First World War—that is, at the time of a war caused in no small part by a German emperor, Wilhelm I., who nervously steered into confrontations and crises instead of pursuing a more temporizing politics.[53] I am leaving out here the fittingly breathless, climactic design of Walser's second and final part—suffice it to say that the striking repetitiveness ventriloquizes the *rolling* sound of *Grollen*: the rumbling resentment of the death-drive, an anger that cannot let go, precisely because it has to be repressed. The rolling rage makes itself audible through *amplificatio* in the form of double constructions: the narrator not only excessively repeats words ("very, very bad," "boys ... with boys," "grown-ups with grown-ups, mature ones with mature ones, and I want to say, nations with nations," a resentment

---

53 In *Vossische Zeitung* on November 15, 1915. Walser's small prose piece could thus be read as the Swiss counter-narrative to the dominant affect-theory claim about the First World War, namely that it was "the age of nervousness" that brought about that war; see Joachim Radkau, *Das Zeitalter der Nervosität: Deutschland zwischen Bismarck und Hitler* (München: Hanser, 1998).

"that broadens and broadens, finds no end, becomes more and more urgent, more and more hurtful") but also indulges in the superfluousness of numerous pleonasms ("gentle and humble," "to the others, to the villains," "[s]ecret, gritty grudge, deep, silent raging," "vengeance or revenge," "enslaving and dishonoring"). In spite of Morgenstern's critique of Walser's style, in "The Hatchitti" repetitiveness is absolutely to the point in that the linguistic echoing emulates the feeling of being stuck, not being able to let go—in German *nachtragend*.

So primal is this feeling that language, too, retreats to its fundamental functions: the verbs resign to "being" ("O, such a Chitti *is* horrendous. Secret, gritty grudge, deep silent raging *are* something very, very bad"), adjectives to the distinction between "good vs. bad," and the sentence construction contents itself with the most basic combination of conjunction, subject, and verb ("and that is ..."):

> ... and that widens and widens .... Yes, that is the Chitti, the Hatchitti, the secret, unburied and quietly hidden rumbling; that doesn't want to come to rest, cannot leave well alone, cannot sleep, and that, right, o you fellow men, that is sad, that is bad.[54]

Just like that, we have proceeded from the comedy of children's play to the world-historical tragedy of war: a tragic violence, which results from the inability to let comedy be comedy and to do what every Walserian anti-hero teaches us to do: to laugh in the face of aggression instead of holding grudges.

I have waited until this last chapter to address Norbert Elias' famous claim that the repression of emotions is a direct result of the civilization process, although some might expect a study like this on *Ambiguous Aggression: Flirtation, Passive Aggression, Domestic Violence (German Realism and beyond)* to lend itself to a reading of and through Elias' hypothesis.[55] But if this book has aspired to one thing, it is to demonstrate that literature strives against the linearity of historical narration and that the affects of realism and modernism are neither one-way-streets nor simply disconnected from one another. "The Hatchitti" is an opportunity to try to get one's head around the confusing after-life of realist affects. If, for instance, one were to assume that a dialect word like "Chitti" was closer to a, however phantasmatic, origin of language than "stupid High German" (to quote from one of Walser's letter to his sister

---

54 " ... und das weitet und weitet sich, ... Ja, das ist die Chitti, die Hutchitti, das heimliche, unbegrabene und still verborgene Grollen; das will nicht zur Ruhe kommen, kann sich nicht zufrieden geben, kann nicht schlafen, und das, nicht war, o ihr Mitmenschen, das ist traurig, das ist bös."
55 Norbert Elias, *Über den Prozess der Zivilisation*, 2 vol. (Frankfurt/M.: Suhrkamp, 2010 [1939]).

Fanny[56]), and that therefore the dialect phrase *Chitti* were better suited to mediate "the raw affect of aggression," then Walser deconstructs this assumption at the same time that he gives cause for it. This is because *chitti*—this seemingly primal, chthonic anger—already presents a *repressed* form of aggression, one that is paradoxically as much nature as it is part of culture, which is to say the primal is the repressed or the hybrid.

The etymologies of the two words most central to the "Hatchitti" reflect and intensify this ambiguity insofar as *Chitti* signifies both aggression and laughter. The word in the text that functions as a translation of "Chitti" is *Grollen* ("the secret, unburied and quietly hidden rumbling"); yet, the etymology of *Grollen* turns out to be just as ambiguous as *Chitti*: *Grollen* describes a paradoxical form of muteness or repression that, according to the *Grimmsches Wörterbuch*, derives from roaring (*grölen*—to roar; to bawl), which means *Grollen* embodies one of those instances in German language of which Hegel is so fond because the meaning of a word includes its opposite.[57] The simultaneity of opposite meanings contradicts the successive temporality of the genetic sublimation-paradigm as proposed by Elias, Freud, and Nietzsche, insofar as according to the logic of sublimation everything begins with screaming aggression, then civilization takes its course and represses aggressions until aggression is silenced or at least dimmed down to the sound of ironic laughter (Odradek's "laughter without lungs"?). We could even go so far as to say that the etymologies of *Chitti* and *Grollen* are of a circular temporality: for not only does the narrator deplore that humanity has made no progress in its cultivation of affects but that even moderated aggression (*Grollen*) still leads to war; even more extremely ambiguous: the etymologies of the two key terms as well as the storyline present laughter not only as a reaction to aggression but as its very cause.

Dissimulation ("A Slap in the Face, Etc.")

A man and a woman deeply engaged in conversation, a flirtation of sorts, if indeed the sound of lyrical language is to be trusted—for the paragraph kicks off with rhyme, the language of love's redundancy. He is talking and she is taking in every word of his babbling until, at some point, he utters "a certain little word" ("ein gewisses Wörtchen") and the woman almost gives way under the weight of this word. "Although I have made many mistakes with women I have never used this certain little word with them," the narrator faults. Of course, the reader of "A

---

56 Walser, "An seine Schwester Fanny. Februar/März? 1904," *Briefe*, 22–23, at 23.
57 See Hegel's "Vorrede zur zweiten Auflage der Logik," *Wissenschaft der Logik* (= *Werke in 20 Bänden. Theorie Werkausgabe*, vol. 5, ed. Eva Moldenhauer and Karl Markus Michel) (Frankfurt/M.: Suhrkamp 1970–71), 20–21.

Slap in the Face, Etc." ("Eine Ohrfeige und Sonstiges [1925]"[58]) wants to know, what did the man say to the woman? And the narrator relishes our curiosity—why else would he torture us and make us wait for the word? All the narrator gives to us to decode the scene are visual cues from the woman's face:

> Over her face twitched a silent, quiet, muted agony, which amused me. Yeah, I'm malicious. She would have liked best to deal a blow to the object of her amazement but she couldn't do it. She gazed into space, as if to gain composure in some angle. Her excitation was delicate and terrifying; trivial and at the same time horrifying.[59]

From a narrative point of view we are dealing with a simultaneously realized and unrealized internal focalization: realized insofar as the first-person narrator is never described from the outside, unrealized because the narrator remains rather private (e.g., we do not even know the narrator's gender with certainty, although the vast majority of Walser's texts are told from the viewpoint of persons of male gender).[60] Instead of letting us into his or her emotional life the narrator prefers to delve into the psyche of a person in his immediate surrounding, a woman. If indeed we can rely on the narrator's, possibly unreliable, observations then the aggression that he describes bears some familiarity with the kind of *domestic violence lite* that we have encountered in this book several times: suppressed aggression, female aggression, aggression that must remain invisible, the type of exasperated anger

---

58 Robert Walser, "Eine Ohrfeige und Sonstiges," in *Die Rose* (= *Sämtliche Werke*, vol. 8) (Zurich/Frankfurt/M.: Suhrkamp, 1986), 49–65, at 57–58. In the introduction to her translation of Walser's *The Robber* (Lincoln, NE: University of Nebraska Press, 2000), v–xiii, Susan Bernofsky writes on the time around the publication of *The Rose*: "While the previous decade had seen the appearance of nine of his fourteen books, by 1920 publishers' interest in his work had waned and in the years that followed he was able to publish only a single volume, *Die Rose* (*The Rose*, 1925), a collection of stories. The newspapers and magazines in whose feuilleton pages his work had frequently appeared began to send rejections. Walser's editor at the *Berliner Tagblatt* even reported having received letters from angry readers threatening to cancel their subscriptions if the 'nonsense' didn't stop" (vi).
59 "Über ihr Gesicht zuckte eine stille, leise, verhaltene Qual, woran ich mich amüsierte. Ich bin eben boshaft. Am liebsten hätte sie dem eben Angestaunten eins versetzen mögen, war dazu aber außerstande. Sie schaute ins Leere, wie in irgendeinem Winkel Fassung einzufangen. Ihre Erregung war zart und furchtbar; belanglos und zugleich entsetzlich." Ibid.
60 Gérard Genette concedes that a fully realized internal focalization is a rare thing and that strictly speaking only interior monologue qualifies as such: *Narrative Discourse: An Essay in Method*, trans. Jane E. Lewin (Ithaca, NY: Cornell University Press, 1980 [1972]), 193.

that showed through in the letters by Felice, Milena, and Fontane's wife in the chapter on passive aggression. What is new in "A Slap in the Face, Etc." is that in the brief moment, in which the woman struggles to contain her anger, she appears to die a small death, a *petite mort*, suggested by the strangely erotically charged vocabulary (*zucken, Qual, Erregung, zart*). This particular eroticism has a spiritual dimension, which resonates with Walser's interest in mysticism; I would even dare to compare the woman's excitation—her silent, twitching *admiratio* ("Anstaunen") when confronted with the word that has not even yet arrived at its reader—to the inverted orgasm of a Baroque saint, the ecstasy of Saint Teresa de Avila. But still, why, of all people, would the famously "virginal"[61] Walser evoke the language of the obscene to depict a scene in which nobody makes a scene? At the risk of shamelessly psychologizing Walser, one might want to return at this point to Elias Canetti's diagnosis that Walser's texts bear traces of suppressed anxiety.[62] And if we feel that there is something to Canetti's intuition, then we would want to add one further anxiety to be suppressed, namely that of losing oneself *in* aggression, including sexual aggression.

In "A Slap in the Face, Etc." it is this coerced invisibility that makes the woman appear as a hybrid: half saint, half trapped animal whose glance, like that of Rilke's panther, has become weary from the passing bars ("She gazed into space"). Of course, in the case of a woman, these bars are "merely" symbolic: a woman could be paradoxically *fassungslos* ("uncontainable," "bewildered," "not getting a grip") as a result of being *trapped* in the symbolic order; that is, of not being allowed *as a woman* to express her anger. Instead, she has to avert her gaze and to stay on the lookout for a corner in the room that would allow her to regain her composure (*die Fassung wieder erlangen*) before she makes eye contact again with her oblivious male counterpart. It is only the penetrating gaze of the first-person narrator who informs us of "her inner fight ... to vindicate herself"—an "exertion" that otherwise ironically goes by unnoticed.

---

61 W. G. Sebald speaks of Walser's "virginal innocence" (like Agamben) in "Le Promeneur Solitaire: A Remembrance of Robert Walser," 120. Hans Dieter Zimmermann interprets Walser's chastity in the context of his interest in pietism and as a form of monastic life: "Walser und die pietistische Ethik," in *"Immer dicht vor dem Sturze ..." Zum Werk Robert Walsers*, ed. Paolo Chiarini and Hans Dieter Zimmermann (Frankfurt/M.: Athenäum, 1987), 237–251, at 244.
62 Canetti, "Aufzeichnungen zu Robert Walser (1973)," 12: "The peculiarity of *Robert Walser* consists in the fact that he never spells out his motives. He is the most hidden [*versteckteste*] of all poets. He is always well, he delights in everything. But his *Schwärmerei* is cold because it leaves out part of his personality, and that is why it is also uncanny. Everything becomes his *outer* nature and what actual matters about this person [*das Eigentliche an ihr*], the most inner [*das Innerste*], the anxiety, he denies his whole life."

The word finally arrives at its destination: "GOT IT?" (*BEGRIFSCH?*) is written in all-caps at the center of the page, exhibiting the vulgarity of an advertisement. "It is the cruel gift of the malignant word," notes Denise Riley in *Language as Affect*, "to linger and echo as if fully detached from its original occasion, whose authoritative hostility I might by now, having recognized it as such, have dethroned."[63] In Walser, too, the malignant word becomes the real Other. "He said something very simple," Walser's narrator records, "and after this simple thing that his comprehension spouted off he asked her from the height of it: 'GOT IT?'" A meta-question of sorts: did you get what is so aggressive about asking someone whether they got it? Did my question insult you? Was the answer too obvious? Obviously, to ask about the obvious insults our intelligence. In Walser's "Some Words about Writing a Novel" the poetic function is said to depend on latency, i.e., on "what is not said [*Ungesagtheiten*]."[64] Making the obvious explicit is at the opposite pole of the introverted female aggressivity of Walser's "A Slap in the Face, Etc." It is this latency of aggression that triggers our hermeneutic frenzy; maybe it even triggers Walser's writing. The very same latency that is first yanked out into the open by the man and then ridiculed as a surface phenomenon in the narrator's final words: "While I observed this, I read a 'woman's magazine' [*Frauenblatt*]."

In spite of this, the latency of "A Slap in the Face" is powerless, impotent; the imagined flat, open female hand, which dreams of slapping the man's face, is juxtaposed with a male fist that "comprehends" (*begreift*). Given that we have already broached the topic of fetishism in Walser's writing style, it is noteworthy that in German philosophical discourse there are hardly any other terms with as much of a fetish function as the words *Begriff* and *begreifen*. Philosophers are smitten with the flexibility of the term, the ambiguous character of which shall exemplify both the incomparable physicality of the German language and its speculative reach. *Begriff*—what other word could more aptly show how German is both abstract and concrete, the only true language for philosophy, as both Hegel and Heidegger cried out ecstatically?[65] Still, there have

---

63   Riley, *Impersonal Passion*, 16.
64   Robert Walser, "Einige Worte über das Romanschreiben," *Wenn Schwache sich für Starke halten*, 181–182, at 182.
65   According to Hegel, the ideal precondition for thinking is a language rich in logical terms; Hegel assumes that "the German language has in this regard many advantages to other modern languages" ("die deutsche Sprache hat darin viele Vorzüge vor den anderen modernen Sprachen," "Vorrede zur zweiten Auflage der Logik," 20) in that it is both abstract and concrete. Similarly, Heidegger in *Einführung in die Metaphysik* (Tübingen: Max Niemeyer, 1966 [1956]), which heads back to a lecture series given in 1935) not only calls the Germans "the metaphysical *Volk*" (29) but in his reflections "Zur Etymologie des Wortes ‚Sein'" Heidegger also argues that the Greek language "besides German (is) both the mightiest and the most spiritual" (43).

been quieter voices, like that of Anselm Haverkamp who emphasized the almost *übergriffige* (molesting) manner, "the aggressive grasping [*Begreifen*], gripping [*Zugreifen*], getting a grip on something [*in den Griff Nehmen*] of the German *Begriff*."[66] Or Georges-Arthur Goldschmidt who ironized the acclaimed physicality of German, which "seems to come much closer to immediate understanding," by making it climax pornographically:

> German up to its most innermost part is bound to the body's gestures and desires. ... Not without reason we say that one speaks *mit dem Brustton der Überzeugung* [literally: with the chest-tone of conviction]; there is no text, no speech, in which one would hold one's breath; the panting, the up and down, the jerky breath, that the guilty teenager tries to hide: from this rhythm the German language begins to raise its voice.[67]

For Walser, the first half of the twentieth century makes this latently (sexually) aggressive potential of the German language manifest. Walser's essay "Die deutsche Sprache" (1919) is a eulogy for a once-beloved female German language that has turned ugly and hateful: "She lost all her gracefulness, sounded dry, hard, and silly and served almost exclusively for purposes of harshness or sharpness."[68] Coming back to our seemingly banal scene, one could say that the Swiss German *Begrifsch* ("Got it?," high-German *Begreifst du?*) plays on the relation between the concrete and the abstract and violently inquires as to whether the female opposite is capable of abstraction, of grasping (*begreifen*) an idea—that is: whether the woman can indeed have a concept (*Begriff*) of, well, anything at all. Whereas the man has such a firm grasp on the concept of aggression that it even slips away from him, the hand of the woman is left empty. And if that were not enough, it actually requires the voice of the male narrator to ventriloquize the latent, impotent female aggression with sadistic amusement.

---

66 "In the post-Latin forms of the Roman languages (English, French) the aggressive *Begreifen* ('grasping'), *Zugreifen* ('gripping'), *in den Griff Nehmen* ('getting a grip on something') of the German *Begriff* is *conception*: a passive receiving rather than something that has been actively grasped and turned into concepts. Thus, 'to conceive of' is not a form of comprehension that would straightaway grasp but a receiving 'execution' of something given." Anselm Haverkamp, "Begreifen, bildlich," in *Diesseits der Oder. Frankfurter Vorlesungen* (Berlin: Kadmos, 2008), 161–178, at 165–166.

67 Georges-Arthur Goldschmidt, *Quand Freud voit la mer: Freud et la langue allemande I* (Paris: Buchet Chastel, 2006), 21.

68 "Sie verlor all ihren Liebreiz, klang trocken, hart und albern und diente fast ausschließlich zu Barschheits- und Schneidigkeitszwecken." Walser, "Die deutsche Sprache," *Träumen*, 394–395, at 394. The text first appeared in the *Neue Zürcher Zeitung* in May 1919.

And yet, the word that initiates the woman's interrogation—*BE-GRIFSCH?*—the concept of concepts, allegorizes itself in the end. Maybe we even hear the word tailing off with a sh-sound, the kind of slurring that becomes perceptible when words slide together: "Do you understand what I'm saying even when I slurthesewordstogether?" There is a shutting up, a literal inarticulateness at the heart of this comprehension, a hint of healing female aggression, of telling the mansplainer to sch-ut up.

Resentment ("Childish Revenge" and "Coffeehouse-Performance")

For the writer of withdrawal, whose "Disappearing Acts"[69] encompasses his style as well as his life, the prose piece (*Prosastück*) presents a natural choice in that it can serve as a literary hiding-place of sorts. The prose piece allows the self-conscious Walser, who by the way became canonized for this genre, to pursue his writerly passion without being intimidated and silenced by the novel as the epitome of "high Art" or *kleos*: instead, prose pieces are doomed to vanish on account of their smallness as well as their fugitive temporality; usually, the prose piece sees the light of the daily press only briefly in order to then be forgotten.[70] Still, there is something in Walser's way of writing that resists this invisibility and that is the repetitive character of his texts. Michael Niehaus pointedly remarks that "Robert Walser's prose-texts realize the 'idea' of the prose-piece—albeit (paradoxically) not as single pieces but in their seriality."[71] Alone in his time in Bern, Walser authored more than a thousand prose pieces. If one reads these texts one will notice how Walser works through the same affect-constellation again and again, with a sense of contentment possessed only by fetishists. This peculiar writing situation affords a reader ample affective material: with multiple stages of literary production that allow us to speculate as to how aggression (on the diegetic as well as extra-diegetic level) might have been repressed or sublimated in the movement from one prose piece to the next and how simultaneously the semantic ambiguity as well as the affective ambivalence increased.

---

69 Lerner, "Robert Walser's Disappearing Acts."
70 "As a feuilleton-writer Robert Walser made himself known, as a feuilleton-writer he remained unknown. This is because the author-subject is just as fugitive as the feuilleton." Peter Utz, "Zu kurz gekommene Kleinigkeiten. Robert Walser und der Beitrag des Feuilletons zur literarischen Moderne," in *Die kleinen Formen in der Moderne*, ed. Elmar Locher (Bolzano: Sturzflüge, 2001), 133–166, at 156.
71 Michael Niehaus, "Das Prosastück als Idee und das Prosastückverfassen als Seinsweise: Robert Walser," in *Kleine Prosa*, ed. Thomas Althaus et al. (Tübingen: Max Niemeyer, 2007), 173–186, at 184.

Without any further ado, let us look at what might well be the cruelest prose piece in Walser's œuvre. Its title is "Kindliche Rache. Ein Miniaturroman"[72] ("Childish Revenge: A Miniature Novel"), published in the *Prager Presse* in June of 1926—according to Jochen Greven one of the most productive and successful years for Walser.[73] This productivity seems to have resulted in no small part from the hardships that Walser experienced upon his relocation to Bern in 1919, "only with a few francs in his pocket, a ridiculed, unsuccessful author."[74] Kerstin Gräfin von Schwerin reminisces that "in Bern Walser veritably exploited his immediate everyday surroundings"[75] in order to write about them, often for feuilletons. The year 1926 was one year after his last book *Die Rose* was published, and three years before he decided to enter the psychiatric clinic in Waldau.

As every act of revenge responds to an earlier incident, the origin of the "Childish Revenge" is in question; the incident, which must have set in motion the wheel of repetition, is presented as a moment of public debasement occurring in the artist's sanctum—the coffeehouse. One author insulted another, who remains nameless and therefore could have been any other writer, including our first-person narrator or maybe even Walser himself; after all, as Stephan Kammer points out, the moments of "local and temporal deixis"[76] in "Childish Revenge" imbue the prose piece with a sense of "reality." So here is the public rebuke in a nutshell:

> Of what avail was it for the author that he once in a coffeehouse dismissed a colleague maybe with just too much vehemence by throwing into his surprised face the accusation of being a weakling [*Schwächlingshaftigkeit*]?[77]

---

72 Walser, "Kindliche Rache. Ein Miniaturroman" was reprinted in the posthumous essay-collection *Zarte Zeilen* (*Gentle Lines*), 296–299, which at times is not so gentle; the prose pieces in *Zarte Zeilen* all stem from Walser's Berner time: *Sämtliche Werke*, vol. 18: *Prosa aus der Berner Zeit, 1926* (Zurich/Frankfurt/M.: Suhrkamp, 1986).
73 Jochen Greven, "Nachwort des Herausgebers," Walser, *Zarte Zeilen*, 329–336, at 329.
74 Carl Seelig, *Wanderungen mit Robert Walser*, 108.
75 Kerstin Gräfin von Schwerin, "Prosa der Berner Zeit," in *Robert Walser Handbuch*, ed. Lucas Marco Gisi, 196–206, at 199.
76 Stephan Kammer, "Poetologie der Lektüre—Lektüre der Poetologie: Robert Walsers *Kindliche Rache*," *Text & Kontext. Zeitschrift für germanistische Literaturforschung in Skandinavien* 54 (2007): 107–125, at 112.
77 "Was nützte dem Schriftsteller, daß er einst in einem Kaffeehaus einen seiner Kollegen mit vielleicht nur zu viel Wucht abgetan hatte, indem er ihm den Vorwurf der Schwächlingshaftigkeit ins überraschte Gesicht schleuderte?" Walser, "Kindliche Rache. Ein Miniaturroman," 298.

The rendition of the events that directly succeed this original aggression follows the script of karmic retribution: the aggressor was left by his beautiful young wife, after which he married his servant, with whom he had a child who soon "died off" and—now the prose piece switches into the traumatic present tense—leaves its parents heartbroken; the father writes a book entitled *Childish Revenge*:

> He forgot that after all we are all so-to-speak weak, and because my watch cautions me that it is almost ten o'clock and I am used to hitting the hay on time, I abruptly, i.e. imperiously, cut off and break off the tightly-constructed life-novel with the remark that the sweet, dear little child of the peaceloving, culturedoing people only thus died off.
>
> The pain of the long-suffering parents is immeasurable. The mother goes on acting as if she were senseless, in that she seems hardly able to do anything other than to press her lips together. The father, however, is busy with the invention of a new book, that presumably will be terribly difficult to read, and whose title in all probability will be: "Childish Revenge." The high sense is that the child takes revenge on those whose joy-of-life it was assigned to be by withdrawing from them again, just after it had showed itself to them.[78]

If one judges Walser according to his techniques of withdrawal then one can call this text a little masterpiece. Thanks to his ability to turn aggression ambiguous, what would otherwise perhaps strike one as a truly sick fantasy of revenge—because it resorts to the most despicable deed of retaliation, the killing of an infant—appears as something that one can mock and draw a lesson from. If we are to believe Walser's story (and how else should we relate to a piece of fiction?), then it stages neither the revenge of author nor character nor even, strictly speaking, that of the child, but stages rather the child's revenge *as imagined by its father*, who interprets his child's death as an aggression directed at him.

---

78 "Er vergaß, daß wir ja alle sozusagen schwach sind, und da mich ein Blick auf die Uhr belehrt, daß es zehn Uhr ist und ich gewöhnt bin, mich rechtzeitig in die Federn zu begeben, so schneide und breche ich den straffaufgebauten Lebensroman jäh, d.h. gebieterisch mit der Anmerkung ab, daß den friedliebenden, kulturtreibenden Leutchen das herzige, liebe Kindchen nur so wegstarb. Der Schmerz der schwergeprüften Eltern war unermeßlich. Die Mutter gebärdet sich noch in einem fort wie unsinnig, indem sie beinahe nicht anderes zu tun imstande scheint, als die Lippen zusammenzupressen. Den Vater aber beschäftigt die Erfindung eines neuen Buches, das vermutlich entsetzlich schwierig zu lesen sein wird, und dessen Betitelung aller Wahrscheinlichkeit nach lauten dürfte: ‚Kindliche Rache.' Der hohe Sinn ist der, daß sich das Kind an denen, deren Lebensfreude es auszumachen berufen ist, dadurch rächt, daß es sich ihnen, kaum, daß es sich ihnen gezeigt hat, wieder entzieht." Ibid.

One could also say: the father monopolizes the position of suffering and thus becomes the object of critique. What makes this tone possible is the meta-poetological framing of the story, which Stephan Kammer defined as a "narrative metalepsis":[79] the prose piece adopts its title "Childish Revenge: A Miniature-Novel" from a (meta-)fictional book allegedly authored by the childless father.

It is only if one reads Walser's prose piece with the misanthropic skepsis of which it is worthy that the possibility arises that aggressions may have been multiply displaced. In fact, the chain of projection could reach as far back as to the author himself, to Walser. If we were to assume that—hypothetically speaking—the author himself might have been the victim of a public humiliation in a coffeehouse in Bern, then Walser could have assigned the task of righting this wrong to his narrator who could have then referred "his" aggression to the character of the dying child who takes revenge on its needy parents—the last link would be the father himself, who is brilliantly made to draw all aggression upon him, like a magnet, by being depicted as exploiting the infant's death for his own literary career. According to this reading, Walser would have committed the perfect crime, i.e., one that leaves no trace and thus leaves us to speculate.

Then, in July 1926—that is, only one month after "Childish Revenge" had appeared in the *Prager Presse*—another prose piece was published, this time in the *Berliner Tageblatt*: "Coffeehouse Performance" ("Kaffeehausauftritt").[80] Here, a first-person narrator recalls someone's demeaning remark that he was no longer of any service to his country:

> I was viciously attacked on account of alleged weakness. Vicious attacks, however, are themselves weak. Of course, I don't name the one who attacked me with a viciousness that bespoke of a not quite fitting worry. I understood the attacker, who was it out of worry, why I immediately excused his viciousness. I was forceful enough to do this. You see, he was worried that I wasn't a force anymore.[81]

---

79 Stephan Kammer, "Poetologie der Lektüre—Lektüre der Poetologie: Robert Walsers Kindliche Rache," *Text & Kontext. Zeitschrift für germanistische Literaturforschung in Skandinavien* 54 (2007): 107–125, 113.

80 Both feuilleton-texts are contained in the collection *Zarte Zeilen* (*Gentle Lines*); although more than two-hundred pages separate the two pieces, which appear in reverse chronological order at that, there are strong indicators for their connectedness.

81 "Ich wurde wegen angeblicher Schwäche heftig angegriffen. Heftiges Angreifen ist aber selber schwach. Ich nenne ihn selbstverständlich nicht, der mich mit einer Heftigkeit angegriffen hat, die von einer nicht ganz passenden Besorgnis zeugt. Ich verstand den Angreifer, der dies aus Besorgtheit war, sehr gut, weshalb ich seine Heftigkeit sogleich entschuldigte. Ich fand hierzu die nötige Kraft. Er besorgte nämlich, ich sei jetzt keine Kraft mehr." Walser, "Kaffeehausauftritt," *Zarte Zeilen*, 28–31, at 29.

The maneuvers in "Coffeehouse Performance" resemble a fencing-match, in which the *épée* seems to come from all sides and nowhere. If there is aggression (as indicated by the categories "attack[er]" and "vicious[ness]")—then the first-person narrator is eager to keep this aggression extremely ambiguous. Instead of indulging in the fantasy of a "Childish Revenge" that entails the attacker's abandonment by his wife and the death of his child, "Coffeehouse Performance" turns dissimulation up to the point of vertigo: the narrator expresses empathy with his "attacker," concern about safeguarding his anonymity, and claims to "understand," even "apologize" for his allegations.

But which allegations, really? Walser's narrator refuses to identify with the object of his investigation, purporting instead that he became the target of an aggression without, however, reciprocating it: "I actually didn't notice much hereof. Others notice and establish these things much quicker than I do, who doesn't perceive it out of humility." The almost comical insistence on not having noticed the attack is itself noteworthy insofar as this contestation cunningly circumvents a structural problem posing itself for any victim of ambiguous aggression—that is, the epistemological problem of whether one can take a critical approach towards the aggression of which one is the object. Even the father of psychoanalysis in the course of interpreting his dream about Irma's injection first had to admit, in order to satisfy the demands of scientificity, to feelings of revenge toward former clients and colleagues, who dared to be critical of his treatment, in order then "to work through" his aggression and to reach an allegedly "objective" interpretation.[82]

Given that many of the prose pieces in *Zarte Zeilen* emulate a juridical tone it seems apt to translate the epistemological question into legal language: Walser's narrator finds himself in the middle of a dispute about an ambiguous aggression, in which he must decide between two mutually exclusive arguments, none of which would allow him to get "justice." If the narrator claims that the attack was so severe that it made him angry then he is dismissed because he might be too angry to judge the case rationally—there is no plaintiff. If, however, the plaintiff is not angry then the attack cannot have been so bad—there was no attack. What this logic comes down to is that an injured subject has no objectivity and a not-injured subject has no grounds for a claim.[83]

---

82 Sigmund Freud, "Die Methode der Traumdeutung. Die Analyse eines Traummusters," in *Die Traumdeutung* (= *Studienausgabe*, vol. 2, ed. Alexander Mitscherlich a.o.) (Frankfurt/M.: Fischer, 2000), 126–140.
83 One might hear in Walser's "Coffeehouse Performance" more harmless, quotidian resonances with Jean-François Lyotard's *The Differend: Phrases in Dispute*, trans. Georges Van Den Abbeele (Minneapolis: University of Minnesota Press, 1988 [1983]), 9: "I would like to call a *differend* [*différend*] the case where the plaintiff is divested of the means to argue and becomes for that reason a victim."

Walser's narrator "solves" this problem by bringing in "others" as witnesses who noticed the attack, while he himself exposes more virtuous emotions.

A second objection: why, if there was nothing outrageous about the attack, bother writing about it? The narrator reasons: "I am informing the public of this case because I think it's interesting in itself." What is truly interesting is the formulation "interesting in itself," because it snuggles up to Kant's definition of the beautiful as disinterested pleasure.[84] If Walser's narrator had succeeded in defusing a story of public slander into *interesseloses Wohlgefallen* then aggression would have turned into beauty and we would have in front of us a rare case of successful sublimation. Thus, the question is: is sublimated aggression still aggression? Nietzsche would nod. "Coffeehouse Performance" is a study of ressentiment in the extreme, a perpetual transformation of values, "the *slave's revolt in morality*," as Nietzsche thunders in disgust,[85] or with Deleuze, "Ressentiment is revolt, the victory of the weak *as* weak."[86] In Walser's prose piece, the vicious turns out to be the weak, viciousness is worry, attacks are a result of worry, i.e., of disavowed love for the Other; equally, the narrator's ability to excuse his enemy proves his own force. He is forceful on account of his lack of force. In effect, the aggressor's "worry" is not only matched but surpassed by the narrator's own worry for the aggressor's "soul" and "salvation." When at the end the narrator lets slip that a female friend mocked the attacker's book as boring, our narrator milks the story for its moral:

> He too didn't succeed in everything he undertook, what sincerely made me happy for the sake of his soul because a soul takes damage [*eine Seele nimmt Schaden*] if it makes too complementary

---

84 For "disinterested pleasure," see Immanuel Kant, *Critique of the Power of Judgement*, trans. Paul Guyer and Eric Matthews (Cambridge: Cambridge University Press, 2000 [1790/1793]), §2–5. Michael Niehaus writes in "Das Prosastück als Idee und das Prosastückverfassen als Seinsweise," 178, that although Walser mostly chooses the first person, he ironizes this position. At the same time, Niehaus acknowledges that Walser's narrators speak in unison with themselves, from the position of disinterestedness. I would add that therein lies Walser's literary mastery: in his capacity to convince the reader simultaneously of his irony and his sincerity.

85 Friedrich Nietzsche's, *On the Genealogy of Morals*, trans. Carol Diethe (Cambridge a.o.: Cambridge University Press, 2007 [1887]), 145; see the reflection on Nietzsche's art of passive aggression in the chapter on passive aggression, p. 44. Carl Seelig, Walser's guardian, reports that Walser argued that Nietzsche suffered an inferiority complex and that his concept of master-morality (*Herrenmoral*) was deeply offensive to women: the "perfidious revenge of someone unloved." "24. Juli 1944," *Wanderungen mit Robert Walser*, 81–84, at 83.

86 Gilles Deleuze, *Nietzsche and Philosophy*, trans. Hugh Tomlinson (London/New York: Continuum, 2005 [1962]), 109.

experiences by succeeding in anything that it begins. My Christian sentiments rejoice that he too sits or stands there as disputable [*anfechtbar*], so to speak.

The formulation "to take damage" (*Schaden nehmen*), due to its materiality, interrupts as a rhetorical *inconcinnitas* the otherwise elevated, figurative tone of caritas for a brother's "soul." Just like in *The Assistant* (with the word *verziehen*), another context would offer itself more naturally, namely that of *Schadenfreude* about the fake parrhesiast, the armchair-Luther who cannot help but sit, a *Schadenfreude* that laughs at its own sublation into the catalogue of Christian virtues.

Ambivalence (The Robber)

Many readers of Walser have pointed out—with a thrill that only the policing of small perversions affords—that pain and pleasure go together in Walser's life and letters. But to look for (sado-)masochistic tendencies in Walser is like searching for aquatic mammals in *Moby-Dick*: it is harder to not see them than to be blinded into seeing them. After all, it is not so much for the so-called perversions (i.e., not just the author's desire to be mothered with all that it entails: to be fed, spanked, loved, rejected) that we need Walser. Rather it is for the sake of his unparalleled tolerance for ambivalence, an affective spectrum so broad that it causes the three ambiguous aggressions—flirtation, passive aggression, domestic violence—to start blurring with one another into one complicated, emotional assemblage.

Max Brod and Stefan Zweig praised Walser as "sensitive," even "the sensitive one" ("feinfühlig"[87] and "den Feinfühligen"[88]) and accordingly Brod demanded from Walser's readers that they had to "feel through" his prose. One way to understand the description of a literary author as *feinfühlig* is by translating this notion into the psychoanalytic vocabulary and to take it as attestation for Walser's capacity to let opposite affects co-exist alongside one another. For Melanie Klein "ambivalence" is just that: to develop a psyche in which "loved and hated" objects are split "on planes which gradually become increasingly nearer and nearer to reality."[89] Walser takes the next step by destabilizing the whole notion of "feeling" and rearranging emotional reactions in the spirit of ambivalence: thus if people normally treat feelings "as if they were grounded in the things themselves," as Robert Musil notices, then Musil lauds Walser for describing a theater fire not as "a terrible misfortune" but

---

[87] Stefan Zweig, "Grosse kleine Welt," *Über Robert Walser* 1 (1937): 139.
[88] Max Brod, "Kommentar zu Robert Walser (1911)," *Über Robert Walser*, 1, 78–83, 79.
[89] Melanie Klein, "A Contribution to the Psychogenesis of Manic-Depressive States," *International Journal of Psychoanalysis* 16 (1935): 145–174, at 172–173.

instead as "a superb misfortune or a well-deserved one," or even as "a delightful misfortune."⁹⁰ Therefore to focus solely on sadomasochistic fantasies in Walser's writing means reducing this generous ambivalence, what Sontag called "the variety of mental weather in Walser's stories and sketches,"⁹¹ to the limited co-existence of pain and pleasure.

Take Walser's brief text on Keller's *Romeo and Juliet of the Village*. Walser here deploys the utmost linguistic ambiguity to reenact Keller's own tolerance for ambivalence—an ambivalence that nowhere else becomes more palpable than in the depiction of the contradictory affects of the crowd in *Romeo and Juliet*.⁹² If Klein defines ambivalence as constituted by oppositions in the psyche that slowly merge with one another, then Walser stages a similar linguistic procedure by the repeated use of oxymoron: he remarks that Keller makes ordinary people appear "more simple and more significant" by combining "heavyweight and grace"; Walser calls the two lovers, whom the village people "pitied and envied," "the fortunate unfortunate"—and concludes that he felt "silently proud" that through the process of reading Keller's novella he was able to fathom his national history and realize how important "obedience and enjoyment" were.⁹³ Walser, though, does not only emulate stylistically Gottfried Keller's broad affective spectrum—he also

---

90 Robert Musil, "Die *Geschichten* von Robert Walser (1914)," *Über Robert Walser*, 1, 89–91, at 89.
91 Sontag, "Walser's Voice," viii.
92 Gottfried Keller describes the reaction of people at the fair when they see the lovers Vrenchen and Sali dancing together as follows: "Die Verwunderung dieser Zuschauer war ganz seltsam gemischt aus Mitleid mit dem Unglück, aus Verachtung der Verkommenheit und Schlechtigkeit der Eltern und aus Neid gegen das Glück und die Einigkeit des Paares," *Romeo und Julia auf dem Dorfe*, 127. In his reading Robert C. Holub highlights that there is "a great deal of ambiguity and doubt—although not necessarily a lack of realism—surrounding Sali's and Vrenchen's motives for their double-suicide." "Realism, Repetition, Repression: The Nature of Desire in *Romeo und Julia auf dem Dorfe*," *MLN* 100, no. 3 (April, 1985): 461–497, at 472.
93 "[D]ie Alltagsgestalten wurden *simpler und bedeutender* .... Besonders schön war mir die Stelle, wo der Dichter, die Feder mit einem aus *Schwergewicht und Grazie* überaus reizvoll vereinigtem Können handhabend, sich über den Unsegen nebenher verbreitet, den Aneignung unrechten Gutes aufs Menschenleben nach sich ziehen muß, und ebenso schön, wenn nicht rührender, das Einfügen oder Anmerken, welches andeutet, wie die Trinker in der romantisch gelegenen Vagantenbude Vreneli und Sali, *die beglückten Unglückseligen*, um ihrer *sichtlich-tiefen* Neigung willen, so ehrlich *bemitleideten wie beneideten*. Ich war quasi auf mich *still-stolz* geworden, daß ich trotz viel inzwischen Erlebtem, immer noch, ganz wie in früheren Jahren, dem Lauf und den Windungen des Geschichtsstromes ... nachzugehen vermochte, fühlend, wie wichtig solches *Gehorchen und Genießen* nicht für mich allein, sondern für Landsleute überhaupt sei....." (my emphasis). Walser, "Die Kellersche Novelle," *Die Rose*, 23–25, at 24–25.

divines Keller's *lived* capacity for aggression, which, to Walser's mind, sets Keller apart from other authors of his time:

> The unmerited comfort, in which our generation has lived since the turn of the century, has led to a pedantry [*Oberlehrerhaftigkeit*] that is sometimes downright repulsive to me. Every demon is petted to death. How entirely different was Gottfried Keller! I am convinced that in him too something of a scoundrel lived.[94]

Still, what do we make of this quote *in praise of aggression* after all that we have read about teasing, sublimating, dissimulating, repressing? Toward the end of his life, Walser (as cited here in conversation with his guardian Carl Seelig in 1945) returns to his earlier plea for aggressiveness, a plea that he already formulated with fervor in the letter to his melancholic sister, with which we started our reflections on ambiguous aggression in Walser.

Kai Evers has recently offered an overview of a number of bizarrely brutal, even cruel passages from Walser's micrographic writings—a kind of violence, which, as Evers warns his readers, "does not fit Walser's popular image."[95] It is hence no coincidence that I, too, in my final analysis draw from the microscripts, namely from the novel fragment *The Robber* (ca. 1925, published 1972); my hope is that this text will help us in bringing together and heightening the contradictions that characterize Walser's changing attitude towards aggression. *The Robber* is famously difficult to navigate due to its labyrinth-like formal structure, which encompasses the multi-dimensionality and mobility of affect.

> And there lived again a discontent wife that started lamenting [*ein Klagelied ... anstimmen*] about her husband's prissiness [*Bravheit*] by writing a story in which her husband strung himself up and then published the ungainly story. Once it came out in print she gave it to her husband to read who, however, was so prissy and courteous, that it didn't cross his mind to be angry at her. Rather he gave her a shoddy, little bonhomous-kiss [*Gutmütigkeitsküßchen*]. What murderously-peaceful [*mordsfriedliche*] people there are. She

---

94 Carl Seelig, "23. September 1945," *Wanderungen mit Robert Walser*, 96–98, at 97; in German: "Die unverdiente Geborgenheit, in der sich unsere Generation seit der Jahrhundertwende befindet, hat eine autorliche Oberlehrerhaftigkeit hervorgerufen, die auf mich manchmal geradezu abstoßend wirkt. Jeder Dämon wird totgetätscht. Wie ganz anders war doch Gottfried Keller! Ich bin überzeugt, daß auch ein Schuft in ihm lebte."
95 Kai Evers, "Robert Walser and Violence: Strange Excursions into the Microscripts," in *Robert Walser: A Companion*, ed. Samuel Frederick and Valerie Heffernan (Evanston, IL: Northwestern University Press, 2018), 229–249, at 229.

fainted. Believe me. Deplorable women who have husbands who cannot get angry.⁹⁶

The quote above contains in *mise en abyme* another allegorical scene of reading and writing, which is the result of the literary text incorporating another (fictional) literary text, and thus implicitly giving instructions on how to (not) read itself, or at least reflecting on the conditions of its genesis. Walser's prose pieces "Childish Revenge" and "Coffeehouse Performance" already raised questions of whether writing in revenge counts as sublimation and if sublimated aggression still is aggression. *The Robber* reiterates the question in a hilariously polemical manner—superficially, the anecdote above follows Freud's sublimation script in "Creative Writers and Day Dreaming" ("Der Dichter und das Phantasieren"): instead of killing her apathetic husband, the commendable wife sits down and writes a story. Only in this story she makes him commit suicide—and not just any kind of suicide but a suicide that comes close to a medieval mirror-punishment, in that the "death by hanging" that the "discontent wife" inflicts on her husband would probably also have bestowed on her husband a post-mortem erection—the futile index for a desired sexual aggression that appears to have been previously missing. Whoever deems this interpretation too extreme should follow Evers' example and study Walser's prose piece "With Anger about Her Anger She Was Green" ("Vor Wut über ihre Wut war sie grün," 1928), which describes a wife castrating her partner and then eating his penis, with which he used to "play around."⁹⁷ But even to the woman eating his penis, sliced up like a sausage, the man reacts only with apathy, as Evers records: "the man exhibits no signs of pain, shock, or trauma. ... The fear of castration turns out to have been baseless."⁹⁸

Likewise, in *The Robber* the husband reads the story of his own death with perfect indifference and replies with nothing more than a kiss. Again, note Walser's use of oxymoronic composites in this scene ("little bonhomous-kiss" [*Gutmütigkeitsküßchen*]; "murderously-peaceful" [*mordsfriedlich*]), which, like the composites in the letter to his sister

---

96 "Und da lebte wieder eine unzufriedene Gattin, die ein Klagelied auf die Bravheit ihres Mannes anstimmte, indem sie eine Geschichte schrieb, worin sich ihr Gatte aufknüpfte, und die unschöne Geschichte veröffentlichte. Als sie im Druck herauskam, gab sie sie ihrem armen Mann zu lesen, der aber so brav und artig war, daß ihm gar nicht einfiel, ihr zu zürnen. Vielmehr gab er ihr ein schäbiges Gutmütigkeitsküßchen. Was es doch für mordsfriedliche Leute gibt. Sie fiel in Ohnmacht. Glaub's wohl. Bedauernswerte Frauen, die Männer haben, die nicht zornig werden können." Walser, *Der Räuber*, 114.
97 Robert Walser, "Vor Wut über ihre Wut war sie grün," in *Aus dem Bleistiftgebiet*, vol. 5, ed. Bernhard Echte (Frankfurt/M.: Suhrkamp, 2003), 124–125.
98 Kai Evers, "Robert Walser and Violence: Strange Excursions into the Microscripts," 238–239.

136   Ambiguous Aggression

Lisa, graphically present the violence of the familial or conjugal bond. We could easily draw further parallels to Walser's œuvre; for just like the woman in "The Slap in the Face Etc." the wife in *The Robber*, too, does not have the emotional resources at her disposal that would allow for an angry outcry over male indifference; instead, she is forced to turn the aggressive energy inward and to implode—she faints. But this fainting still manages to shake up the metaphorology of fainting: from now on, we will always have to wonder whether a woman's passing out is not actually caused by accrued anger.

Still, we have to ask ourselves, what went wrong; that is, why did the wife's plan to shake up her husband not work out? Maybe the wife's ambiguous aggression was still too latent. Or, maybe she did not take into consideration that *not* getting angry might be the most aggressive and therefore most effective way to provoke aggression (thus, the infuriating quality of "Coffeehouse Performance," albeit, or indeed because of, its merciful tone). The robber fulfills his own (un-)ethical demand and promptly gets shot by his lover Edith, but quickly recovers from the incident. But we have to be careful not simply to conflate "not being angry" and thereby driving someone up the walls with teasing, insofar as teasing implies pretending. In comparison, the man who insults the woman by underestimating her intellect ("Got it?"/"Begriffsch?," "The Slap in the Face, Etc.") as well as the husband in *The Robber* belong to a different species of people who simply "cannot get angry." From Walser we learn that nothing is more aggravating than such a sincere lack of aggression:

> Some people complain about the rudeness of their fellow humans. But basically they don't want us to shed our rudeness. For them it's all about lamenting, complaining, being discontent. But I would rather be a vigorous brute than a complainer. The rude ones often are also the subtlest. The complainer feels that and begrudges the good packaging in which the rude ones wrap the treasure of their delicacies. The subtle ones coat their rudeness with a layer of subtlety.[99]

If "Coffeehouse Performance" showed us how resentment has the capacity to transvaluate "negative" into "positive" (or "socially

---

99 "Manche beschweren sich über ihrer Mitmenschen Grobheit. Aber im Grunde wünschen sie gar nicht von uns Abwerfung der Grobheit. Es kommt ihnen bloß aufs Klagen, Beschweren, Unzufriedensein an. Ich will aber lieber ein tüchtiger Grobian als ein Klageführer sein. Die Gröbsten sind oft auch gerade die Feinsten. Die Beschwerdeführer fühlen das und mißgönnen den Groben die gute Packung, womit sie den Schatz ihrer Zartheiten einhüllen. Die Feinen umhüllen ihre Grobheiten mit einer Schicht von Feinheit." Walser, *Der Räuber*, 97.

accepted") affects, then *The Robber* brings this Nietzschean process of transvaluation to the extreme—to the point of radical ambivalence, that is. Whereas in the previously quoted passage the narrator joined the laments of the "discontent" wife ("Deplorable women who have husbands who cannot get angry"), in this last citation from *The Robber* complaining (*Beklagen, Beschweren*) is revealed to be a secret pleasure for certain people. In "Critique of Pure Complaint" Aaron Schuster contends that complaining is driven by a "desire for unsatisfied desire," which Lacan associates with the hysterical position.[100] But whereas Schuster grasps complaining as a communal practice,[101] Walser's narrator perceives of it, on the contrary, as a hypocritical distancing from the humanity of one's *Mitmenschen* ("Some people complain about the rudeness of their fellow humans [*Mitmenschen*].") Interestingly Schuster, in his otherwise remarkably multi-perspectival meditation on the subject, does not address the case of a person complaining to the immediate subject of their complaint. This is precisely the scenario that Walser plays out here; the gist that we can take from *The Robber* in this regard is that complaining—like melancholia—is not just pure passivity or metaphysical impotence (to which the genre of the litany is closer) but rather a form of disputation or argument. What links complaining to melancholia is the "spirit of gravity" (*Geist der Schwere*) antagonized by Zarathustra ("And when we sweat, then do people say to us: 'Yea, life is hard to bear!' But only man himself is hard to bear!"[102]). Note that the German word for "complaining" (*beschweren*) still bears this weight (*die Schwere*). Just as in the letter to his melancholic sister in *The Robber*, Walser stays alert to this active, aggressive side and marks it through two further oxymoronic composites: "Klageführer" and "Beschwerdeführer." Given that the year from which *The Robber* emanated, 1925, is also the year when the title *Il Duce* (in German, *der Führer*) became notorious for Mussolini and more largely for fascism, it does not require a particularly subtle reading to draw the conclusion that Walser's small theory of complaint deconstructs oppositions of active and passive, and thereby goes beyond good and evil.

With this, we have returned at the end of this chapter to Max Brod's assertion that after Nietzsche there had to be a Walser. Walser's *The*

---

100 See Aaron Schuster, "Critique of Pure Complaint," in *The Trouble with Pleasure: Deleuze and Psychoanalysis* (Cambridge, MA: MIT Press, 2016), 1–26, at 1.
101 Ibid., 2: "The basic ethical stance of the complainer is to avoid shaming or embarrassing the other by revealing his or her lack."
102 "Und schwitzen wir, so sagt man uns: 'Ja, das Leben ist schwer zu tragen!' Aber der Mensch nur ist sich schwer zu tragen!" Friedrich Nietzsche, "Vom Geist der Schwere," in *Also sprach Zarathustra. Ein Buch für Alle und Keinen* (= *Kritische Studienausgabe*, vol. 4, ed. Giorgio Colli and Mazzino Montinari) (München: dtv, 1999), 241–245, at 243.

Robber employs Nietzsche's techniques in order to constantly invert, transvaluate, and eventually deconstruct those oppositions that structure our vocabulary of affects as well as our thinking about them. If the narrator announces that the rude ones shall be the subtle ones[103]—or more exactly, that the rude ones *are* already subtle because they "package" their "delicacies," then—within barely three brief sentences—he has undone several presumptions: 1) the complainer is not less aggressive than the person about whom he complains; 2) "rude vs. subtle" (or "coarse vs. fine" = *fein* vs. *grob*) is not a stable opposition: the rude ones are subtle, the subtle ones, rude—but whoever expects from this a simple inversion will be proven wrong because the narrator continues, without a blink, that the subtle ones still use *subtlety* to hide their rudeness; 3) this means there simply is no way *not* to be aggressive (not even, or especially not, melancholia or complaint); but there is also no way to be *really* aggressive (not even, or especially not, brutality). This is because the (subtle) brutes/(brutally) subtle people are doing their fellow men a service by gifting them their aggression: they recognize the Other in his or her being (see the desire of the discontent wife) and they sacrifice themselves for taking on the role of the aggressor and of subsequently becoming themselves the object of an unacknowledged aggression, in the form of complaint. The aggressor eventually ethically surpasses the complainer so that the narrator polemicizes at another point in the novel: "Making reproaches can become an addiction that one can ridicule and the one who is corrected is spiritually better off than the one who corrects."[104]

What happens to the sentence "The rude ones are often also the subtlest" if we replace the word "ambiguous" with "subtle" and "aggressive" with "brute"? Pretty simple: "The ambiguous ones are often also the most aggressive." If you have followed me up to this point then you might well have noticed this shift, this slow but steady merging, occurring between realism and modernism. In Walser, ambiguous aggression becomes ubiquitous—to the point where "ambiguity" and "aggression" can no longer be told apart. I take this point of convergence, where the concept through which we defined literature has itself dissolved in the course of the experiment, as the appropriate moment to come to an end with my reflections on ambiguous aggression.

---

103 *Grob*—rude, rough, unsubtle; *fein*—subtle, fine, delicate.
104 "Das Vorwürfemachen kann zur Sucht werden, die man belachen kann, und ein Korrigierter ist seelisch stets besser dran als ein Korrigierender, der eigentlich immer nichts als ein Leidender ist …. Sich kritisieren lassen müssen, das hat etwas in sich, was sehr belustigt stimmt." Walser, *Der Räuber*, 132.

Six Conclusion

The sequence of chapters in this book has been characterized by a steady increase of aggressivity—from flirtation via passive aggression to domestic violence; that is, we have moved from an aggressive ambiguity with a certain *frisson* to one bereft of any such playfulness. This increase in aggression mirrors, to a certain extent, our historical situation: at the moment in time in which this book is coming to an end, its topic of *Ambiguous Aggression* has become both timely and untimely—timely because it neatly fits into discussions about "communities of affect," "microaggressions," and #MeToo; untimely, because with the Trump presidency and the rise of right-wing movements like *Alternative für Deutschland* across Europe, we have entered a period in which hate speech and bullying appear to have replaced more subtle aggressions. Even an extreme ambiguous aggression such as domestic violence only gains attention in the media if it can be linked to yet another mass shooting.

Although one might deduce from this that the days of ambiguity are over, the rhetoric of white supremacy actually makes ample use of latent aggression. We have seen that ambiguous aggression affords one with the questionable comfort of engaging in aggression without taking responsibility for it. Therefore—unless someone is speaking from a position of real inferiority or powerlessness—ambiguous aggression testifies to a certain cowardice on the side of the speaker and is capable of invoking fear of losing one's bearings on the side of the recipient. Ambiguous aggression today means gaslighting and dogwhistling: the most bleak example of gaslighting could be Trump's de-realizing claim that Puerto Rico's dead did not die; examples for dogwhistling (coded speech intended to appeal to bigots and hate-groups but to which persecuted minorities are necessarily also attuned) include Bannon's talk of "globalists" whereby he attacks Jews, and Trump's reference to the "inner-city" population whereby he targets communities of color, and finally our shared, disconcerting habituation to hearing on a daily basis in the twenty-first century of "deportations" again.

To those who hear echoes of previous times, the philologist Victor Klemperer's insights into the changes the German language underwent during the Third Reich (the *Lingua Tertii Imperii, LTI*) prove uncannily topical: in the analyses Klemperer, a Jew, secretly wrote down in order to keep sane, he asks as a not-so-fun fact of the day: "What is the punctuation mark most frequently used by the Nazis?" Contrary to what one might believe, it was not the exclamation mark:

> Instead the LTI makes use ad nauseam of what I would call ironic inverted commas. ... Because the LTI particularly loathes neutrality, because it always has to have an adversary and always has to drag this adversary down. ... Chamberlain and Churchill and Roosevelt are always only "statesmen" in ironic inverted commas, Einstein is a "research scientist", Rathenau a "German" and Heine a " 'German' writer."[1]

It would be easy to continue this list with contemporary examples, such as Trump calling Obama a "president" in air-quotes or referring to Judge James Robart of Washington, who put a hold on the travel ban, as a "so-called judge." Like the Nazi quotation marks, those of today have to be read as attempts to intimidate and terrorize people by presenting their existence, and indeed their essence, as merely hypothetical; that is, as something that may just as well be eliminated.

Thus, although the common conception is that there is nothing ambiguous about German aggression and its historical record of full-blown hatred at the scale of mass destruction, the reality is messier. Just think of the idyllic names of concentration camps: Buchenwald, Birkenau, Sonnenburg ... The idyll, the literary scholar and trauma expert Judith Kasper puts forward for consideration, "is, just like the language of the camps, a false language, but as a false language it is always the only language we have ... [,] a little picture, a blinding appearance that does not make stop before Auschwitz."[2] Or take another account of Nazi propaganda, this time from Sebastian Haffner's *Germany: Jekyll and Hyde* (1940); according to Haffner there existed:

> two very contradictory kinds of propaganda. The one, intended to lure more Nazis ..., woos with brutality, ruthlessness, hardness, fanaticism, with outspoken plans for world subjection. In a word, it is cynical and honest. The other is meant "for the people"....

---

[1] Victor Klemperer, *Language of the Third Reich: LTI – Lingua Tertii Imperii, A Philologist's Notebook*, trans. Martin Brady (New York: Continuum, 2010), 67–68.

[2] Judith Kasper, *Der traumatisierte Raum. Insistenz, Inschrift, Montage bei Freud, Levi, Kertéxz, Sebald und Dante* (Berlin: de Gruyter, 2016), 154–155.

> "We" love peace with the patience of lambs. We are prepared to contract pacts of non-aggression with every state.[3]

Ambiguous aggression touches upon denial here; it actually enables denial, i.e., "to commit murder but not to know it ...; to enjoy the fruits of wrong-doing and to be cheated only of a bad conscience."[4]

So what variation of the *Sonderweg*, which path to the Shoah, does *Ambiguous Aggression* map out, if any? Are the literary scenes discussed here—ranging from Droste-Hülshoff to Kafka—proof of a steady swelling of aggression during the nineteenth and early twentieth centuries? Do they exemplify a historical logic according to which the kind of temporary moderation of aggression promulgated by Stifter's *sanftes Gesetz* was doomed to fail? As we have seen from the three examples of Nazi propaganda, spectacular forms of aggression run parallel with more perfidious forms. Given that the same is true of political discourse nowadays, one is left to wonder whether US affect theory of the last decade also offers itself to interpreting realist and modernist literature, because both periods—the late nineteenth/early twentieth century and the millennium—preceded fascist times. This would mean that an intensification of ambiguous aggression or resentment could be taken as a litmus test for a more general rise of aggression, an aggression on the verge of eruption.

After this spirited historicization, it is time to de-historicize the previous claims and to reflect upon language as such and its relation to both ambiguity and aggression:

> We are, all of us, accustomed to speaking badly of language— *These ambiguous words* (such as "make" [*machen*]) *are like striking several flies with one blow* ... (Freud, letter to Fliess, December 22, 1897). The disposition to strike and strike dead, which, however, subtly, is connected with philology, can hardly be explained other than through the fact that language itself is perceived as brutalization. To reduce massive affects to miniscule noises and scratches requires an expenditure of psychic and somatic tension that easily turns against the desired result of reduction, against language, speaking, the speakers. Logoclasm belongs to language as misology to philology. Instead of fearing an everthreatening collapse of sublimation, one should warm to the thought that language represents an indeed elastic but also exceedingly fragile barrier of sublimation that can be broken through at any time through gestures, facial expression, infamies, fisticuffs, and

---

3 Sebastian Haffner, *Germany: Jekyll and Hyde* (New York: Continuum, 2005 [1940]), 74.
4 Ibid., 76.

worse. And is broken through in every sentence, every syllable, every pause. Violence belongs to the structural unconscious of our language because violence channels its way to consciousness.[5]

The meta-reflection stems from Werner Hamacher's *Minima Philologica*, which also de-nationalizes the question of language's violent ambiguity—with the caveat, of course, that Hamacher is a *German* philosopher-theorist; that is, someone whose idea of language was certainly influenced by the *"Totschlägergesinnung"* of German language. But it is just as pertinent that Hamacher's thinking over the years developed in intimate dialogue with literature. And though we have seen that ambiguous aggression is not a prerogative of the literary realm, but rather happens every day and anywhere (including politics), nowhere is its concentration higher than in literature. Literature, in this sense, does not serve to illustrate a claim but is "embodied theory."[6] And maybe German literature, indeed, has something to teach us in this respect, for there exists an awareness in the German language that violence may arise from the attempt both to reduce ambiguity and to intensify it: from the desire for both univocality and polysemy. That is, aggression lies in the urge to literalize[7]—Celan's "grave in the sky" (*"ein Grab in den Lüften"*)—as well as in the ambiguity of ambiguity, which was on display here in readings of Droste-Hülshoff, Stifter, Keller, Storm, Fontane, Walser, Kafka, and others.

---

5   Werner Hamacher, "84," *Minima Philologica*, trans. Catherine Diehl (New York: Fordham University Press, 2015), 91–92; "Wir sind allesamt schlecht auf die Sprache zu sprechen.—*Diese zweideutigen Worte* [wie „machen"] *sind gleichsam mehrere Fliegen auf einen Schlag …* (Freud an Fließ, 22.12.97)—Die Schläger- und Totschlägergesinnung, die sich, wie subtil auch immer, mit der Philologie verbindet, läßt sich kaum anders als dadurch erklären, daß das Sprechen selbst als Brutalisierung empfunden wird. Massive Affekte auf winzige Laute und Kritzeleien zu reduzieren, erfordert einen Aufwand an psychischer und körperlicher Anspannung, der sich leicht gegen das erwünschte Resultat der Reduktion kehrt, gegen die Sprache, das Sprechen, die Sprechenden. Der Logoklasmus gehört zur Sprache wie die Misologie zur Philologie gehört. Statt einen Sublimierungskollaps zu fürchten, sollte man sich mit dem Gedanken anfreunden, daß die Sprache eine zwar elastische, aber äußerst fragile Sublimierungsschranke darstelle, die jederzeit durch Gestik, Mimik, Infamien, Handgreiflichkeiten und Schlimmeres durchbrochen werden kann. Und in jedem Satz, jeder Silbe, jeder Pause durchbrochen wird. Gewalt gehört zum strukturell Unbewußten unsrer Sprache, weil Gewalt ihr den Weg zum Bewußtsein bahnt." Werner Hamacher, "84," in *95 Thesen zur Philologie* (Frankfurt/M.: roughbooks, 2010), 89–90, at 89.
6   Paul Fleming makes a similar point about the status of examples, or rather paradigms, in Freud's *Psychopathology of Everyday Life*: "Beside Oneself: Parapraxis as a Paradigm of Everyday Life (Freud)," in *Exemplarity and Singularity: Thinking through Particulars in Philosophy, Literature, and Law*, ed. Michèle Lowrie and Susanne Lüdemann (New York: Routledge, 2015), 192–202, at 193.
7   Of this the Baroque mourning play still teaches us, as do Kleist and Büchner; see Barbara N. Nagel, *Der Skandal des Literalen. Barocke Literalisierungen bei Gryphius, Kleist, Büchner* (München: Wilhelm Fink, 2012), 155–158.

Bibliography

Adorno, Theodor W. *Minima Moralia: Reflections of Damaged Life*, translated by E. F. N. Jephcott. London/New York: Verso, 2005.
Adorno, Theodor W. *Minima Moralia. Reflexionen aus dem beschädigten Leben*. Frankfurt: Suhrkamp, 2001 [1951].
Agamben, Giorgio. *The Coming Community*, translated by Michael Hardt. Minneapolis/London: University of Minnesota Press, 2003 [1990].
Apter, Emily. "Transatlantic Feminism Post-DSK Affair." *Public Books* (November 13, 2012). http://www.publicbooks.org/transatlantic-feminismpost-dsk-affair/.
Aristotle. "Poetics." In *Aristotle in 23 Volumes*, translated by W. H. Fyfe, vol. 23. London: William Heinemann Ltd. 1932.
Auerbach, Erich. *Mimesis. Dargestellte Wirklichkeit in der abendländischen Literatur.* Bern: Francke, 1994 [1946].
Barker, Emma. "Reading the Greuze Girl—The Daughter's Seduction." *Representations* 117 (2012): 86–119.
Barthes, Roland. "The Reality Effect (1968)." In *The Rustle of Language*, translated by Richard Howard, 141–148. Berkeley/Los Angeles: University of California Press, 1989.
Bateson, Gregory. "Toward a Theory of Schizophrenia." In *Steps to an Ecology of Mind*, 201–227. Chicago, IL/London: University of Chicago Press, 2000 [1972].
Beizer, Janet. *Ventriloquized Bodies. Narratives of Hysteria in Nineteenth-Century France*. Ithaca, NY/London: Cornell University Press, 1994.
Benjamin, Walter. *Gesammelte Schriften*, 7 vols., edited by Rolf Tiedemann and Hermann Schweppenhäuser. Frankfurt/M.: Suhrkamp, 1972–1991.
Benjamin, Walter. *One-Way Street and Other Writings*, edited by Michael W. Jennings, translated by Edmund Jephcott. Cambridge, MA: The Belknap Press of Harvard University Press, 2016.
Benjamin, Walter. *Reflections: Essays, Aphorisms, Autobiographical Writings*, edited by Peter Demetz, translated by Edmund Jephcott. New York: Schocken Books, 1986.
Berbig, Roland. "Vom Nörgeln und Nöhlen. Eine beiläufige Betrachtung zu Fontane und Kempowski." *Fontane Blätter* 95 (2013): 120–134.
Berlant, Lauren. *The Female Complaint: The Unfinished Business of Sentimentality in American Culture*. Durham, NC/London: Duke University Press, 2008.
Blanchot, Maurice. "Literature and the Right to Death." In *The Work of Fire*, translated by Lydia Davis, 300–344. Stanford, CA: Stanford University Press, 1995 [1981].
Blanchot, Maurice. "Wiederholung und Verdoppelung. Notiz über Literatur und Interpretation," translated by Elsbeth Dangel. *Neue Rundschau* 99 (1988): 121–130.

Bibliography

Bloch, Ernst. "Pippa geht vorüber." In *Spuren*, 82–84. Frankfurt/M.: Suhrkamp, 1985 [1910–1929].

Bloch, Ernst. "Pippa Passes." In *Traces*, translated by Anthony A. Nassar, 59–61. Stanford, CA: Stanford University Press, 2006.

Born, Jürgen. *Kafkas Bibliothek. Ein beschreibendes Verzeichnis. Mit einem Index aller in Kafkas Schriften erwähnten Bücher, Zeitschriften und Zeitschriftenbeiträge.* Frankfurt/M.: Fischer, 1990.

Börner, Mareike. *Mädchenknospe—Spiegelkindlein. Die Kindfrau im Werk Theodor Storms.* Würzburg: Königshausen & Neumann, 2009.

Böschenstein, Renate. "Das Rätsel der Corinna. Beobachtungen zur Physiognomie einer 'realistischen' Figur aus komparatistischer Perspektive." In *Verborgene Facetten. Studien zu Fontane*, edited by Hanna Delf von Wolzogen and Hubertus Fischer, 224–246. Würzburg: Königshausen & Neumann, 2005.

Brinkema, Eugenie. *The Forms of the Affects.* Durham, NC/London: Duke University Press, 2014.

Brod, Max. *Über Franz Kafka.* Frankfurt a.M.: Fischer, 1974.

Browning, Robert. *Pippa Passes.* New York: Dutton, 1906 [1841].

Bürger, Peter. *Theorie der Avantgarde.* Frankfurt am Main: Suhrkamp, 1974.

Burke, Edmund. *A Philosophical Enquiry into the Origins of our Ideas of the Sublime and Beautiful*, edited by Adam Phillips. Oxford: Oxford University Press, 1990.

Campe, Rüdiger. *Affekt und Ausdruck. Zur Umwandlung der literarischen Rede im 17. und 18. Jahrhundert.* Tübingen: Niemeyer, 1990.

Caruth, Cathy. "The Falling Body and the Impact of Reference (de Man, Kant, Kleist)." In *Unclaimed Experience: Trauma, Narrative, and History*, 73–90. Baltimore, MD/London: Johns Hopkins University Press, 1996.

Coetzee, J. M. "The Genius of Robert Walser." *The New Yorker*, November 2, 2000.

De Laclos, "Pierre-Ambroise-François Choderlos. Les Liaisons dangereuses." In *Œuvres complètes*, edited by Laurent Versini, 3–386. Paris: Gallimard, 1979 [1782].

De Man, Paul. "Semiology and Rhetoric." In *Diacritics* (fall 1973): 27–33.

Deleuze, Gilles. "Humor, Irony & the Law." In *Masochism: Coldness and Cruelty & Venus in Furs*, translated by Jean McNeil, 81–90. New York: Zone Books, 1991 [1967].

Deleuze, Gilles. *Nietzsche and Philosophy*, translated by Hugh Tomlinson. London/New York: Continuum, 2005 [1962].

Derrida, Jacques. "Purveyor of Truth," *Yale French Studies* 52 (1975): 31–113.

Detering, Heinrich. *Kindheitsspuren. Theodor Storm und das Ende der Romantik.* Heide: Boyens, 2011.

Downing, Eric. *Double Exposures: Repetition and Realism in Nineteenth-Century German Fiction.* Stanford, CA: Stanford University Press, 2000.

Droste-Hülshoff, Annette von. *Die Judenbuche, Historisch-kritische Ausgabe*, vol. VI, edited by Winfried Woesler. Tübingen: Max Niemeyer, 1978.

Droste-Hülshoff, Annette von. *The Jew's Beech*, translated by Lionel and Doris Thomas. In *German Novellas of Realism*, vol. 1, edited by Jeffrey L. Sammons, 88–132. New York: Continuum, 1989.

Elias, Norbert. *The Civilizing Process: Sociogenetic and Psychogenetic Investigations*, translated by Edmund Jephcott. Oxford/Malden, MA: Blackwell, 1990 [1939].

Elias, Norbert. *Über den Prozess der Zivilisation*, 2 vol. Frankfurt/M.: Suhrkamp, 2010 [1939].

Empson, William. *Seven Types of Ambiguity*. New York: New Directions, 1966 [1930].
Empson, William. *The Structure of Complex Words*. Cambridge, MA: Harvard University Press, 1989 [1951].
Ferenczi, Sándor. "Confusion of Tongues Between the Adults and the Child: The Language of Tenderness and the Language of Passion," translated by Michael Balint. *International Journal of Psychoanalysis* 30 (1949): 225–230.
Fleming, Paul. "Beside Oneself: Parapraxis as a Paradigm of Everyday Life (Freud)." In *Exemplarity and Singularity: Thinking through Particulars in Philosophy, Literature, and Law*, edited by Michèle Lowrie and Susanne Lüdemann, 192–202. New York: Routledge, 2015.
Fontane, Emilie and Theodor. *Der Ehebriefwechsel*, 3 vols. In *Grosse Brandenburger Ausgabe*, edited by Gotthard and Therese Erler. Berlin: Aufbau-Verlag, 1998.
Fontane, Theodor. *Briefe*, vol. 3: *Briefe an Mathilde von Rohr*, edited by Kurt Schreinert und Charlotte Jolles. Berlin: Aufbau, 1963.
Fontane, Theodor. *Frau Jenny Treibel, Short Novels and Other Writings*, edited by Peter Demetz, translated by Ulf Zimmermann. New York: Continuum, 1982.
Fontane, Theodor. *Grosse Brandenburger Ausgabe*, edited by Gotthard Erler. Berlin: Aufbau-Verlag, 1997.
Fore, Devin. *Realism after Modernism: The Rehumanization of Art and Literature*. Cambridge, MA/London: MIT Press, 2015.
Freud, Sigmund. *Civilization and Its Discontents*, translated by James Strachey. New York/London: Norton, 1961 [1930].
Freud, Sigmund. *Studienausgabe*, edited by Alexander Mitscherlich, Angela Richards, and James Strachey, 10 vols. Frankfurt/M.: Fischer, 2000.
Freud, Sigmund. *Zur Einführung des Narzißmus, Gesammelte Werke*, edited by Anna Freud a.o., vol. 10. London: Imago Publishing, 1946.
Freud, Sigmund. *Zur Psychopathologie des Alltagslebens (Über Vergessen, Versprechen, Vergreifen, Aberglaube und Irrtum)*. Berlin: S. Karger, 1912.
Frevert, Ute. *Emotions in History—Lost and Found*. Budapest/New York: Central European University Press, 2011.
Galen of Pergamum. *On the Passions and Errors of the Soul*, translated by Paul W. Harkins. Columbus, OH: Ohio State University Press, 1963.
Genette, Gérard. *Narrative Discourse: An Essay in Method*, translated by Jane E. Lewin. Ithaca, NY: Cornell University Press, 1980 [1972].
Geulen, Eva. "Legislating Education: Kant, Hegel and Benjamin on 'Pedagogical Violence,'" *Cardozo Law Review* 26 (2004/05): 943–956.
Gisi, Lucas Marco (editor). *Robert Walser Handbuch. Leben – Werk – Wirkung*. Stuttgart: Metzler, 2015.
Goethe, Johann Wolfgang von. *Unterhaltungen deutscher Ausgewanderten*. In *Werke. Vollständige Ausgabe*, vol. 6. Stuttgart: Cotta, 1958.
Goethe, Johann Wolfgang von. *The Recreations of the German Emigrants*, translated by Thomas Carlyle. London: John C. Nimmo, 1903.
Goldschmidt, Georges-Arthur. *Quand Freud voit la mer : Freud et la langue allemande I*. Paris: Buchet Chastel, 2006.
Goodstein, Elizabeth S. *Georg Simmel and the Disciplinary Imaginary*. Stanford, CA: Stanford University Press, 2017.
Gordon, Linda. "The Politics of Sexual Harassment (With a New Introduction)." In *Where Freedom Starts: Sex, Power, Violence, #MeToo*, 102–126. New York: Verso, 2018.

Grawe, Christian. "Lieutenant Vogelsang a.D. und Mr. Nelson aus Liverpool. Treibels politische und Corinnas private Verirrungen in 'Frau Jenny Treibel'," *Fontane-Blätter* 38 (1984): 588–606.

Gross, Daniel M. *Uncomfortable Situations: Emotion Between Science and the Humanities*. Chicago, IL: Chicago University Press, 2017.

Haffner, Sebastian. *Germany: Jekyll and Hyde*. New York: Continuum, 2005 [1940].

Hahn, Barbara. "'Weiber verstehen alles à la lettre'. Briefkultur im beginnenden 19. Jahrhundert." In *Deutsche Literatur von Frauen*, vol. 2, edited by Gisela Brinker-Gabler, 13–26. München: C.H. Beck, 1988.

Hamacher, Werner. *95 Thesen zur Philologie*. Frankfurt/M.: Roughbooks, 2010.

Hamacher, Werner. *Minima Philologica*, translated by Catherine Diehl. New York: Fordham University Press, 2015.

Hauptmann, Gerhart. *Bahnwärter Thiel*. In *Sämtliche Werke. Centenar-Ausgabe*, vol. 6, edited by Hans-Egon Hass, 35–68. Berlin: Propyläen, 1963.

Hauptmann, Gerhart. *Flagman Thiel*, translated by Adele S. Seltzer. In *German Novellas of Realism*, vol. 2, edited by Jeffrey L. Sammons, 304–330. New York: Continuum, 1989.

Haverkamp, Anselm. "Begreifen, bildlich." In *Diesseits der Oder. Frankfurter Vorlesungen*, 161–178. Berlin: Kadmos, 2008.

Haverkamp, Anselm. *Latenzzeit. Wissen im Nachkrieg*. Berlin: Kadmos, 2004.

Hegel, G. W. F. "Vorrede zur zweiten Auflage der Logik." In *Werke in 20 Bänden. Theorie Werkausgabe*, vol. 5, edited by Eva Moldenhauer and Karl Markus Michel, 20–21. Frankfurt/M.: Suhrkamp, 1970–1971.

Hegel, G. W. F. *Elements of the Philosophy of Right*, edited by Allen W. Wood, translated by H. B. Nisbet. Cambridge: Cambridge University Press, 1991 [1820].

Hegel, G. W. F. *Phenomenology of Spirit*, translated by A. V. Miller. Oxford: Oxford University Press, 1977 [1807].

Heidegger, Martin. *Einführung in die Metaphysik*. Tübingen: Max Niemeyer, 1966 [1956].

Heine, Heinrich. *Deutschland. Ein Wintermärchen*. Stuttgart: Reclam, 1974 [1844].

Helfer, Martha B. "'Wer wagt es, eitlen Blutes Drang zu messen?': Reading Blood in Annette von Droste-Hülshoff's *Die Judenbuche*," *The German Quarterly* 71, no. 3 (summer 1998): 228–253.

Hertling, Gunter H. "Adalbert Stifter's 'Forewords' to *Bunte Steine* in English: His Poetics, Aesthetics, and Weltanschauung," *Modern Austrian Literature* 32, no. 1 (1999), 1–21.

Hobus, Jens. "'Was soll ich mit Gefühlen anfangen, als sie wie Fische im Sand der Sprache zappeln und sterben zu lassen?' Emotionen als ästhetisches Phänomen im Werk Robert Walsers." In *Sentimentalität und Grausamkeit. Ambivalente Gefühle in der skandinavischen und deutschen Literatur der Moderne*, edited by Sophie Wennerscheid, 229–241. Berlin: LIT, 2011.

Hohendahl, Peter Uwe and Ulrike Vedder. *Herausforderungen des Realismus. Theodor Fontanes Gesellschaftsromane*. Freiburg i.Br.: Rombach, 2018.

Holub, Robert C. "Realism, Repetition, Repression: The Nature of Desire in *Romeo und Julia auf dem Dorfe*," *MLN* 100, no. 3 (April, 1985): 461–497.

Holz, Arno and Johannes Schlaf. *Papa Hamlet*. Stuttgart: Reclam, 1963 [1892].

Honnefelder, Gottfried. *Der Brief im Roman. Untersuchungen zur erzähltechnischen Verwendung des Briefes im deutschen Roman*. Bonn: Bouvier, 1975.

Huyssen, Andreas. *After the Great Divide: Modernism, Mass Culture, Postmodernism*. Bloomington: Indiana University Press, 1986.

Huyssen, Andreas. *Bürgerlicher Realismus*. Stuttgart: Reclam, 1974.

Bibliography   147

Iser, Wolfgang. "Das Komische: Ein Kipp-Phänomen." In *Das Komische*, edited by Wolfgang Preisendanz and Rainer Warning, 398–402. Munich: Wilhelm Fink, 1976.
Jakobson, Roman. *Language in Literature*, edited by Krystyna Pomorska and Stephen Rudy. Cambridge, MA: Harvard University Press, 1997.
Jameson, Fredric. *The Antinomies of Realism*. London/New York: Verso, 2015 [2013].
Jesenská, Milena. *Die Briefe von Milena*, edited by Alena Wagnerová. Frankfurt/M.: Fischer, 2005.
Johnson, Barbara. "The Frame of Reference: Poe, Lacan, Derrida," *Yale French Studies* 55, no. 56 (1977): 457–505.
Kafka, Franz. *Briefe 1902–1924*. Frankfurt/M.: Fischer, 1958.
Kafka, Franz. *Briefe an Felice und andere Korrespondenz aus der Verlobungszeit*, edited by Erich Heller and Jürgen Born. Frankfurt/M.: Fischer, 1967.
Kafka, Franz. *Briefe an Milena*, edited by Jürgen Born and Michael Müller. Frankfurt/M.: Fischer, 2011.
Kammer, Stephan. "Poetologie der Lektüre—Lektüre der Poetologie: Robert Walsers *Kindliche Rache.*" *Text & Kontext. Zeitschrift für germanistische Literaturforschung in Skandinavien* 54 (2007): 107–125.
Kant, Immanuel. *Critique of the Power of Judgement*, translated by Paul Guyer and Eric Matthews. Cambridge: Cambridge University Press, 2000 [1790/1793].
Kantorowicz, Ernst H. "The Sovereignty of the Artist: A Note on Legal Maxims and Renaissance Theories of Art." In *Selected Studies*, 352–365. New York: J. J. Augustin, 1965.
Kasper, Judith. *Der traumatisierte Raum. Insistenz, Inschrift, Montage bei Freud, Levi, Kertéxz, Sebald und Dante*. Berlin: de Gruyter, 2016.
Kaye, Richard A. *The Flirt's Tragedy: Desire without End in Victorian and Edwardian Fiction*. Charlottesville VA: University of Virginia Press, 2002.
Keller, Gottfried. *Die Leute von Seldwyla*, vol. 1. In *Sämtliche Werke. Historisch-Kritische Ausgabe*, vol. 4, edited by Walter Morgenthaler. Zürich: Stroemfeld, 2000.
Keller, Gottfried. *Seldwyla Folks: Three Singular Tales*, translated by Wolf von Schierbard. New York: Brentano's Publishers, 1919.
Kerr, Katharina (editor). *Über Robert Walser*, vol. 1. Frankfurt/M.: Suhrkamp, 1978.
Klein, Melanie. "A Contribution to the Psychogenesis of Manic-Depressive States," *International Journal of Psychoanalysis* 16 (1935): 145–174.
Klemperer, Victor. *Language of the Third Reich: LTI – Lingua Tertii Imperii, A Philologist's Notebook*, translated by Martin Brady. New York: Continuum, 2010.
Klemperer, Victor. *LTI. Notizbuch eines Philologen*. Stuttgart: Reclam, 2007 [1947].
Kluge, Alexander. *Fontane, Kleist, Döblin, Büchner. Zur Grammatik der Zeit*. Berlin: Wagenbach, 2004.
Kontje, Todd. *A Companion to German Realism: 1848–1900*. Woodbridge: Boydell and Brewer, 2002.
Kornbluh, Anna. *The Order of Forms: Realism, Formalism, and Social Space*. Chicago, IL: University of Chicago Press, 2019.
Kotzebue, August von. *Die Leiden der Ortenbergischen Familie*, vol. 2. Frankfurt/Leipzig: Kummer, 1804 [1785].
Kreienbrock, Jörg. *Kleiner. Feiner. Leichter*, Zurich: Diaphanes, 2010.
Lane, Christopher. "The Surprising History of Passive-Aggressive Personality Disorder," *Theory & Psychology* 19, no. 1 (2009): 55–70.
Lausberg, Heinrich. *Handbook of Literary Rhetoric*, edited by David E. Orton and R. Dean Anderson. Leiden/Boston/Köln: Brill, 1998 [1960].

Lerner, Ben. "Robert Walser's Disappearing Acts." *The New Yorker*, September 3, 2013.
Levine, Caroline. *Forms: Whole, Rhythm, Hierarchy, Network*. Princeton, NJ: Princeton University Press, 2015.
Liebrand, Claudia. *Ich und die Anderen. Fontanes Figuren und ihre Selbstbilder*. Freiburg i.Br.: Rombach, 1990.
Longinus. "On Sublimity." In *Classical Literary Criticism*, edited by D. A. Russell and Michael Winterbottom, 143–187. Oxford/New York: Oxford University Press, 1989 [1972].
Luhmann, Niklas. "Jenseits von Barbarei." *Modernität und Barbarei. Soziologische Zeitdiagnose am Ende des 20. Jahrhunderts*, edited by Max Miller and Hans-Georg Soeffner, 219–230. Frankfurt/M.: Suhrkamp, 1996.
Luhmann, Niklas. "Sozialsystem Familie." In *Soziologische Aufklärung*, vol. 5, 196–217. Wiesbaden: Verlag für Sozialwissenschaften, 2005.
Luhmann, Niklas. *Love as Passion: The Codification of Intimacy*, translated by Jeremy Gaines and Doris L. Jones. Stanford, CA: Stanford University Press, 1998 [1982].
Lukács, Georg. "Erzählen oder beschreiben? Zur Diskussion über Realismus und Naturalismus (1936)." In *Begriffsbestimmung des literarischen Realismus*, edited by Richard Brinkmann, 33–85. Darmstadt: Wissenschaftliche Buchgesellschaft, 1969.
Lyotard, Jean-François. *The Differend: Phrases in Dispute*, translated by Georges Van Den Abbeele. Minneapolis: University of Minnesota Press, 1988 [1983].
Malinow, K. L. "Passive-Aggressive Personality." In *Personality Disorders: Diagnosis and Management*, edited by J. R. Lion, 121–132. Baltimore, MD: Williams & Wilkins, 1981.
Massumi, Brian. "The Autonomy of Affect," *Cultural Critique* 31 (autumn 1995): 83–109.
Matt, Peter von. "Wer hat Robert Walsers Briefe geschrieben?" In *'Immer dicht vor dem Sturze …' Zum Werk Robert Walsers*, edited by Paolo Chiarini and Hans Dieter Zimmermann, 98–105. Frankfurt/M.: Athenäum, 1987.
Matt, Peter von. "Wie weise ist Walsers Weisheit?" In *Robert Walsers 'Ferne Nähe'. Neue Beiträge zur Forschung*, edited by Wolfram Groddeck, 35–47. München: Wilhelm Fink, 2007.
Mecklenburg, Norbert. *Theodor Fontane. Realismus, Redevielfalt, Ressentiment*. Stuttgart: Metzler, 2018.
Miller, Alice. *The Drama of the Gifted Child. The Search for the True Self*, translated by Ruth Ward. New York: Basic Books, 1997 [1979].
Morgan Wortham, Simon. "*Flirtations: Rhetoric and Aesthetics This Side of Seduction* (review)," *Oxford Literary Review* 39, no. 1 (June, 2017): 141–145.
Mueller, James R., Katharine Doob Sakenfeld, and M. Jack Suggs (editors). *The Oxford Study Bible. Revised English Bible with the Apocrypha*. New York: Oxford University Press, 1992.
Müller-Seidel, Walter. "Fontane—Der Stechlin." In *Der deutsche Roman vom Barock bis zur Gegenwart: Struktur und Geschichte*, edited by Benno von Wiese, 146–189. Düsseldorf: Bagel, 1965.
Nagel, Barbara Natalie. *Der Skandal des Literalen. Barocke Literalisierungen bei Gryphius, Kleist, Büchner*. München: Wilhelm Fink, 2012.
Nagel, Barbara Natalie, Daniel Hoffman-Schwartz, and Lauren Shizuko Stone. *Flirtations: Rhetoric and Aesthetics This Side of Seduction*. New York: Fordham University Press, 2015.
Nagel, Barbara Natalie. "Flirt als semiotische Krise bei Henry James, Thomas Mann, Jean Genet," *Figurationen* 2 (2018): 25–42.

Nägele, Rainer. "Keller's Cellar Vaults: Intrusions of the Real in Gottfried Keller's Realism." In *Rethinking Emotion: Interiority and Exteriority in Premodern, Modern and Contemporary Thought*, edited by Rüdiger Campe and Julia Weber, 187–201. Berlin: de Gruyter, 2014.
Neswald, Elizabeth. "Körpermaschinen". In *Thermodynamik als kultureller Kampfplatz. Zur Faszinationsgeschichte der Entropie 1850–1915*, 310–318. Freiburg i.Br.: Rombach, 2006.
Neumann, Gerhard. "Theodor Storms 'Psyche'. Ein Wahrnehmungsmodell des Realismus." In *Wirklichkeit und Wahrnehmung. Neue Perspektiven auf Theodor Storm*, edited by Elisabeth Strowick and Ulrike Vedder. Bern: Peter Lang, 2013.
Ngai, Sianne. *Ugly Feelings*. Cambridge, MA/London: Harvard University Press, 2005.
Niehaus, Michael. "Das Prosastück als Idee und das Prosastückverfassen als Seinsweise: Robert Walser." In *Kleine Prosa*, edited by Thomas Althaus et al., 173–186. Tübingen: Max Niemeyer, 2007.
Nietzsche, Friedrich. *Kritische Studienausgabe*, 15 vols, edited by Giorgio Colli und Mazzino Montinari. München: dtv, 1999.
Nietzsche, Friedrich. *On the Genealogy of Morals*, translated by Carol Diethe. Cambridge: Cambridge University Press, 2007.
Nietzsche, Friedrich. *The Will to Power*, edited and translated by Walter Kaufmann and F. J. Hollingdale. New York: Random House, 1967.
Nollendorfs, Cora Lee. "'… kein Zeugniß ablegen': Woman's Voice in Droste-Hülshoffs *Judenbuche*," *The German Quarterly* 67, no. 3: 325–337.
Osterkamp, Ernst. "Dämonisierender Realismus. Bemerkungen zu Theodor Storms Erzählkunst." In *Wirklichkeit und Wahrnehmung. Neue Perspektiven auf Theodor Storm*, edited by Elisabeth Strowick and Ulrike Vedder. Bern: Peter Lang, 2013.
Panofsky, Erwin. *The Life and Art of Albrecht Dürer*. Princeton, NJ: Princeton University Press, 1955 [1943].
Parker, Rozsika. *The Subversive Stitch. Embroidery and the Making of the Feminine*. London: I.B. Tauris, 1984.
Parkinson, Anna M. *An Emotional State: The Politics of Emotion in Postwar West German Culture*. Ann Arbor, MI: University of Michigan Press, 2015.
Pfeiffer, Joachim. *Die zerbrochenen Bilder. Gestörte Ordnungen im Werk Heinrich von Kleists*. Würzburg: Königshausen & Neumann, 1989.
Phillips, Adam. "Worrying and Its Discontents." In *On Kissing, Tickling, and Being Bored: Psychoanalytic Essays on the Unexamined Life*, 47–58. Cambridge, MA: Harvard University Press, 1993.
Phillips, Adam. *On Flirtation*. Cambridge, MA: Harvard University Press, 1996.
Pickar, Gertrud Bauer. "The Battering and Meta-Battering of Droste's Margreth: Covert Misogyny in *Die Judenbuche*'s Critical Reception," *Women in German Yearbook* 9 (1994): 71–90.
Plamper, Jan. *The History of Emotions: An Introduction*. Oxford: Oxford University Press, 2015.
Plug, Jan. *They Have All Been Healed: Reading Robert Walser*. Evanston, IL: Northwestern University Press, 2016.
Pott, Hans-Georg. *Die Wiederkehr der Stimme. Telekommunikation im Zeitalter der Post-Moderne*. Wien: Sonderzahl, 1995.
Povinelli, Elizabeth A. *Economies of Abandonment: Social Belonging and Endurance in Late Liberalism*. Durham, NC/London: Duke University Press, 2011.
Preisendanz, Wolfgang. "Voraussetzungen des poetischen Realismus in der Erzählkunst des 19. Jahrhunderts." In *Formkräfte der deutschen Dichtung*, edited by Hans Steffen, 187–210. Göttingen: Vandenhoeck & Ruprecht, 1963.

Quintilian. *Institutes of Oratory; or, Education of an Orator*, translated by John Selby Watson. London: George Bell and Sons, 1907.

Quiring, Björn. *Shakespeare's Curse: The Aphorias of Ritual Exclusion in Early Modern Royal Drama*, translated by Michael Wrinkler and Björn Quiring. New York: Routledge, 2014.

Rabinbach, Anson. *The Human Motor: Energy, Fatigue, and the Origins of Modernity*. Berkeley/Los Angeles: University of California Press, 1992 [1990].

Radkau, Joachim. *Das Zeitalter der Nervosität: Deutschland zwischen Bismarck und Hitler*. München: Hanser, 1998.

Rancière, Jacques. *The Politics of Aesthetics: The Distribution of the Sensible*, translated by Gabriel Rockhill. New York: Continuum, 2007 [2000].

Richter, Jean Paul. *Vorschule der Aesthetik: Nebst einigen Vorlesungen in Leipzig über die Parteien der Zeit*, vol. 1. Stuttgart/Tübingen: Cotta, 1813.

Riley, Denise. *Impersonal Passion: Language as Affect*. Durham, MD/London: Duke University Press, 2005.

Rose, Jacqueline."I Am a Knife," *The London Review of Books* 40, no. 4 (February 22, 2018): 3–11.

Rosenberg, Jordy. "The Daddy Dialectic." *The Los Angeles Review of Books*, March 11, 2018, https://lareviewofbooks.org/article/the-daddy-dialectic/ (last retrieved March 19, 2018).

Schlaffer, Hannelore. "Die gesprächige Ehe," *Fontane-Blätter* 67 (1999): 75–91.

Schlegel, Friedrich. *Kritische Friedrich-Schlegel-Ausgabe. Erste Abteilung: Kritische Neuausgabe*, vol. 2, edited by Ernst Behler, Jean-Jacques Anstett, and Hans Eichner. München: Schöningh, 1967.

Schlegel, Friedrich. *Theorie der Weiblichkeit*, edited by Winfried Menninghaus. Frankfurt/M.: Insel, 1983.

Schor, Naomi. *Reading in Detail: Aesthetics and the Feminine*. New York/London: Methuen, 1987.

Schuster, Aaron. "Critique of Pure Complaint." In *The Trouble with Pleasure: Deleuze and Psychoanalysis*, 1–26. Cambridge, MA: MIT Press, 2016.

Sebald, W. G. "Le Promeneur Solitaire: A Remembrance of Robert Walser." In *A Place in the Country: On Gottfried Keller, Johan Peter Hebel, Robert Walser and Others*, translated by Jo Catling, 117–153. New York: Penguin, 2015.

Seelig, Carl. *Wanderungen mit Robert Walser*. Frankfurt/M.: Suhrkamp, 2017.

Seneca. "On Anger (De Ira)." In *Moral Essays*, vol. I. translated by John W. Basore. Cambridge, MA: Oxford University Press, 1928.

Sharma, Meara. "Claudia Rankine on Blackness as the Second Person." *Guernica*, November 17, 2014, https://www.guernicamag.com/interviews/blackness-as-the-second-person/.

Siegert, Bernhard. *Relays: Literature as an Epoch of the Postal System 1751–1913*, translated by Kevin Repp. Stanford, CA: Stanford University Press, 1999 [1993].

Silverman, Kaja. *Male Subjectivity at the Margins*. New York/London: Routledge, 1992.

Simmel, Georg. "Die Koketterie." In *Philosophische Kultur. Über das Abenteuer, die Geschlechter und die Krise der Moderen. Gesammelte Essais*, 81–98. Berlin: Klaus Wagenbach, 1983 [1929].

Simmel, Georg. "Flirtation." In *On Women, Sexuality, and Love*, edited and translated by Guy Oakes, 133–152. New Haven, CN/London: Yale University Press, 1984.

Simmel, Georg. "Zur Psychologie der Frauen (1890)." In *Schriften zur Philosophie und Soziologie der Geschlechter*, edited by Heinz-Jürgen Dahme and Klaus Christian Köhnke, 27–59. Frankfurt/M.: Suhrkamp, 1985.

Bibliography 151

Smith, Zadie. "F. Kafka, Everyman," *New York Review of Books* 55, no. 12 (July 17, 2008).
Sontag, Susan. "Walser's Voice." In *Selected Stories*, translated by Christopher Middleton, vii–ix. Manchester: Carcanet New Press, 1982.
Sprengel, Peter. *Gerhart Hauptmann. Bürgerlichkeit und großer Traum. Eine Biographie*. München: C.H. Beck, 2012.
Stewart, Kathleen. *Ordinary Affects*. Durham/London: Duke University Press, 2007.
Stiemer, Hendrik. *Über scheinbar naïve und dilettantische Dichtung. Text- und Kontextstudien zu Robert Walser*. Würzburg: Königshausen & Neumann, 2013.
Stifter, Adalbert. *Granite*, translated by Jeffrey L. Sammons. In *German Novellas of Realism*, vol. 1, edited by Jeffrey L. Sammons. New York: Continuum, 1989.
Stifter, Adalbert. "Preface to *Many-colored Stones*," translated by Jeffrey L. Sammons. In *German Novellas of Realism*, vol. 1, edited by Jeffrey L. Sammons, 1–6. New York: Continuum, 1989.
Stifter, Adalbert. *Werke und Briefe. Historisch-kritische Gesamtausgabe*, edited by Alfred Doppler and Wolfgang Frühwald. Stuttgart: Kohlhammer, 1982.
Storm, Theodor. *Paul the Puppeteer with The Village on the Moor and Renate*, translated by Denis Jackson. London: Angel Books, 2004.
Storm, Theodor. *Sämtliche Werke: Novellen 1867-1880*, vols. 2 and 3, edited by Karl Ernst Laage. Frankfurt/M.: Deutscher Klassiker Verlag, 1987.
Storm, Theodor. *The White Horse Rider*, translated by Stella Humphries. In *German Novellas of Realism*, vol. 2, edited by Jeffrey L. Sammons. New York: Continuum, 1989.
Suter, Martin. *Die Lebensquelle. Lebensphilosophie und persönlicher Mythos im Spätwerk Robert Walsers*. Bern: Peter Lang, 1984.
Terada, Rei. *Feeling in Theory: Emotion after the "Death of the Subject"*. Cambridge, MA: Harvard University Press, 2003.
Threadcraft, Shatema. "North American Necropolitics and Gender: On #BlackLivesMatter and Black Femicide," *South Atlantic Quarterly* 116, no. 3 (July 2017): 553–579.
Utz, Peter. "Robert Walser." In *Deutsche Dichter des 20. Jahrhunderts*, edited by Peter Utz and Hartmut Steinecke, 197–211. Berlin: Erich Schmidt, 1994.
Utz, Peter. "Zu kurz gekommene Kleinigkeiten. Robert Walser und der Beitrag des Feuilletons zur literarischen Moderne." In *Die kleinen Formen in der Moderne*, edited by Elmar Locher, 133–166. Bolzano: Sturzflüge, 2001.
Vedder, Ulrike. *Geschickte Liebe. Zur Mediengeschichte des Liebesdiskurses im Briefroman "Les Liaisons dangereuses" und in der Gegenwartsliteratur*. Köln: Böhlau, 2002.
Vinken, Barbara. "L'abandon de Félicité – *Un cœur simple* de Flaubert." In *Le Flaubert Réel*, edited by Barbara Vinken and Peter Fröhlicher, 141–164. Tübingen: Max Niemeyer, 2009.
Vinken, Barbara. *Unentrinnbare Neugierde. Die Weltverfallenheit des Romans*. Freiburg i.Br.: Rombach, 1991.
Virgil. *Aeneid 1-6. English and Latin*, translated by H. R. Fairclough. Cambridge, MA: Harvard University Press, 1999.
Vischer, Friedrich Theodor. "Theorie des Romans." In *Theorie des bürgerlichen Realismus*, edited by Gerhard Plumpe, 240–247. Ditzingen: Reclam, 2009.
Walser, Robert. *Sämtliche Werke in Einzelausgaben*, 20 vols. Zurich/Frankfurt/M.: Suhrkamp, 1985–1986.
Walser, Robert. *Aus dem Bleistiftgebiet*, edited by Bernhard Echte. Frankfurt/M.: Suhrkamp, 2003.

Walser, Robert. *Briefe*, edited by Jörg Schäfer and Robert Mächler. In *Das Gesamtwerk*, vol. XII/2, edited by Jochen Greven. Geneva: Kossodo, 1975.

Walser, Robert. *The Robber*, translated by Susan Bernofsky. Lincoln, NE: University of Nebraska Press, 2000.

Walser, Robert. *The Assistant*, translated by Susan Bernofsky. New York: New Directions, 2007.

Wedemeyer, Arnd. "Herrschaftszeiten! Theopolitical Profanities in the Face of Secularization," *New German Critique* 105, no. 35/3 (autumn 2008): 121–141.

Wegmann, Nikolaus. *Diskurse der Empfindsamkeit. Zur Geschichte eines Gefühls in der Literatur des 18. Jahrhunderts*. Stuttgart: Metzler, 1988.

Widhammer, Helmuth. *Die Literaturtheorie des deutschen Realismus (1848–1860)*. Stuttgart: Metzler, 1977.

Wolff, Larry. *Postcard from the End of the World: Child Abuse in Freud's Vienna*. New York: New York University Press, 1995 [1988].

Woolf, Virginia. *Jacob's Room*. Brooklyn, NY: Melville House, 2011 [1922].

Zimmermann, Hans Dieter. "Walser und die pietistische Ethik." In *'Immer dicht vor dem Sturze ... ' Zum Werk Robert Walsers*, edited by Paolo Chiarini and Hans Dieter Zimmermann, 237–251. Frankfurt/M.: Athenäum, 1987.

Žižek, Slavoj. *The Parallax View*. Cambridge, MA: MIT Press, 2006.

Index

Acker, Kathy 69
Adorno, Theodor 14, 45, 96
aesthetics
   of ambiguity 11, 51
   of flirtation 15, 21, 27–8
   of life 106
   of passive aggression 43
   of realism 4, 8 n.27
   of violence 73, 76–8, 88, 94, 98
affect
   affect theory 2, 5–7, 13–15, 41, 103–4, 139, 141
   aggressive 46, 76, 119–21, 124
   and ambiguity 11–16, 37, 44, 126, 132–3 *see also* 'ambivalence'
   critical capacity of 70, 104, 138–9
   hollowness of 56, 83
   layers of 110–11, 134, 137
   in realism 2, 5–9, 76, 120
   regulation of 104, 106–7, 114 *see also* 'moderation'
Agamben, Giorgio 105, 123 n.61
ambiguity
   of affect 10, 133 *see* 'ambivalence'
   of aggression 7, 121, 141–2
   everyday 43, 63 *see also* 'parapraxis'
   expenditure and scarcity of 58, 60, 133, 138
   as frightening 20, 58
   of literature xii, 6–7, 11–12, 16–17, 51–2, 69–70, 126
   polysemy 37, 52, 98, 142
   reduction of 51, 70, 100, 105, 116, 142 *see also* 'rhetoric, literalization'
   of violence 78, 82, 88, 92, 96–8, 101, 139
ambivalence 2, 5, 6, 12, 16, 104 n.7, 107, 126, 132–3, 137
anger 10, 14 n.49, 85, 104, 111, 113, 115, 117–19, 121–3, 135–6
anti-Semitism 44, 139–40
Aristotle 75
Auerbach, Erich 4

Bachmann, Ingeborg 76
Barthes, Roland 4 n.12, 8, 49, 88 n.39
Bateson, Gregory 56, 81, 81 n.25, 92
Baudelaire, Charles 3, 35 n.47
Bauer, Felice 2, 11, 61, 64
Begriff 124–5, 136
belatedness 1, 12, 16, 52, 86
Benjamin, Walter 3, 14, 15, 21–2, 32–4, 37, 39, 84, 85 n.30, 94–6, 105, 114 n.38
Berlant, Lauren 12, 14, 53, 108–9
binding 26, 73, 81, 98, 110–13, 116 *see also* 'double bind'

blindness 82, 89, 104
Bloch, Ernst 3, 15, 21–2, 32, 34–5, 37
Brinkema, Eugenie 6, 12, 14
Büchner, Georg 142 n.7
Burke, Edmund 27–8

Campe, Rüdiger 7
Canetti, Elias 103
capitalism 21, 42
Celan, Paul 142
censorship 68, 84
Chemaly, Soraya 72
Christianity 44, 75, 83, 132
comical *see also* irony
  the comical 50, 56 n.34, 67–8, 102 n.74, 130
  humor 58–9
  laughter 13, 44, 114, 119–21, 132
  the ridiculous 95, 117, 119
complaining 12, 14, 20, 52, 55–7, 62, 108–9, 136–8
compound words 110–13
critical theory 15, 19, 22
cursing 16, 107–9

death
  death-drive 26, 77, 99, 119
  death threats 65
  and melancholy 104, 107, 113
  of a child 89–95, 128–30
  of a lover 134–5
  of a woman 85, 93–4
  petite mort 123, 135
Deleuze, Gilles 6, 7 n.26, 115, 131
De Man, Paul 59, 68
denial 73–4, 89, 91, 141
Derrida, Jacques 52
detail 8, 14, 88
dialogue 44, 52, 89–90 n.41, 94, 95
Dickens, Charles 3, 5, 49
Döblin, Alfred 96
dogwhistling 139
double bind 56–7, 59, 75, 92, 110, 115–16

Downing, Eric 4 n.13, 49 n.14, 80
Droste-Hülshoff, Annette von 2, 77–8

Elias, Norbert 11, 120
emotion
  German 12–15, 53
  history of 7, 11, 14, 53, 111 n.29
  named emotions 1–2, 6–9
  and rhetoric 75, 85–6
Empfindsamkeit (sensibility) 12, 56
Empson, William 6, 11, 51, 91
energetics 16, 96–9, 101, 106, 111, 136
epistolarity 16, 43, 50–3, 56, 65–6, 69
Erler, Gotthard 53 n.25, 62 n.52, 64
eroticism 22, 24, 28, 30–2, 36, 39 n.56, 41, 53, 123

feminism 13, 20, 41, 72, 77
Ferenczi, Sándor 29 n.34, 81
fetishism 8 n.27, 124, 126
Flatley, Jonathan 12
Flaubert, Gustav 3, 49, 69 n.72
Fontane, Emilie 2, 16, 52–62, 64, 67, 123
Fontane, Theodor 1–3, 9, 10 n.34, 15, 16, 19, 22, 34–41, 48–52, 62–70, 115 n.42, 142
Fore, Devin 4
form, formalism 1–2, 6, 8–11, 15, 41 n.61, 42, 46, 60, 79, 87, 88 n.39, 92, 95, 100, 106–7, 111, 134
Freud, Sigmund 11, 12, 14, 15, 22, 28, 38, 63, 73, 81, 83, 84 n.29, 88, 96, 101, 108 n.22, 116, 121, 130, 135, 141, 142 n.5
Frevert, Ute 7, 14 n.49, 111 n.29

gaslighting 139
gender 15, 21, 23, 26 n.22, 27, 33, 39, 45, 68–9, 100, 122

Index

genre *see also* epistolarity
   lyrical 34, 36, 50, 87, 121
   novel 3, 12, 13, 16, 22, 35, 39–41, 48–50, 52, 55, 60, 69, 96, 98, 102, 107, 109–10, 114–15, 117–18, 124, 126–9, 134, 137–8
   novella 27, 29, 33–4, 39, 77, 79, 82, 89, 91, 93–4, 133
   prose piece 4, 90, 114, 115, 117, 119 n.53, 126–31, 135
   rhythm 1 n.2, 93, 125
   sonnet 87
Goethe, Johann Wolfgang von 55, 93–4
Goldschmidt, Georges-Arthur 125
Gordon, Linda 20
grammar
   parataxis 40
   pronoun 98, 100, 116
   punctuation 112, 140
   subjunctive/ *irrealis* 55, 62
   Syntax 16, 79, 86–7

Hamacher, Werner 142
Hasenclever, Walter 79
hate-speech 124, 139
Hauptmann, Gerhart 2, 16, 62 n.52, 79, 89–98
Haverkamp, Anselm 76 n.12, 125
Hegel, G. W. F. 11, 45, 55, 72 n.2, 85 n.30, 121, 124
Heidegger, Martin 14, 124
Heine, Heinrich 50, 102, 140
Helfer, Martha 78
Helmholtz, Hermann von 97
Hesse, Hermann 104
hierarchy 1 n.1, 13
Hobus, Jens 104 n.7
Holz, Arno 79, 94 n.56
Huyssen, Andreas 3 n.8, 4 n.9

idyll 45, 112, 140
impotence 112, 137

innocence 16, 83–4, 105, 123 n.61
interpretation
   conflict of 4, 49, 52, 65–6, 77, 82
   hermeneutics 7, 48, 51, 69, 68–70, 124
   identificatory 28, 104 *see also* 'rhetoric, literalization'
   pleas for 52, 58–9
   (un-)readability 5, 6, 7, 67, 69, 73, 83
irony
   infinite 24, 59, 70, 106 *see also* 'interpretation'
   performative 44, 57, 86
   sarcasm 5, 6, 7, 67, 69, 73, 83
   in Walser 106, 111–13, 115 n.41, 117, 121, 123

Jakobson, Roman 3 n.8, 11, 51, 88 n.39
Jameson, Fredric 2, 7, 76
Jean Paul Richter 28 n.31, 55
Jelinek, Elfriede 76
Jesenská, Milena 2, 66–8
Johnson, Barbara 52, 66

Kafka, Franz 2–4, 11, 16, 43, 49, 52, 59, 60–70, 105 n.16, 106, 112 n.32, 118, 141–2
Kammer, Stephan 127, 129
Kant, Immanuel 1, 21, 28 n.31, 131
Kasper, Judith 140
Kaye, Richard A. 22
Keller, Gottfried 3, 5, 6, 12, 15, 16, 22, 32–4, 36, 39, 79, 83–4, 96, 99–100, 102 n.74, 116, 133–4, 142
Kipnis, Laura 20
Klein, Melanie 132
Kleist, Heinrich von 14, 25, 76, 87 n.37, 94, 113 n.36, 142 n.7
Klemperer, Victor 125, 140
Kluge, Alexander 58

Kornbluh, Anna 1
Kotzebue, August von 76
Kracauer, Siegfried 3
Kraus, Chris 69
Kreienbrock, Jörg 12, 103

Lacan, Jacques 52, 137
Laclos, Pierre-Ambroise-François Choderlos de 36, 69
latency 13 n.44, 16, 67, 83, 91, 124, 125, 136, 139
law 9–10, 20, 29–31, 47, 84–5 n.30, 87 n.37, 94, 99, 114–15, 130
Le Guin, Ursula 76
Lenz, J. M. R. 76
Levine, Caroline 1
Longinus 1, 85–7
love *see also* 'epistolarity'; 'melancholy'
    flirtation 28, 32, 35–6
    historicity of 1–2, 46–7, 53, 84, 122
    and passive aggression 45–7, 54, 60, 62, 66, 118, 131
Luhmann, Niklas 46, 53, 72 n.2, 92, 94, 99
Lukács, Georg 7, 8 n.27, 88

martyrdom 56, 96
Marx, Karl 14, 97
mass-shooting 72, 139
Massumi, Brian 6
master/slave dialectic 45, 114, 131, 131 n.85
Matt, Peter von 112
media 13, 19, 64, 75, 139
    immediacy 6, 60, 65, 92, 106, 117, 129
    mediation 1, 31, 39, 121
melancholy 29, 107–8, 108 n.22, 109–11, 113, 134, 137–8
Merkin, Daphne 19
#MeToo 19–21, 139
microaggressions 13

Miller, Alice 81
moderation 9, 10, 97, 121, 141 *see also* 'sublimation'
modernism 2–9, 12, 15, 17, 45–6, 49 n.15, 53, 79, 96, 103, 120, 138, 141
Morgan Wortham, Simon 26
Morgenstern, Christian 118
Musil, Robert 96, 132

Nägele, Rainer 83–4
narcissism 66, 82
narratology 79, 81–2
    diegesis 81, 88, 91, 126
    focalization 8, 122
National Socialism 17, 89
Ngai, Sianne 12, 14
Niehaus, Michael 126, 131 n.84
Nietzsche, Friedrich 10–12, 14, 15, 44–6, 105–6, 117, 121, 131, 137–8

Obama, Barack 140
ordinariness
    everyday aggression 13, 43, 117
    life 2, 118 n.51
    of realism 1–2, 13–14, 21, 75–7, 133
    triviality 43, 46, 71, 122
Ovid 36, 40

pacifism 16, 104
parapraxis 63, 142 n.6
Parker, Rozsika 39
Parkinson, Anna M. 13
Parnes, Ohad 92
performativity 50, 88, 98, 112
perversion 83, 132
Petrarch 6
Phillips, Adam 29, 113 n.34
Plug, Jan 103
politeness 16, 43, 58, 103, 106
potentiality 10, 21–2, 23 n.13, 39, 41–2, 77, 115, 125

Pott, Hans-Georg 64
Povinelli, Elizabeth A. 12, 13, 76
Preisendanz, Wolfgang 10 n.34
pretense 50, 105
psychoanalysis 6, 13, 15, 66, 81, 101, 107, 130, 132

queerness 12–13, 15, 21–3, 26, 41
Quintilian 51, 87
Quiring, Björn 112

Rabinbach, Anson 97, 101
Rancière, Jacques 5, 13
Rankine, Claudia 12, 13
realism
   English 3, 5, 39
   French 3, 5, 9
   German 1–22, 26, 35, 41, 44, 48, 49, 75–80, 89, 96, 98, 120, 133 n.92, 138, 141
reiterative imagery 16, 91, 93
repetition 49, 77, 80 n.22, 127
repression 11, 14, 41, 63, 73, 98, 102 n.74, 118–21, 126, 134
resentment 11, 16, 44–5, 47, 104, 107, 119, 126, 136, 141
   ressentiment 13 n.41, 15, 44–5, 105, 131
resistance 6, 9, 42, 44, 45, 69, 102 n.74, 113
rhetoric 1, 7–9, 16, 40, 44, 54, 59, 60, 79, 82, 85, 89, 95, 107, 118, 132, 139
   accumulatio 118
   amplificatio 119
   apotropaia 56, 59
   brevitas 60
   dissimulatio 16, 51–2, 105, 107, 121
   genus humile/sublime 95
   hyperbaton 80, 85–7, 91, 95, 98
   inconcinnitas 95, 132
   literality/literalization 29, 70, 91, 93, 102 n.74, 142

metaphor 57, 84, 102 n.74, 136
pleonasm 120
prosopopeïa 117
Riley, Denise 8, 12, 14, 124
Rohr, Mathilde von 61–2
Romanticism(German) 2, 7, 12, 53
Rose, Jacqueline 41
Rosenberg, Jordy 42
rudeness 15, 83 n.27, 136–8

Sachs, Hans 76
(sado-)masochism 38, 53, 104, 115, 132–3
Schadenfreude 104, 132
Schiller, Friedrich 55
Schlaf, Johannes 79, 94 n.56
Schlegel, Friedrich 55, 111 n.29
Schor, Naomi 14
Schuller, Marianne 103
Schuster, Aaron 56, 137
Schwerin, Kerstin Gräfin von 127
seduction 21, 28, 36, 39, 88, 96, 116
Seelig, Carl 3, 108, 112–13, 127 n.74, 131 n.85, 134
sexual harassment 20, 21, 23, 29, 41
Shakespeare, William 6
Shoah 17, 141
Siegert, Bernhard 64
Silverman, Katja 26
Simmel, Georg 3, 15, 22–6, 29, 31–4
Snediker, Michael D. 12
Sontag, Susan 103–5, 133
Stewart, Kathleen 5, 13
Stifter, Adalbert 2, 9, 10, 16, 79–88, 90, 94, 96–8, 102, 141–2
Storm, Theodor 2, 5, 6, 15, 16, 22–3, 26–31, 36, 39 n.58, 79, 85, 95, 96, 102, 142
sublimation 10, 16, 104, 107, 117, 121, 131, 135, 141 *see also* 'moderation'
symptom 26, 74, 82, 87, 91
system 40 n.60, 44, 64, 88–9, 92–4, 99–101

teasing 16, 37, 107, 114–15, 117–19, 134, 136
Terada, Rei 7
theology 95–6, 98, 102
Threadcraft, Shatema 72
translation 83 n.27, 90–1, 97 n.68, 100, 102 n.74, 121, 132
transvaluation 84, 136–8
trauma 13, 40 n.60, 79, 83, 86, 98, 128, 135, 140 *see also* 'belatedness'
tropes 1, 9, 58, 80, 85–7, 93 *see also under* 'rhetoric'

unaccountability 16, 89, 96, 99
uncanny 65, 83, 93, 118, 123 n.62

Vedder, Ulrike 41 n.61, 69, 92
victimhood 26, 29, 47, 56, 77–8, 96, 101, 118–19, 129–30
  perpetrator 72, 77–8, 101

Vinken, Barbara 39 n.56, 69
Virgil 91
Vischer, Friedrich Theodor 9

Walser, Robert 2–4, 15, 16, 79, 85, 90, 94, 96–138, 142
war 15, 34, 36, 44, 48, 104, 119–21
Weiss, Peter 76
white-supremacy 139–40
Wilhelm I. 119
Willer, Stefan 92
Wittgenstein, Ludwig 14
Wolff, Larry 73
Woolf, Virginia 13
worrying 113 n.34, 129, 131

Žižek, Slavoj 45
Zola, Émile 5
Zweig, Stefan 132

www.ingramcontent.com/pod-product-compliance
Lightning Source LLC
Chambersburg PA
CBHW052049300426
44117CB00012B/2038